At the Heart of the White Rose

At the Heart of the White Rose

Letters and Diaries
of Hans and Sophie Scholl

Edited by Inge Jens

Translated from the German by J. Maxwell Brownjohn
Preface by Richard Gilman

Plough Publishing House

Published by Plough Publishing House
Walden, New York
Robertsbridge, England
Elsmore, Australia
www.plough.com

Plough produces books, a quarterly magazine, and Plough.com to encourage people and help them put their faith into action. We believe Jesus can transform the world and that his teachings and example apply to all aspects of life. At the same time, we seek common ground with all people regardless of their creed.

Plough is the publishing house of the Bruderhof, an international community of families and singles seeking to follow Jesus together. Members of the Bruderhof are committed to a way of radical discipleship in the spirit of the Sermon on the Mount. Inspired by the first church in Jerusalem (Acts 2 and 4), they renounce private property and share everything in common in a life of nonviolence, justice, and service to neighbors near and far. To learn more about the Bruderhof's faith, history, and daily life, see Bruderhof.com. (Views expressed by Plough authors are their own and do not necessarily reflect the position of the Bruderhof.)

23 22 21 20   3 4 5 6

Photographs from the Scholl family collection unless otherwise noted. Front cover: *July 23, 1942. Hans and Sophie Scholl with Christoph Probst (*right*), just before Hans and Christoph's student company left for Russia.* Photograph by George Wittenstein. Title Page: Hans Scholl image © Manuel Aicher. Sophie Scholl image courtesy of Federal Archive of Germany. The American edition of this book was adapted from the original text published in Germany under the title *Hans Scholl, Sophie Scholl, Briefe und Aufzeichnungen,* copyright © 1984 S. Fischer Verlag GmbH Frankfurt am Main.

A catalog record for this book is available from the British Library.
Library of Congress Cataloging-in-Publication Data

Names: Scholl, Hans, 1918-1943, author. | Scholl, Sophie, 1921-1943, author.
 | Jens, Inge, editor. | Brownjohn, John, translator.
Title: At the heart of the White Rose : letters and diaries of Hans and
 Sophie Scholl / edited by Inge Jens ; translated from the German by J.
 Maxwell Brownjohn ; preface by Richard Gilman.
Other titles: Hans Scholl, Sophie Scholl, Briefe und Aufzeichnungen. English
 | Letters and diaries of Hans and Sophie Scholl
Description: Walden, New York : Plough Publishing House, [2017] | Includes
 bibliographical references and index.
Identifiers: LCCN 2016059451 (print) | LCCN 2016059877 (ebook) | ISBN
 9780874860290 (pbk.) | ISBN 9780874860306 (epub) | ISBN 9780874860344
 (mobi) | ISBN 9780874860351 (pdf)
Subjects: LCSH: Scholl, Hans, 1918-1943--Correspondence. | Scholl, Sophie,
 1921-1943--Correspondence. | College students--Germany--Correspondence. |
 Anti-Nazi movement--Germany--Munich. | Universit?at M?unchen--Riot, 1943.
 | Weisse Rose (Resistance group)
Classification: LCC DD247.S375 A4 2017 (print) | LCC DD247.S375 (ebook) | DDC
 943.086092/2--dc23
LC record available at https://lccn.loc.gov/2016059451

Printed in the United States of America

Contents

Foreword

H ANS SCHOLL, born September 22, 1918, executed
February 22, 1943; Sophie Scholl, born May 9, 1921,
executed February 22, 1943. These two names and
two fates are representative of thousands more: representative,
first, of those other members of the White Rose – Willi Graf,
Christoph Probst, Alexander Schmorell, and Professor Kurt
Huber – who were sent to the guillotine; representative, too, of
those White Rose associates whom the Gestapo hunted down
in Freiburg, Hamburg, Ulm, and elsewhere; and representative, last but not least, of all those anonymous Germans who
were forced to atone in prison cells and punishment battalions
because they believed active defense of human rights was more
important than compliance with despotic laws.

Hans and Sophie Scholl's youth precluded their evolving a
completely coherent and consistent view of the world; had they
been precociously sophisticated, they would never have run such
extreme risks. It is also certain that they both felt compelled,
in accordance with the dictates of the time, to disguise their
political sentiments with Brechtian guile, camouflaging them in
esoteric asides and allusions intelligible only to insiders. Thus
their political scope, their romantic idealism, their wealth of
contradictions, their framing of rebellious ideas in an intimate,
familiar idiom, endow the letters with a representative quality.

Two young people were voicing what thousands of their own kind, mainly older schoolchildren and university students, were thinking. On them, political education and an acquaintance with the liberal counterforces of art, religion, and scholarship, imposed an obligation to preach resistance, not in the cloud-cuckoo-land of the mind, but in the here and now of everyday life under fascism, and to do so in language whose aesthetic nature was itself expressive of political dissent.

The following letters and other writings by Hans and Sophie Scholl have therefore been selected for their mode of expression as well as their content — for the "how" as well as the "what." This, it is hoped, will help to paint a more vivid picture of their characters and personal development during the five and a half years that elapsed between the beginning of the correspondence in 1937 (no earlier letters have survived) and their deaths in 1943.

Neither Hans nor Sophie Scholl could have guessed that their private letters would someday be read by people other than those to whom they were addressed. If these documents have nonetheless been made public — after due deliberation, be it noted — it is not simply that their authors' eventual martyrdom lends special weight to every word, however trifling, but above all because the sincerity, spontaneity, and literary density of these letters, with their unmistakably conversational and unstudied tone, clearly illustrate how young Germans critical of the National Socialist regime thought and felt, how some of them managed, by dint of reading, meditation, and discussion, to break the spiritual quarantine imposed on their country, and how they developed their purely private theories, evolved as an alternative to the prevailing system, into direct political action aimed at public and universal liberation.

Inge Jens

Preface

to the American Edition

I'VE VISITED the University of Munich several times, so I must have seen the street signs that identify the square in front of the main building as "Geschwister-Scholl Platz." But the name meant nothing to me twenty or even ten years ago, for until recently I'd only vaguely heard about the resistance group called the White Rose, after whose leader and his sister the square had been renamed. When I did learn about it I was pierced with admiration and pity.

A handful of students at the university, together with a middle-aged philosophy professor, begin in the summer of 1942 secretly to write and distribute leaflets urging an end to the war and the overthrow of Hitler, paint words like "Freedom!" on public walls, are caught by the Gestapo, swiftly tried and, in the cases of Hans and Sophie Scholl and Christoph Probst, beheaded the same day, February 22, 1943. (Other executions follow a few months later.)

"Geschwister-Scholl": brother and sister Scholl. The German language, so given to compounds and collective nouns, here achieves a master stroke of compression and evocation. For Hans and Sophie are forever fused in memory by what they did, this medical student nearing the end of his training and this young woman just beginning a war-delayed formal education in philosophy and art. They were dead at twenty-four and twenty-one and so left behind no careers, no "life's work." Yet a life's work is there after all, flowering in a series of actions carried out over the course of only six or seven months, a movement of the spirit that was both emblem and crown of an existence.

What the two of them did in the face of mortal danger becomes even more astonishing in the light of what we now know: that such pockets of resistance as there were in Germany were made up almost entirely either of people with firmly held political beliefs (which the Scholls lacked), remnants of the old Left mainly, or those who were motivated by an aristocratic contempt for the Nazi barbarians or dread of a Germany devastated in defeat. Apart from scattered church figures like Dietrich Bonhoeffer, it was rare for anyone to risk his or her life out of almost purely religious motives and much rarer still for such persons to be as young as were the Scholls and nearly all their fellow-conspirators.

Hans and Sophie are made ready for their valiant doomed enterprise by a childhood and youth in a deeply humane if not especially religious family. The earliest letters printed here reflect their parents' moral fineness and the loving atmosphere of their home. At nineteen Hans writes to them that "few people can look back on such a fine, proud boyhood" as his and tells his mother that "you've a quiet fervor, an unfailing warmth." (Their father, a pacifist in World War I, will later be imprisoned for several months for having been overheard referring to Hitler as "the scourge of God.")

The family – there are two other daughters and another son – is devoted to music, literature, and art, and, balancing that in the best tradition of German humanism, to nature, the outdoors. Sophie writes at eighteen to her boyfriend, an army officer named Fritz Hartnagel, about a camping trip: "Who would have thought it possible that a tiny little flower could preoccupy a person so completely that there simply wasn't room for any other thought, or that I could have turned into the earth, I liked it so much." Later she writes to her father: "The sight of the mountains' quiet majesty and beauty makes the reasons people advance for their disastrous doings seem ludicrous and insane."

From his letters and a diary he kept while serving as a medical orderly on the Russian front (he's profoundly attracted to the Russian people and land) a portrait of Hans takes shape that shows him as earnest, generous, high-minded, with a questing if not original intelligence. Of his vocation for medicine he writes unexceptionally to his parents that "tending the sick is a great and humanitarian occupation," and tells his girlfriend, Rose Nägele, that "I must go my own way, and I do so gladly. I'm not anxious to avoid a host of dangers and temptations. My sole ambition must be to perceive things clearly and calmly." Yet he also thinks of himself as something of a neurasthenic – "There's a kind of mad melancholy underlying everything [in me]" – and indeed as the times grow worse a sort of reality-induced neurosis does seem to take hold of him: "The war may have distorted a lot of things in my brain."

Sophie, who adores her brother, is more complex, wittier, more the artist (she passionately loves music and has a talent for it). "The sun felt obliged to put its head out and send us its hottest rays," she writes to Fritz Hartnagel. "Perhaps it did so out of curiosity." And she tells him in another letter that "establishing contact with someone new is a momentous occurrence, a simultaneous declaration of love and war." Although one's admiration for Hans never falters, it's Sophie who breaks your heart. Photographs of Hans show an exceedingly handsome clean-cut young man, while those of Sophie reveal a girl without conventional beauty – her nose is too broad and her chin is a little long – but one from whose face shines a deep intelligence and a transfiguring kindness.

But maybe I'm reading into some of this. So affecting are these letters and diaries that it's impossible to maintain a coolly objective view of their authors; one's esteem for them, one's pity and, it's not too strong a word, one's love, keeps "editing" their story to a level of revelation and moral beauty it doesn't always, on the face of it, express. But that's just the point: our knowledge of their fates shapes our response, making even the most mundane details of their correspondence, their matter-of-fact diary entries, the most informal of snapshots take on a heartrending significance.

As the war goes on and rumors of German atrocities, especially the death camps, reach Munich, the Scholls' letters, and even more their diaries, grow more agitated and despairing. "My pessimism gets worse every day," Hans writes in his diary. "Skepticism is poisoning my soul." And Sophie tells a friend, "I realize that one can wallow in the mind . . . while one's soul starves to death. This wouldn't have occurred to me once upon a time." It's at the intersection of recognition, horror, and longing that their religious interests, which for both of them had been mild and peripheral, begin to expand and move toward the center.

Hans's "conversion" process is more intellectual than Sophie's, his spiritual growth being nurtured in large part by books. Many of these are by French Catholics, among them Léon Bloy, Paul Claudel, Georges Bernanos, and Etienne Gilson (ten years later these same writers would play a central role in my own temporary conversion to Catholicism). For both Hans and Sophie another strong Catholic influence comes from their friendship with the elderly writer and editor Carl Muth, and from Theodor Haecker, whose books had been banned but who would read from them to members of the White Rose. In the end, neither Hans nor Sophie actually joined the Church, although one of the six executed conspirators was an ardent Catholic and another was baptized just before his death.

On December 7, 1941 (the day of Pearl Harbor), Hans writes to Rose Nägele: "I'm thinking of you on this second Sunday of Advent, which I'm experiencing as a wholehearted Christian for the first time in my life." Yet some months later he writes in his diary: "O God of love, help me to overcome my doubts. I see the Creation, your handiwork, which is good. But I also see man's handiwork, our handiwork, which is cruel."

He has of course been caught in that central crisis of faith which so many religious persons have undergone in this century, faced with the intolerable question: What sort of God would permit evil on such a scale? But he moves past it into acceptance of the mystery. In October 1942, after the first leaflets have been disseminated, he writes to his parents out of what may or may not be an intimation of his impending martyrdom but is in any case chilling for us to come upon: "I am reading . . . a history of the Church. I find the chapter on the persecution of the Christians especially interesting."

Sophie is more intuitive, less schooled; full of a self-doubt which strikes me as the rarest kind of humility, she struggles with anguished hope toward a point of affirmation and peace. "I'd so much like to believe that I can acquire strength through prayer," she writes in her diary. "I can't achieve anything by myself." And in another entry: "I've decided to pray in church every day, so God won't forsake me. Although I don't yet know God and feel sure my conception of him is utterly false, he'll forgive me if I ask him." And then in the loveliest of self-effacing gestures she writes: "I pray for a compassionate heart, for how else could I love?"

Everything moves toward fatality. But the Scholls have come to know who they are and what they must do. Hans had written in his diary: " . . . Something *must* come because all values can never be destroyed." And Sophie had told a friend, Lisa Remppis, that "I think we at last have a chance to prove ourselves – and preserve our integrity." The fourth White Rose leaflet ends with these words: "We will not be silent. We are your bad conscience. The White Rose will not leave you in peace!"

On February 17, 1943, Sophie writes to Lisa: "I've just been playing the Trout Quintet . . . listening to the andantino makes me want to be a trout myself . . . in that piece of Schubert's you can positively feel and smell the breezes and scents and hear the birds and the whole of creation cry out for joy . . . it's sheer enchantment." The next day Hans and Sophie Scholl are in the hands of the Gestapo.

The nearly irresistible temptation is to ask questions like these: Why were there so few of them, why didn't more people speak and act against the terror the way the Scholls did? You can find answers, ultimately unsatisfying but at least fulfilling the duty of historical inquiry. To resist meant to turn against your own country, which wasn't true in France, say, or Holland or Norway. Surveillance was ferocious. Most young people were away in the army or in heavily regimented war work. Clandestine communications were immensely difficult. And so on.

It seems to me that to go on in this line of reasoning is at some point to lose the Scholls and their fellow-resisters, to convert them into statistics. They were exceptional, to be sure, but that isn't how they ought to live in our consciousness. Victims and transcenders of a monstrous era, they occupy an exemplary status, testifying to human possibility, to courage, grace, and self-sacrifice. The dominion of spiritual and moral truth can't be quantified. In a radio address after hearing of their deaths, Thomas Mann said: "Good, splendid young people . . . you shall not be forgotten." The goodness and splendor of Hans and Sophie, Geschwister-Scholl, are permanent, not contingent, existing serenely now beyond the dreadful history of which they were an infinitesimal part and to which they said no.

Richard Gilman
New York
March 1987

The Scholl parents, Robert and Magdalena

The Scholl children, Ludwigsburg; *back:* Inge, Hans,
Elizabeth, *front:* Sophie and Werner, 1930–31

Hans Scholl

1937–1939

Born in Ingersheim on September 22, 1918, Hans Scholl was nearly fourteen when he moved to Ulm in 1932 and nearly fifteen when Hitler came to power. He joined the Hitler Youth in the fall of 1933 and rose to command a squad. Two years later he resigned and, together with some friends of his, formed an independent youth group affiliated with the Bündische Jugend, dj-1/11,[1] a group banned by the National Socialists.

He continued to keep in touch with this group when, after graduating from secondary school in 1937, he was sent to Göppingen Camp to do his spell of compulsory service in the Reicharbeitsdienst (RAD), or State Labor Service.

All young people had to join the RAD, initially for a period of six months. Predominantly employed in manual tasks, RAD members wore uniforms and were organized along military lines. The preliminary training aspect of their activities assumed growing importance as time went by, and they were ultimately absorbed into the German war machine.

To his mother, Göppingen, May 4, 1937

Dear Mother,

I got your parcel. The rolls were delicious.

This is meant to be a birthday letter, but I don't know what to write about. I'll probably be coming home on Sunday. I realize it must seem ages to you since I left. From my own point of view, these four and a half weeks have passed in a flash.

I've changed a bit, I suppose. Inwardly and outwardly. It doesn't mean I've renounced my old principles and perceptions. I've taken another step up the ladder. This place is a mine of experience.

I'm putting my heart and soul into my work, believe me – I never shirk. The main external changes in me are shorter hair, a heavy tan, and a more relaxed expression.

So much for the general situation.

It's good for youngsters like us to get away from home for once. There's an old proverb: never leave home, and you'll never go back there.

We're forever singing with all our hearts, though, and it's a comfort to be able to vent your innermost feelings, if only in song.

> Long is the way back to the homeland,
> Far, so far,
> There near the stars above the rim of the woods,
> Old times laugh . . .

And now, tons and tons of happy returns on your birthday.

Your devoted son,
Hans

To his sister Inge, Göppingen, October 8, 1937

Dear Inge,

I got your joint parcel. Many thanks for my birthday present.[2] I can't read the George book yet. To absorb his words properly I'll need time and endless peace and quiet. Stefan George is immensely hard to understand, but we can get an inkling of him and his towering, unassailable, solitary grandeur.

Our duties here are very monotonous. In the evenings we sit around the big table in our barrack room and read. All kinds of books, each to his taste. I became engrossed in Knittel's exciting *Via Mala*.[3] Now I've finished it.

It's our farewell party tomorrow night [celebrating completion of his service in the Arbeitsdienst]. I'm off to Stuttgart on Sunday. I'd have loved to go to the Furtwängler[4] [concert], but the only seats left cost 8 or 10 marks.

I hope you're all well.

Lots of love,

Hans

After completing his stint in the Arbeitsdienst in mid-October 1937, Hans Scholl was drafted. A keen horseman since boyhood, he applied to join the cavalry at Bad Cannstatt, on the outskirts of Stuttgart.

Late in the fall of 1937, while Hans was undergoing his basic training, a nationwide campaign was launched against members of the banned youth movement Bündische Jugend (dj-1/11) and its sympathizers. Hans's brother Werner and his two sisters, Inge and Sophie, were arrested in the course of this witch hunt. Sophie was released at once, but Inge and Werner had to spend a week in the Gestapo jail at Stuttgart. Hans, whose military status exempted him from the direct jurisdiction of the civil authorities, was not detained for questioning until later in December.

To his mother, Bad Cannstatt, November 27, 1937

My dear Mother,

Everything turned up here safely. I was delighted, having been looking forward to it so much. Many thanks for your letter. The bible quotation[5] is wonderful. It helped to restore my composure. Now I hope we can all be happy again. We don't mean to feel like martyrs,[6] even though we may sometimes have reason to, because we won't let anyone impugn our purity of sentiment. Inner strength is our most powerful weapon. That's what I always tried to impress on my youngsters [the boys in the dj-1/11] in the old days. Our communal excursions and evening get-togethers helped us to acquire that strength, and we'll never, ever forget those trips. We certainly had a boyhood worthy of the name!

And that's my dearest wish: that in spite of all the difficulties and all the mudslinging,[7] this sentiment should live on in the hearts of my former comrades.

We won't be getting any home leave yet next Sunday, from the look of it. Today I saw the film *Patriots*.[8] I doubt if the coming week will produce much in the way of news.

Fondest love,

Hans

To his parents, Bad Cannstatt, December 12, 1937

Dear Parents,

I received your parcel, for which many thanks. I got back to Cannstatt safely and have settled in again very well. This afternoon I was invited home by a comrade from Stuttgart. We had some interesting assignments last week. Wednesday was field training, Thursday marksmanship (I scored two 12's out of three shots), and Friday a night exercise complete with full equipment. Saturday we just cleaned our things. I've now had myself measured for a pair of trousers by a reputable Stuttgart tailor.

They're going to cost 48 marks – a fortune! They're the same as the officers wear (because I'll most probably become an officer in the reserve). It was the last piece of cloth the tailor had, so I was lucky from that angle. He complained a great deal about the shortage of cloth. He has a lot of orders, and he can't meet them all. The trousers will be ready on Thursday, but I can only pick them up if I pay cash because we aren't allowed to run up debts in the squadron. So please, Father, if you possibly can, send me the money. . . .

Hans's arrest may have occurred within hours of writing the preceding letter. He was lucky to find a staunch advocate in his squadron commander, Rittmeister (cavalry captain) Scupin, who urged that the investigation be speedily concluded and pressed for his release from custody. This is attested by Scupin's two letters to Robert Scholl, Hans's father.[9] Having drawn the authorities' attention to his family by becoming a youth leader in the dj-1/11, Hans Scholl felt to blame, as well, for the earlier arrest of his brother and sister.

To his parents, Detention Prison, Stuttgart, December 18, 1937

Dear Parents,

Now that a day has gone by since Father visited me, I want to write to you both. Thank you so much for coming, Father. You brought me fresh hope. I'm so immensely sorry to have brought this misfortune on the family, and I was often close to despair during my first few days in detention. I promise you, though, I'll put everything right. When I'm free again, I'll work and work – that and nothing but – so you can look on your son with pride again.

I have plenty of time to think now and the whole of my sunny boyhood passes before my eyes in the brightest colors. First childish play, then serious work, then tireless exertion on behalf of a community. Few people can look back on such a fine, proud boyhood. And now I've regained confidence in my future. I've regained faith in my own strength, and ultimately I owe that strength to you two alone. Only now am I fully alive to my father's desire, which he himself possessed and passed on to me, to become something great for the sake of mankind.

Don't lose your gaiety, Mother, I entreat you, because your children need it so badly. What matters most is that Christmas should remain a joyful family occasion.

I think of you both so much.

Yours,

Hans

P.S. . . . Give my love to Lisl, Inge, Sophie, and Werner [Hans's sisters and brother].[10] They wouldn't let me have Sophie's Christmas present, unfortunately. Please send me my English textbooks, at least the ones from my senior grades. Vocational training books are allowed here. Send me some other textbooks too, but you'll have to write a covering letter saying I need them for my job in later life, or I won't get them.

Let's hope I'll be home again soon!

Thanks to Rittmeister Scupin's efforts, Hans Scholl was released from the detention prison early in January, although he remained under investigation, which often bore heavily on his spirits.

To his parents, Stuttgart, January 6, 1938

Dear Parents,

I got safely back to barracks at three o'clock Monday morning, having taken a cab from the station. I slept like the dead for a few hours before going on duty. At 7 a.m. we were driven to the rifle range at Dornhalde. I had to make up for the two firing practices I'd missed. I didn't do particularly well, generally speaking, but I completed all my firing sequences. In the afternoon we started driving lessons. A lot more snow had fallen by the time I woke this morning. It went on snowing all morning, and it's still snowing even now. I don't think Stuttgart has ever seen so much snow. We're on duty this Sunday, but I'm sitting in the barrack room reading and writing.

I'll bet there's some good skiing at Ulm, too.

My thoughts often turn to that lovely, happy spell of furlough, and I'm already looking forward to the day when I can come home again. The thing is, I'm quite a different person "at home" than I was before. I can't find the words to convey my gratitude to you both, because words fail you when you're so completely overwhelmed by emotion. But maybe I've become more of a man in recent days than I'd once have thought possible. And when I look back on this period later on, I'll know whom to thank for helping me to survive it.

Fondest love,
Hans

To his sister Inge, Bad Cannstatt, January 18, 1938

Dear Inge,

Afraid I can't come to Ulm today because the whole squad has been confined to barracks. Is all well with you and the others? I do hope so. I'm not too bad. I often forget the whole thing and act carefree and exuberant, but then the dark shadow looms up again and makes everything seem dismal and empty. When that happens, all that keeps me going is the thought of a future that'll be better than the present. You've no idea how much I look forward to going to university. . . .

I very much hope to be able to come to Ulm next Sunday. I itch to see and talk with you all once more. This place is just a charade. . . .

Lots of love,
Hans

To his mother, Bad Cannstatt, January 22, 1938

Dear Mother,

Thank you for your letter. I feel a sort of duty to answer it. You've a quiet fervor, an unfailing warmth, that may well be the greatest thing anyone can encounter in this life. I'm still young. I lay no claim to age and experience, but above and beyond the flickering blaze of my youthful soul, I sometimes detect the eternal breath of Something infinitely great and serene. God. Fate.

Your letters convey so much about that secure stronghold, and don't imagine that your words pass me by. What a mother says sticks, like it or not.

All my love,

Hans

The "subversive activities" charge still pending against Hans Scholl for his dj-1/11 activities was coupled with one alleging a "foreign exchange offense." His sister Inge recalls that this had some basis in fact. While on a trip abroad with his youth group in the summer of 1936, Hans had stuffed a big Nivea Cream can with German currency and smuggled it across the Swedish frontier, because the Ulm party was traveling without authorization from the Reich Youth Directorate and had consequently been refused a foreign exchange allowance. It is probable that the Gestapo "stumbled on" this incident while questioning the members of Hans's group, who were in their midteens. (Proceedings were dropped in July 1938 under the terms of a general amnesty proclaimed to mark the annexation of Austria.) Hans found some pleasant distraction during this tense time in visits to Leonberg, home of the Remppis family, who were friends of the Scholls. The daughter, Lisa, was on particularly close terms with Hans and Sophie.

To his parents, Bad Cannstatt, March 3, 1938

Dear Parents,

First, many thanks for the parcel and Mother's letter and card.

I'm in much better shape than I was. You mustn't worry that I'm brooding too much. I've a vague feeling that everything is going to turn out all right. I look forward immensely to the day when all will be forgotten and I'll be a different person again.

My whole body, every sinew, every vein of it, yearns for life. I must use my energy to the full.

Last Monday, when I came out of court, I sneaked into a nice café and wrote you from there. Then I took the bus to Leonberg, where we spent an enjoyable evening. I was back in barracks just before midnight. Tuesday and Wednesday passed without incident, but I felt terribly apprehensive when Thursday came. However, nothing happened that day either, and by Thursday evening I'd completely calmed down again. On Friday I told our lieutenant the whole story. He's entirely on my side, but a lieutenant of his kind holds some pretty naïve views, even if his father is a lawyer. Our CO's away at present. All the noncoms know about the foreign exchange business by now, of course, which is why I'm going to transfer to another squadron as soon as possible. I don't want to go to Bruchsal [11] in any case.

I'm room senior at present (even though I'm the youngest).

Saturday afternoon I went to the deer park with Lisa [Remppis]. She's very much looking forward to visiting Ulm.

Today I heard Schubert's *Unfinished* at the Liederhalle.

They're giving Beethoven's 9th next Sunday and Monday, but Werner must come that day (Sunday) all the same!

When Hitler came to Stuttgart, we mounted an honor guard. He drove along the ranks so I saw his blurred face at very close quarters. . . .

Our furlough is scheduled to start on Father's birthday.

All my love,

Hans

On March 12, 1938, German troops entered Austria.

To his parents, Bad Cannstatt, March 14, 1938

Dear Parents,

Since we haven't gone off to Austria like the rest, worse luck, I've finally found the time to write to you.

Your parcel arrived on Friday, Mother. Many thanks!

Our duties last week were leisurely in the extreme. All we did was get our vehicles and guns ready, and then it came to nothing. Our heated imaginations built all kinds of castles in the air: nights on the town in Vienna, strolls beside the Danube. In fact, only regular tank regiments marched in, and the majority of those were Bavarian troops. The A25 from Korn-westheim (the same arm of service as us) and the Ludwigsburg antiaircraft boys were lucky enough to go on this pleasure trip. How will it all end, though? A lot of saber-rattling goes on here. In general, I refrain from commenting on political develop-ments. My head feels heavy. I don't understand people anymore. Whenever I hear all that anonymous jubilation on the radio, I feel like going out into a big deserted plain and being by myself.

I spent Saturday evening at Leonberg. In Lisa [Remppis] I've found a person I can love wholeheartedly. Don't misunder-stand me, though. I realize Lisa's half a child still, and I'm not depriving her of her childishness. I can't philosophize with her. She's so natural and fresh, and that's just what I need. . . .

I found Gerhart Hauptmann's play *Michael Kramer*[12] very heartening. I'm reading a few chapters of Rilke's *Aufzeichnungen des Malte Laurids Brigge* every night.

Fondest love,

Hans

To his parents, Bad Cannstatt, March 28, 1938

Dear Parents,

I've just come from the district court. All they did was take down my personal particulars. I asked the official what would happen next. He told me I'll be served with the indictment in the next few days, and then the trial will open. They send the indictment via regimental headquarters. That's what I find the unpleasantest part. If only it was over at last!

Fondest love,

Hans

P.S. I went to the palmist.[13] He said I should wait and see what happens. I've nothing to fear. He also told me I'd be lucky in everything in later life. Women are another matter (ha ha). One other important point: he said this business will be settled in the very near future.

Hans Scholl finally received the indictment on the "subversive activities" charge on April 25, 1938. He wrote to his parents the same day. "I received the indictment today. The boys have been released under the amnesty, thank God. . . . Application is being made to put Ernst Reden on trial and remand him in custody. . . . I'm not afraid of going on trial. Even if I can't justify myself in open court, I can justify myself to myself."

To his sister Inge, Stuttgart, June 11, 1938

Dear Inge,

Many thanks for your letters. It's only now that I've summoned up the peace of mind to write to you, and even now I don't feel like being profound. You know what I've been through in the last few days. That puts me under an obligation to thank you all, and you especially.

I had a glorious vacation at Ulm. We went swimming in the Iller nearly every day. The party usually consisted of Fritz, Anneliese, Erika, Sophie, Werner, Lisl, and myself. One morning I got up before sunrise (it was Lisa's birthday) and watched the birds on a deserted Danube marsh. Another time we spent the evening at Erika's and she played to us. It was very beautiful, because it was so personal. . . .

I'm doing a lot of fencing.[14] I've now acquired a foil of my own. I've a great deal of respect for my fencing master. Yesterday I bought a book on Renée Sintenis.[15] I plan to give it to Lisa. I read it from cover to cover at a sitting. I can thoroughly recommend it to you. Its views on the modern woman are simply splendid.

I'm spending tomorrow with Lisa.

I'll write again soon.

Yours,

Hans

To his sister Inge, Stetten, June 27, 1938

Dear Inge,

Our squadron is back in the training area again. We've already been on a field exercise lasting several days. I'm in a billet for the first time since I joined up. That's an important chapter in our military career. When you've been slogging hard all day and come back to a nice billet in the evening, tired out, dirty, and sweaty, to find the table set and the bed made up, it's really glorious.

I haven't been home for quite a while. Something always crops up. I've spent a lot more time at Leonberg instead. . . .

I often see Mathilde[16] in Stuttgart. We've already become close friends, in fact, not that I meant us to. It just happened that way.

I'll probably hike down to the Danube Valley a couple of times in the next few days and swim there. I love the scenery, just as I love alpine scenery too.

I'll pay you a visit when I get some furlough after maneuvers.

I keep a rosebud in my breast pocket. I need that little flower because it's the other side of the coin, far removed from soldiering but not at odds with a soldierly frame of mind. You should always carry a little secret around with you, especially when you're with comrades like mine.

Lots of love,

Hans

P.S. Can you let me have the camera for a couple of weeks? I'll return it as soon as maneuvers are over. . . .

To his parents, Stetten, June 28, 1938

Dear Parents,

We've already settled in comfortably on the Heuberg. Having steeled myself to endure sweltering heat, I was pleasantly surprised. The sun shines all day long, but "a cool breeze is blowing!" The scenery is exceptionally beautiful. Our trip to the Heuberg and three days of maneuvers have been a novel experience. I'm always cheerful and in good spirits these days.

We fired off some live ammunition this afternoon. My ears are still buzzing. . . .

In other respects I might be on the moon at present. Politics, etc., don't exist on the Heuberg. I haven't seen a paper for weeks. What are things coming to?

We chew over military matters the whole time, of course, and debate what form this or that development will take in the next war. Very few of my comrades stop to wonder why there should be a war at all. The majority would march blindly off without a word, animated by a certain curiosity or spirit of adventure. The masses . . . I detest the concept more and more.

No need to send me any laundry, Mother.

All my love,

Hans

On September 30, 1938, Britain, France, Italy, and Germany signed the so-called Munich Agreement. To preserve the peace, the Western Powers had acquiesced in what Hitler claimed to be his last territorial demand and sanctioned the Third Reich's annexation of Czech frontier areas with predominantly German-speaking inhabitants. After ratification of the agreement, on October 1, 1938, German troops marched into the Sudetenland.

To his sister Inge, Bruchsal, October 21, 1938

My dear Inge,

Now that all the excitements of recent weeks are over, I've the time to write to you. I don't find letter writing easy, though.

I've never been such a patriot, in the true sense, as I was in the early days of October this year. Only when you're compelled to wonder if the Fatherland still means as much as it may once have done – only when you've lost all faith in banners and speeches because prevailing ideas have become trite and worthless – does true idealism assert itself.

Thank you so much for the splendid birthday present.

I look forward to seeing you again at Ulm in November.

My squadron moved to Bruchsal yesterday. I myself and a few other members of the regiment are being assigned to the hospital at Ludwigsburg[17] on November 1st. I'll then be able to begin my studies[18] in the spring of 1939.

Last week I sat my reserve officer's exam.

I brought the Wiechert book from a friend of Wiechert's in Stuttgart. It's the last copy of this edition and won't be reprinted. He told me that W. is free again, but his latest book is banned from publication.[19]

The fall has taken possession of our hearts, too. It's irresistible, but never mind – spring will come around again!

See you soon!

Yours,
Hans

Hans Scholl completed his basic military service on November 1, 1938, but had to qualify for permission to study medicine by attending an army medical corps course. He was assigned to the base hospital at Tübingen.

To his parents, Tübingen, November 4, 1938

Dear Parents,

I'm now at Tübingen. There isn't much to tell, really. All we've done to date is twiddle our thumbs for a day or two. I've been assigned as an officer's orderly. Later on I'll go to the various departments. We switch around every two weeks. We haven't had our corporal's pay yet, I'm afraid, and we temporarily had to shell out the rail fare from Bruchsal to Tübingen, so please send me some money so I can come home Sunday (provided I'm not on duty). . . .

I like it at Tübingen.

Fond love,
Hans

To his parents, Tübingen, November 8, 1938

Dear Parents,

I'm back into my routine again, though I don't think I have a routine in the conventional sense. Every day brings me something new, every morning the new day wears a different face, and at night, when you briefly sum it all up in your mind, you realize you've gained yet another new experience, absorbed a new image, encountered another fellow creature – yes, and above all nature, which makes more mature people of us.

I read Binding's book[20] about Goethe's influence on the present and thoroughly endorse your views, Father.

A profound experience held me spellbound today. It almost took my breath away for a moment, and I briefly felt everything go black before my eyes. E.K.v.B.[21] died last night, and I was present when they performed an autopsy on him. You have to forget all personal factors at such a moment. You mustn't reflect that you knew the person once, that you spent whole days in his company – even that a small proportion of our long life marched in step with his. And now they're ripping that person's body open and looking for the cause of his death.

Yes, the fall has arrived, and one mustn't blind oneself to the fact. That bleak word means more than just the falling of withered leaves, more than wild, windswept skies – more, too, than the delicate veils of mist that enshroud everything in melancholy. It means dying itself. The dying [you] can't evade because you're still young and believe in the return of spring. You have to pass through this process of dying, which doesn't, after all, mean death itself.

I'd like to spend a moment alone with Dore[22] and say something consoling, but I can't.

Last night I attended a philosophical lecture on the Hellenistic age (Professor Rückert[23]). . . .

I probably won't be coming to Ulm next Sunday.

Fond love,

Hans

To his father, Tübingen, November 21, 1938

. . . I'm quite enjoying the hospital at present. I'm already learning a few things. We have one or two very nice doctors who are doing their reserve course here. I'm trying hard to pick up all I can. Last week I stood in for a nurse who'd gone on leave for a few days. . . .

To his parents, Tübingen, December 6, 1938

Dear Parents,

Thank you for your big parcel. I'm now equipped with everything I'll need till I can finally come to Ulm again.

It's very sad not to be able to celebrate Christmas with the family, but there's a fundamental difference between now and last winter. Tending the sick is a great and humanitarian occupation, and a healthy person like me should be glad and grateful for the chance to help others, so even this Christmas will be a festive occasion for me.

All the same, I hope to be able to visit Ulm once before Christmas.

I'm in a very contented atmosphere at present. We have time to think of ourselves and live better than we did in barracks. . . .

Today I watched an operation. It was extremely interesting. I didn't feel queasy, not even for a moment, the way people say you do. Here as elsewhere, you've simply got to have the right mental approach.

I won't be needing any more laundry before Christmas. The stores have issued me a lot of shirts and underpants, which is a great improvement.

I had to get up twice in the night. Then I slept with the patients, who woke me at 4 a.m. because they were in such pain. I don't feel tired, though. I'm determined to fight fatigue. It's all a question of habit, nothing more. . . .

To his parents, Tübingen, December 8, 1938

Dear Parents,

I won't be able to come home next Sunday either, so please send me the papers I need for Munich. They're as follows: graduation diploma, certificate of Aryan descent, Hitler Youth report. I'll send in my application from here. I doubt if the summer semester of 1939 will be too heavily subscribed. Most [of the applicants] will probably be ex-servicemen.

In my [last] letter I forgot to thank you for the 20 marks, Father. I do so now. They'll come in very handy.

Today I watched an appendectomy. I haven't had any real time off for two weeks, but the time passes quickly. A friend is helping me with my Latin.[24] It's going pretty well so far. I wish you all a really enjoyable Sunday.

Yours,

Hans

To his parents, Tübingen, December 18, 1938

Dear Parents,

Another Sunday has gone by, the fourth in Advent, and I wasn't at home. I haven't been idle, but things are quite different at home. Today I went for a grand walk in the bitterly cold, crystal-clear winter air. I love this weather so much, I can't stay cooped up in a warm room. I expect you celebrated this last pre-Christmas Sunday in a fitting manner.

It's all so different from a year ago, but I can't help brooding on the year that has gone by since then. Have I really improved? Have all my efforts borne fruit and resulted in progress? Many things have changed, but there are times when you feel petty and ridiculous in your human frame. You'd like to shake off all your constraints and enter another world, free and lucid.

I'm so much looking forward to my Christmas furlough. It's lousy, not being able to spend Christmas Eve at home, but there's nothing to be done. I'll celebrate just the same. You can, even on your own.

I would urge Werner to see to the skiing equipment. All the skis should have the old dirt scraped right off and then be freshly tarred. Straps greased, etc. Inge will handle the rest. She's best at it, after all.

Is it really true about Kammerer[25] (Jewish lackey, etc.)? A friend told me.

I shall be writing to Captain Scupin for Christmas. I don't have his home address, so I'll write to his official address.

I'll write again before Christmas.

> Fond love,
> Hans

After successfully completing his course at Tübingen – a postcard to his parents dated January 12, 1939, casually states: "We passed our exam, by the way" – Hans Scholl enrolled in April as a full-time student at Munich's Ludwig Maximilian University for the summer semester of 1939.

To his parents, Munich, April 17, 1939

Dear Parents,

Inge's parcel just turned up. Many thanks.

My first two days of work are over. You can't imagine how happy I am in my new existence. I'm really coming to life again.

There's a couch in my room. I was pleased about it to begin with, but now it's become useless to me, because I won't have time to pamper myself.

The best lecture to date was one of the compulsory lectures on botany. Zoology is very interesting too, though, and I'll most probably enroll for the (3-hour) zoology practicals on Friday afternoons. If I told my classmates everything I've put my name down for, they'd call me crazy. That means my tuition fees will be about 25 marks more than theirs, but it's definitely worth it. Knowledge is power. I'm enjoying Greek. At many lectures I'm the only medical student. All the rest are philosophers.

I really ought to have a complete edition of Nietzsche for my Nietzsche studies. Maybe you could get one secondhand somewhere, Father. . . . If not, forget about it and I'll make do with the library. I should also have an edition of Plato. There are so many things one ought to have. Today I bought myself a Greek textbook. Please send me my tracksuit right away, Mother, and the sweater. It's still quite chilly, sitting in my room at nights.

I've got some flowers in my room now, and a Sintenis picture on the wall, so it's beginning to look quite homey. I'm still short of a few things, though.

I'll try to look up Ernst Wiechert this Sunday. He lives quite near Munich. The Sunday after that I hope to be back in Ulm.

Fond love,

Hans

No evidence of a meeting with Ernst Wiechert has yet been found, but Inge Aicher-Scholl recalls her brother mentioning that he had been profoundly impressed by a brief encounter with Wiechert. The Nietzsche studies Hans referred to became an important topic of conversation. According to Otl Aicher, Friedrich Nietzsche's philosophy was frequently debated by Hans Scholl and his circle of friends from Ulm. Their discussions centered on three points: the interpretation of friendship as a cardinal human virtue, the doctrine of the great individuals whose duty it was to resist all deindividualizing tendencies in the age of the herd, and the doctrine "God is dead." The latter was not construed as an atheistic slogan, but reinterpreted into a prediction that God would die in a church that backed an inhuman regime.

To his parents, Munich, May 6, 1939

Dear Parents,

Delighted with the parcel, just received, and want to thank you right away.

The histology textbook pleased me most of all, of course.

Now I'll have to buy myself an anatomy book as well. That'll cost 16 marks. I'll buy it here. I definitely need these books for my work, I realize that now. Lectures on their own aren't enough. You can't write everything down, and the lectures omit to say a lot of things that would interest one.

It rained again today, really horribly. I came back soaked to the skin and got changed at once. Cycling in this weather is out of the question.

In your next parcel, please send me a few shorthand pads and my raincoat (because of all the rain).

I always keep a careful note of my expenditure (though it's an effort sometimes). I'm not being extravagant, believe me. I've organized things so I can manage fine on 80 pfennigs a day for food. (Provided, of course, that there's no break in food supplies from home like tea, coffee, butter, and so on.)

On top of that I need 20 pfennigs for writing materials and books. Sometimes, of course, biggish items of expenditure crop up when I have to buy myself something new.

What my room needs now is a floor lamp. One's eyes need a decent light, so it wouldn't just be a luxury. This is very important to me because I do a lot of reading at night.

I'd love to come home on Sunday, but I don't know if my finances will run to it. Maybe there's some way of coming, other than by train.

Fondest love,
Hans

*During university vacation Hans Scholl was assigned to "volun-
tary harvesting" in Masuria (East Prussia, now part of Poland).
Inge Aicher-Scholl recalls how batches of students were hauled
off to East Prussia by train. Pinned to one of the freight cars
was a cardboard notice ridiculing the "voluntary" nature of this
vacation work.*

To his parents, Grabnik, July 23, 1939

Dear Parents,

I got to Grabnik (Masuria) after an interminable train
journey. I'm lodging with a farmer who owns around 200 acres.
I have to work hard, but the beautiful countryside and the
horses are ample compensation. I can go riding every day. Still, I
wish these three weeks would soon be up because I'm itching to
take to the road, free and footloose.

If you can possibly send me my knapsack, please put in my
sneakers and sports shirts. I won't get any time to read here.
We work till nine at night. These Masurian farmers can be a
real headache. I've seldom come across a breed of Germans
more obsessed with their own idiosyncrasies. There's a lot of
schnapps drunk here.

It's Sunday today. Everyone's asleep. We fed the horses earlier
on, and I climbed aboard a wonderful mare and rode myself
awake, because I was terribly tired. This afternoon, if it doesn't
rain, I'll stroll down to the lakes for a swim. You can't imagine
how much I long for a bath. The local girls are lovely to look at,
but their homes are as dirty as they themselves are easy on the
eye. We finished cutting the barley yesterday. Next week we'll
get it in.

The atmosphere here in East Prussia is strangely warlike. You
can sense that the fear bred by countless Cossack raids runs
in these people's blood, and that they're ready to defend themselves to the hilt.

I hope I'll soon get another chance to write to you. Wish Sophie a good trip[26] from me. You must have finished berry picking by now, Mother.

Fond love,

Hans

Sophie Scholl

1937–1939

Born on May 9, 1921, Sophie Scholl was in her seventh year at a girls' secondary school at Ulm in November 1937, when the first of these letters was written. As the sister of Hans, who stood accused of subversive activities connected with the banned Bündische Jugend, she had that month been interviewed for the first time by the Gestapo.

Fritz Hartnagel, to whom this first letter is written, was a close friend of the young Scholls. Sophie had met Fritz at the home of Annelies Kammerer, a classmate, in 1937. Four years her senior, Fritz was a budding army officer. In 1938, after graduating from the military academy at Potsdam, he received his lieutenant's commission and was assigned to Augsburg. In the course of time, he and Sophie developed a friendship that meant a great deal to them both.

Also mentioned here are Annelies's parents: Herr Kammerer was the Ulm photographer ostracized for continuing to serve Jewish customers.

Sophie with her friend Erika, during her days in the BDM, 1937

To Fritz Hartnagel, Ulm, November 29, 1937

Dear Fritz,

Don't go getting conceited if we write to you again so soon, but we're bored stiff, and anyway, we've got a favor to ask you. The thing is, Frau Kammerer will be coming to see my mother this week, and then they'll talk about the winter camp and whether or not to let their daughters go. Only we (Scholls and Annelies) will be going. Then we'll bump into you by chance

(Herr Kammerer mustn't get to hear). Could you book us in at the Schindelberg?[27] Then you can book yourselves in at the same place, but so our parents never find out. Could you manage that? Write back as soon as possible, or we'll have to postpone Frau K.'s visit. . . .

The glass door was locked when we got home Saturday morning (it never is as a rule). We quaked and trembled and boldly rang the bell. My father peeked out of the window, thinking it was the Gestapo. He was so agreeably surprised to find it was only us, we didn't get told off.

Inge [Sophie's eldest sister] has her party on December 8th. Will you be coming? As my partner, or better still, with Scharlo.[28] Let us know about Schindelberg promptly.

It's *so* boring here.

Sofie Scholl

To Fritz Hartnagel, Ulm, February 26, 1938

. . . I'm in bed already, and I've even been to sleep and had a dream. I dreamed I was camping (usually I dream I'm on the move). Beside the camp was a big lake. In the evening I went to see a woman who owned a boat. We sailed out across the lake. Night had fallen by then. The sky was completely overcast, and in front of a bank of cloud was the moon, a big, pale disk shedding its light all over the lake. Shedding isn't the right word, actually, because the whole of the lake was such a dull gray. Nothing special about that, but some distance from the moon a little red dot was glowing through the clouds. "That's the sun," the woman told me. "We live in the only place on earth where you can see the sun and the moon at the same time." That's all I remember. They say dreams depend on the noises you hear in your sleep. Maybe it's true. Anyway, I enjoy dreaming. [In dreams] I live in a peculiar world where I'm never entirely happy, but still. Please don't think me dreamy or sentimental. I try hard not to be – in fact I'm very materialistic. . . .

Sophie's letter of April 21 was written the day after Hitler's birthday, celebrated throughout the Reich with parades and demonstrations.

To Fritz Hartnagel, Ulm, April 21, 1938

Dear Fritz,

Although Lisel [Sophie's sister Elisabeth] says this bedroom lighting will ruin my eyesight, here I am writing to you. On her paper, did she but know it. She thinks I'm writing up my diary, but I'd sooner write to you. Does it matter?

It's back to school again, worse luck, so I was beavering away today. I also painted half the kitchen furniture. Maybe it'll still be noticeable when you come. I knew at once you wouldn't come on Wednesday. When you say "maybe" it's as good as saying "I'm pretty sure I won't be coming." Was there a parade at Augsburg too? We watched with the rest of the school. Lisa [Remppis] has gone again, which is a shame. Still, I've got more nice people around me than you do. Will you be coming over sometime in April? Inge's off on the 30th.

Next day:

School's over, but I'm in a foul temper. Whenever I grouch about my family to Annelies she laughs like hell. I was so furious I pinched another three sheets of Lisel's writing paper. She hasn't spotted it yet. I also bit through Inge's necklace, but none of this did anything for my temper, I'm afraid. If you turned up now, I'm sure I'd be in a good mood.

After clearing up the kitchen: You see, work makes life sweet. Inge wasn't in as bad a mood as I thought. She helped me with the washing up, and we concocted some words and music while we were at it. I shall miss her. . . .[29] We've gotten on very well, and I shall definitely be homesick for her. She's looked after me in all kinds of ways, as you know. Who's going to bother about me and my foibles now? I'm growing up myself. I'll go into town with her and we'll try to make the men blush. Because Werner [Sophie's younger brother] says girls blush if a man so much as looks at them.

In school I wrote Lisa a letter and slipped it into the atlas that Werner now has in school with him. He's bound to read it, which will be embarrassing for me. Kismet.

If you aren't coming on Sunday, write to me for once. I always have such a funny feeling. It's as if I can sense every last field and forest between Ulm and Augsburg. . . .

It's so cold here, I can't even go out. That's why I'm feeling so sour. Letter writing is quite fun. I can write to you (you needn't read it) without your interrupting me. That's the boring part of it too, though. I'm just developing a really silly kind of hand-writing – had you noticed? I'd think it was sweet of you if you read the whole of this letter – if you read as far as here. Take care, what I'd like to do best of all now is pinch or bite you to wake you up again. I always do that to Annelies in school when it gets boring. If you have the time and the inclination you can write me some far more boring letters than mine – I'll read them just the same. Hey, you've got to read the sentence before this one.

When I picture you at this moment, I see you grinning, and that's why I'd like to slap you really hard. You're not to grin at me, you hear? Kindly look serious. I think you're still grinning but that would be lousy of you. I wouldn't want anything more to do with you. It's so silly, your not answering me. Even though I've got a vivid imagination, I can't hear you answer properly. How I'd like to slap you! Know something? Take some time off – you can, being a lieutenant – and write to me. You can write anything you like, absolute rubbish even, and I'll read it patiently. If you've read this far, you'll simply have to write to me. If you aren't coming in April, you can at least send your regards to Inge. Lucky this letter is going in an envelope or I'd make utter fools of you and me both. I must mail this now, so so long and best regards and I'll be seeing you or reading you (reading would be nice).

Yours,
Sofie

To Fritz Hartnagel, Ulm, May 23, 1938

. . . Are you ever irritated by the tripe I write? (a) Anger makes a person old and ugly, and (b) you're four years older, four years smarter, four years better, four years worse, and four years more experienced than me. Am I aiming too high? . . .

To her sister Inge, Ulm, July 8, 1938

Dear Inge,

It's remarkable, my writing to you again so soon. I can't wait to get out on the sea. We're going with Herr Kammerer, as you know, and Mother will be writing to you as soon as we know more details. Perhaps you'll get my letter by Sunday. I've just come from Erika's.[30] If I'd known it wasn't suppertime yet, I'd have stayed outside, there's such a splendid gale. It blows your hair forward, and you can lean back comfortably without falling over. A grand storm. I've already been swimming a lot. I can even do a racing dive. Though not perfectly, of course. I've adored being outside lately. It's fun being so small when the trees are so big. I'm looking forward a lot to the heath and the moors. We plan to stay at Worpswede youth hostel.

Annelis Kammerer has gone off to Vienna for four days by car with Herr Kammerer. You'll be seeing her as well in two weeks' time. A pity Erika can't come too. I might have enjoyed Erika's company more, personally, but one mustn't be selfish. Anyway, I realize Erika and Annelies and Lisa would be a bad combination. I see Annelis every day, and it's often quite an effort for me to stomach her at all. In school the other day I simply let fly. We were dissecting a fish in class for Fräulein Fries,[31] whom I admire more and more. It's a very tricky, tiring job, and we were only allowed to do it as a special treat. After three hours I was exhausted. The other three were watching, or not watching as the case may be. "You're lazy as hell," I told them. "Oh, Sofie!" Annelis said irritably. After that she kept on giggling, and when I asked the reason, she said, "At you!" And when I asked why she said, "Never you mind." That really infuriated me. If she had to laugh at me, I told her, she should do it unobtrusively because it wasn't polite. We often have scenes like that. The atmosphere between us is so strained, I keep thinking it's going to snap. I hope Annelis doesn't notice. Sometimes we have such a nice time together, it cancels all our squabbles out. I always tell myself, stick it out till you're over the hump. It would do Annelis good to do the same thing. I find her rather casual these days.

I'm so looking forward to it all, especially the scenery and the sea and seeing you. Are the two Eggers girls[32] coming too? Please write and tell me, also about the island: what kind it's likely to be, camping facilities, etc. We've got four or five shelter halves, if you ever feel like sleeping under canvas yourself. We go camping on the Teufelsmoor too, etc. After the trip I'm going to put in some solid sketching with Erika, and if Mother spends a few days at Backnang, Erika will stay with me. That'll be fun, too.

I don't draw much these days. We learn to draw quite nicely in school, even though our art mistress is mediocre and very young. Still, we've stopped turning out trash, the way we did with Herr Unger.[33] We're definitely making progress. I'd like to go on with art like our teacher. I must stop asking myself so many questions. I'm learning, that's the main thing. The rest should come by itself, shouldn't it? I don't have a sense of vocation or anything like that, but anyone who wants to be an

Sophie Scholl at age eleven or twelve

artist must become a human being first and foremost. From the bottom up. I'm going to try and work on myself. It's very difficult. I'm terribly shallow compared to Erika.

This afternoon I read a fairy story by Kyber:[34] "Alräunchen" – it was very fine. And "Der grosse Augenblick." They're rather sad stories, especially the latter. Have you ever read them?

Did Mother mention when she wrote that Fritz Hartnagel is being transferred to Vienna on August 15?

Biology is tremendous fun these days. I've already dissected an ox eye. And when I did the fish I displayed the inner parts, viscera, organs, etc., so beautifully. The brain and the head as well. The whole of the outer wall had been folded down, and everything lay there looking so neat and firm and functional. And imagine, the heart was still going in and out, in and out, quite slowly and steadily. Fish have golden eyes and lovely, absolutely circular lenses. Awfully nice little creatures. I felt so sorry for them.

I'm going to mail this right away.

Lots of love,
Sofie

To Fritz Hartnagel, Ulm, August 28, 1938

Dear Fritz,

I just received the letter listing all your suspected ailments. Many thanks. For the letter, of course. I'm terribly sorry for you, not that it'll help. Just get better soon.

I'm in bed myself at present. It's around 11 a.m., or getting on for noon. The fact is, term starts tomorrow, and I have to have one last really good lie-in, though I do that nearly every day. I don't need it, either, because I've made a brilliant recovery. I do it just the same, for love of my dear old bed. —This vacation has seemed incredibly short – shorter than the Easter vacation, even though I've seen and done so much. Can you bear me to write at such length? If not, please put this letter away at once. If so, here goes. It was raining when we left, but as soon as we were installed in the car (me up front beside Herr Kammerer, him swathed in masses of clothes and swallowing pills because I had a bit of a sore throat and a temperature), the sun felt obliged to put its head out and send us its hottest rays. Perhaps it did so out of curiosity. We then drove all afternoon till 9:30, when we reached Giessen. Herr Kammerer is a careful driver. I went to the youth hostel, where we hadn't booked. Some boys promptly appeared and offered us candies, which I naturally didn't spurn. There wasn't a bed left, but they fixed us up with some mattresses on the floor. It was all very nice. The next day we drove on to Bremen, or rather Lesum [where Inge was working for the Eggers]. A total of three blowouts en route. I tell you, it took us 1–2 hours to find Franz-Seldtestrasse in that dump. Inge had gone to bed by the time we got there. She greeted us in semi-High German, which sent Lisa into hysterics.

Three days later we set off. We enjoyed everything immensely, especially the North Sea, to the point of nausea. Only Inge and I, that is. Lisa and I went in one trawler, Inge and Annlis and Has [Werner's nickname] in another. It was 3 a.m. and still quite dark when we split up, and Lisa and I were frightfully annoyed when four Hitler Youth leaders and a young married couple joined us because their fisherman was sick. There wasn't a star to be seen by the time we were out among the mud flats, and once we got beyond the islands the sun came up. It was terribly cold, mainly because of the wind, and Lisa and I cuddled the smokestack. We couldn't stand the young married couple. When the wife started throwing up after three hours, we pinched one another with glee. We went on stuffing ourselves with rolls and watching the sea change color. The young husband brusquely ordered us aft. Though indignant, we went. There lay his wife, weeping and weary of life. We tossed her a few consoling words. Then

Sophie at seventeen, 1938

Lisa asked if we could go forward again, and permission was granted. We also had a chat with the boys, who turned out to be very nice. The smallest of them was equally pale and speechless. I was glad that he, at least, was ahead of me in that respect. Then they hauled in the nets for the first time, and we looked on with interest, fingering every little fish and collecting all the crabs together for a crab war. We also gathered up the starfish. The fish, etc., were thrown back into the sea and wolfed by gulls even before they hit the water. The big crabs were boiled right away, and the steam smelled revolting. I was careful not to sit down on principle, but it didn't help. We sang as best we could, anything that came into our heads. Heave-ho and haul away, my hearties – things like that. . . . I suddenly found my mouth full of spit, but I managed to gulp it down. Before long, Gustav and I were draped over the rail side by side. . . . But we sang on lustily afterward and didn't let it show. I hung over the rail another five times until nothing was coming up but gastric juices. It didn't matter a bit, though – we were still in high spirits. In the end everyone lay down on deck like herrings and slept. Sea voyages are fun. . . . We got back at three o'clock. I'm sure Werner told you all about it. A farmer drove us from Wilhelmshaven to Caro- linensiel (that bit we did by car). We told him we came from the south of Germany. He said he had an Austrian refugee lodging with him. Just then a calf ran across the road. "Where did he come from?" asked Inge, meaning the refugee. "That field there," he replied, meaning the calf. "Oh," said Inge, "was he a prisoner of war?" To which the farmer replied, "Here comes another," and another calf ran across the road. Has and I, who were sitting behind, split our sides laughing. There were lots of amusing inci- dents like that. We spent another five days at Worpswede. It was absolutely marvelous. Now I resent not being there. All I've done is talk about our trip. I love wallowing in memories best of all. I could write a big fat book about the trip.

I've been talking about myself all the time. Are you doing much reading while you're ill? I'm reading Thomas Mann's *Buddenbrooks* at present and enjoying it a lot. He takes a very objective view of his characters and paints them as superior types, but not arrogant. Do you know it?

I'm looking forward to the letter you promised me. I know so little about you these days. I guess it must be seven weeks since we saw one another.

Get well soon and lots of love,
Sofie

To Fritz Hartnagel, Ulm, September 24, 1938

Dear Fritz,

It's eight o'clock Saturday evening. Do you realize what a nice time that is? The nicest in the whole week, as a rule, because I can think of tomorrow without the slightest qualm, and as for thinking about the day after that, it's beyond me.

Hans turned up today, and we celebrated his birthday after the event. We still have the whole evening ahead of us. We may spend it at Annlis's. It's absolutely glorious how free we are to dispose of our time. The week has flown by. Time just runs away with me, and I'm staggered at my own effrontery. I'm simply not keeping up with my work. That's to say, work probably isn't the right word, we waste so much time jabbering. I'm sorry for you, having to lie so still. Maybe you can make up for it by improving your knowledge of literature.

We're still having some wonderful fall days here. I often go walking in the woods. The Illerwald is at its loveliest in spring and fall. I also go canoeing with Oskar sometimes, but I'm always so tortured with gnat bites the next day, I spend half the night scratching.

Annlis just called to say her mother has brought up some wine and fizz from the cellar – imagine. Times could be a lot harder.

To be honest, I'd much prefer to spend the evening away on a trip than at Annlis's. I've just been reading one of Inge's letters, and now I'm all nostalgic again. We're very lucky, being able to take off every vacation. I pity all the people who've never enjoyed that kind of experience, but the truth is, I'd begrudge it them. I can't help recalling how Inge and I tramped along the road across the moor, and how we got out the guitar and sang, just like that, and didn't give a hoot about the silly faces of the puzzled passersby.

It's suppertime now, so may I wish you *bon appétit* too?
Also, thank you for your last letter.

Sofie

*Sophie and Fritz had planned a trip to Yugoslavia in the
summer of 1939, but this was thwarted by a foreign exchange
embargo and the banning of foreign travel by young people in the
months immediately preceding the outbreak of war.*

To Fritz Hartnagel, Ulm, July 28, 1939

. . . I just got your letter. I'm not too surprised. I might possibly
have obtained a passport because the Obergau [regional headquarters of the Senior Girls' Hitler Youth organization] might
graciously have granted me permission. The RJF [Reich Youth
Directorate] won't, because there's a total ban on foreign
travel. In other words, young people aren't being allowed to go
abroad at this critical stage. Well, we'd better kiss Yugoslavia
goodbye. . . .

*Instead of going south, they embarked at short notice on a trip
to the north: first to Heiligenhafen on the Baltic, then to the
North Sea coast, and finally to Worpswede, the artists' colony
near Bremen where Sophie had spent some days with her sister
Inge the year before. Then she had made the acquaintance of
Manfred Hausmann, Wilhelm Scharrelmann, Martha Vogeler,
and Clara Westhoff-Rilke. She was now introduced to the paintings of Paula Modersohn-Becker.*

To her sister Inge, Worpswede, August 9, 1939

. . . We've often been to Frau Vogeler's weaving mill.[35] She's a
very friendly woman, and lets us come whenever we like. It's an
interesting place, with plenty to see in the way of furniture and
pictures and fabrics. She also has whole drawers full of Vogeler's

sketches. I find them impressive, but not half as much as I did last year. I'm crazy about Paula Modersohn's work,[36] on the other hand. She developed a tremendously original style for a woman, and her paintings aren't derivative of anyone in particular. You must see them all. After hers, the rest of the pictures in the exhibition just floated past me.

There are some lovely things in Hamburg too, though. Masses of French stuff and a roomful of Corinths.[37] I've seen a great deal in a couple of weeks.

We paid another visit to the Hamme last night – my last with Fritz. The landscape made a deep impression on me, it was so dark and peaceful, but in general I'd prefer to be in the highlands, with South Germans. I can't get close to North Germans, which is why I'm looking forward to Ulm again. . . .

When Fritz had to rejoin his unit, Sophie moved back into the youth hostel at Worpswede. There her decision to return to Ulm earlier than planned was reinforced by an unpleasant incident.

To Fritz Hartnagel, Worpswede youth hostel, August 1939

Dear Fritz,

I'm sending you the two books, also Hanspeter's.[38] It's no good to me now. While we were gone, a man slept in my bed and looked through the books. He proposed to go to the police at once and report us. Frau Ötken[39] managed to stop him because we're her guests, but you know yourself what the Ötkens are like. Now they're taking an interest in my books and becoming very suspicious. Oh, well, we're off tomorrow. It's all to the good.

Many thanks for the cash – it'll come in very handy. The money from my parents hasn't turned up yet.

Now we'll be seeing one another again soon.

Lots of love,

Sofie

To her sister Elisabeth, Ulm, August 19, 1939

Dear Lisl,

You're bound to be surprised that this letter is coming from Ulm, not Worpswede. The fact is, I'd never have done any drawing at Worpswede, and Hanspeter's *Peter Pan*[40] would never have gotten itself illustrated there. Here I have a table of my own — one I can do what I like on. Besides, you know what conclusion I came to at Worpswede? That Württemberg is a thoroughly delightful (scenically) and varied part of the world, and that I know where I am with Swabians. I still don't know how to behave with people from North Germany. But you mustn't think I didn't like Worpswede anymore. The village is nothing special in itself. Its inhabitants are extremely amusing, though some of them put on airs, and a lot of new buildings are going up. But the Hamme, the moor, and the plain are the same as ever. The place has a unique atmosphere at night, all peaceful and melancholy.

I went swimming in the North Sea and the Baltic. I fell in love with the North Sea all over again. The breakers were simply terrific. I'd feel as if I was in seventh heaven, bobbing around on the waves, if only the salt water didn't keep disillusioning me so cruelly.

Inge's off to the Black Forest. She needs it. I may possibly be going to Zurich with Father and Mother. I'd like that, because I could look at some more pictures there. . . .

Two weeks later, on September 1, 1939, Hitler invaded Poland. Britain and France declared war on Nazi Germany two days later. Fritz Hartnagel was assigned to Calw as adjutant of a signals unit attached to the Army Staff on the Upper Rhine front while Sophie prepared for her last semester in school. Herman Vinke, in his The Short Life of Sophie Scholl,[41] *cites Dr. Else*

Fries's statement that, when war broke out and Sophie's friends were drafted, she made them promise never to pull the trigger on another human being.

To Fritz Hartnagel, Ulm, September 5, 1939

Dear Fritz,

Many thanks for your letter. I hope I won't have to wait so long for the next one. There are few things worse than being permanently in the dark about someone, if only about where he is. Did you get my last letter from Ulm? (Frau Vogeler's dress was also sent to you in Munich, but no matter.)

You and your men must have plenty to do now. I just can't grasp that people's lives are now under constant threat from other people. I'll never understand it, and I find it terrible. Don't go telling me it's for the Fatherland's sake.

I hope you're well. Your job isn't all that dangerous, is it?

Hans is still here, which I'm very glad of. I've already started worrying about him.

In other respects, everything goes on here much as usual. Hans and I go swimming every morning. We're also sketching a good deal, doing the old houses on Münsterplatz in color, which gives us a lot of fun. No doubt you'll find that hard to imagine.

School hasn't started yet, of course, and who knows when it will?

I often think of you. Summer seems ages ago. I can hardly believe we spent it together. Remember how we used to sit in that beach chair at Heiligenhafen? Doesn't it make you laugh?

Where exactly are you, or aren't you allowed to say, and what are they giving you to do?

I hope you'll be able to write me soon.

All the best,
Sofie

To Fritz Hartnagel, Ulm, September 19, 1939

My dear Fritz,

Thank you very much for your letters. I was so pleased to get them. I meant to write you one for Sunday, but it wouldn't have reached you in time. How are things at your end? Still quiet? Hans is back at work again.[42] Perhaps you saw that they're going to fit three semesters into one year. Hans has already calculated that he'll be through by the time he's twenty-three and a half. I often went swimming with him while he was here, and we generally sketched together as well. I'm naturally going to finish off *Peter Pan* and the other illustrations,[43] because I don't see why people should be restricted to the grimmest and most ghastly subjects in wartime. Not that the war is particularly noticeable here, aside from the fact that we aren't exactly living off the fat of the land and the city's swarming with soldiers. Incidentally, the other day we saw an airplane swoop on the cathedral and zoom over it a couple of times. It looped the loop, right above the city, and then zoomed off. It was the first enemy plane we'd seen (a French reconnaissance plane). They forced it down near Leipheim.

We aren't giving in to the hope that the war can be brought to a speedy end, even though people here cherish the childish belief that Germany will blockade England into quitting. We shall see.

Lisl is ill at the moment. She had a high temperature yesterday. The weather has changed so quickly. Is it very noticeable where you are? There's no more swimming either. (Important to me!)

One can't talk properly about anything anymore. It all sounds absurd, and it must sound especially so to you. If I tell you that the flowers in the garden are getting brown-rimmed petals because of all the rain – all except the zinnias, which are still a mass of color – it must seem terribly remote to you, mustn't it? When I get some money again, I want to send you

Carossa's *Führing und Geleit*.[44] If you had a little time to spare I'm sure you'd enjoy it.

I hope you'll get some leave this Christmas at least, so I can pay off my debts. And for other reasons.

I'll look forward to getting a reply to this letter. Or is that expecting too much? After all, I've no idea what you do with your time.

Me, I just write to you whenever the mood takes me.

Lots of love,
Sofie

To Fritz Hartnagel, Ulm, October 6, 1939

My dear Fritz,

I'm sorry it's taken me so long to get around to writing another installment, but even though I'm only going to school, there's always plenty to do, what with laundry, window cleaning, etc.

I hope to be able to send you the photos soon. Even photographers are engaged in war work. We've now been back in school precisely two weeks, and today the fall vacation started. Sounds silly, doesn't it? I don't know what I'm going to do during the break – it all depends on Mother. The Nägeles have invited us to their weekend cottage at Murrhardt, and the three of us girls would love to cycle there. Maybe it'll come off. I'm set on the idea, but Mother's putting up some stiff opposition. She keeps reproaching me on account of my nice summer vacation.

Theater and concerts have restarted here. How are things with you? Are you completely cut off from civilian life and entertainment? I hope not. One gathers here that you're still having a reasonably quiet time.

Is there any hope of your getting some leave soon? Maybe it's only just about to start – in fact it's a fair assumption.

Things are bound to come to a head sooner or later. I'm glad Hans is able to go on studying. – Perhaps you'll have to change professions later on.

Goodness, I do find it terribly hard writing letters. It's quite different from talking. I only write so you won't think I forgot because I don't care. I very often think of the summer vacation my mother keeps on about. For instance, the way I slept beside you in the coach from Heiligenhafen to Kiel. I slept so unconcernedly in front of all those people. I often wonder, too, what sort of people you're with and who you're friendly with. You never write about that. Whom do you like best, for instance. Do you ever meet any women or children or girls, working in a prison cell the way you do? (Recently I dreamed that I was in a prison cell myself, incarcerated for the whole of the war. I had a heavy iron ring around my neck – that was the nastiest part of the dream.)

I hope I'll at least get a reply to every other letter of mine. Get your letter writing over quickly. It (your reply) needn't be long.

Does the army make a distinction between Sunday and weekdays? Either way, here's wishing you a nice one.

Yours,
Sofie

To Fritz Hartnagel, Ulm, October 27, 1939

. . . We've just been very peacefully drinking tea (our last, though) at the little round table in the living room, and we even spread some jam on our fruitcake, so you see, it's still just like peacetime. I hope you aren't going short. – I've always taken a great deal of pleasure in our nice apartment, and it's only now I notice what a wrench it is to have to economize. That may sound very superficial, but it matters a lot to me. Even by the North Sea, when we were only moving from place to place for a matter of days, I wound up longing for a bed and a room of my own. And doubly so at Worpswede, with the BDM [female branch of the Hitler Youth].[45] Anyway, we feel incredibly privileged in wartime, compared to you. I wish you could stay with us for a few days, or enjoy the house for a day or two. The next time we went away together, we'd rent some rooms that would be ours for those few days. Rooms we'd decorate ourselves with flowers. And anything we needed to eat, I could cook. (Nice illusion!) Does the idea appeal to you too? Only for a day or two, though, because I couldn't stick one person's company for too long. Don't misunderstand me, but if you spend the whole time with one person, he or she exerts too great an influence on you. Have you ever felt like cutting adrift from absolutely everyone? I think I get very touchy when someone makes demands on me. As you must know yourself, there are hours of solitude that compensate for all the days you've spent pining for someone. That's when ruthlessness (don't misconstrue the word) seems realistic and compassion weak. Not just compassion, but nostalgia too, or whatever you choose to call those emotions. There's every possibility that I'm weak. . . .

To Fritz Hartnagel, Ulm, November 7, 1939

My dear Fritz,

Thank you very much for your sweet letter. I'm always so pleased when you find the time to write to me. I hope you get the mail I send you. Please mention it sometimes in a letter. Do they open it?

If only you had nothing to do all winter but write, even if it was a bit stilted sometimes. I can well understand your needing something now to stop you from getting completely bogged down in your work. You may find the little Mörike book[46] a bit hard to read at present, but not because it's difficult stuff. There are times when I also feel like reading nothing but poetry, which puts so many things in a nutshell, but maybe it's a good thing to summon up the patience to read something else occasionally – something that doesn't directly concern yourself (a lyric poem, for instance). Then you have to pull yourself together and enter a completely different world that may not interest you at all. I think you emerge from it a rather different person afterward. I haven't read the book yet, but I'm very fond of Mörike. His poems are all I know.

I've still got one of the G. Heym illustrations[47] left to do. Hanspeter Nägele, who was here last Sunday, gave me the final nudge I needed to tackle his illustrations, too, in earnest. So it's true to say that my work really starts (modest though it is) when I get home from school.

I'm so glad Hans is still in Munich. I'm quite absurdly anxious about him for no reason at all, because he's in far less danger than you are, for instance. You I can think of with a perfectly easy mind, and I'm glad I can do so the way I want, without any commitment. It's nice when two people keep each other company without promising to meet up at such and such a place, or to stay together forever. They simply travel together awhile, and if their routes happen to diverge, they both go their way in peace. But that's just wishful thinking on my part. In reality, everything follows a far less pleasant course, with a lot of weariness and inertia. . . .

Hans Scholl

1939—1940

*When war broke out in September, Hans Scholl was in the midst
of "voluntary harvesting" in East Prussia. He caught the last
ship home across the Baltic, but his safety for the moment was
assured when he was granted a deferment to study medicine.*

Diary, September 20, 1939

If I didn't restrain myself I'd live entirely in accordance with my
own crazy notions.

    I went out to mail another letter to Thulla. She may get it
tomorrow, or the day after tomorrow at latest. A chill night
wind was blowing in my face outside. The night is very dark,
too, but it isn't a hard, remote kind of darkness – it envelops me
like a cloud. What will Thulla make of my letter when she reads
it? "Deep shadows are veiled in strange indifference," I wrote,
and by deep shadows I meant the war. When I received her
reply to an earlier letter telling me she gathered that I wanted
to go to the front, I knew she hadn't understood at all. It's something quite else, dearest Thulla – something you can't know. I
feel no desire for "heroism" in war. What I seek is purification.
I want all the shadows to melt away from me. I'm searching for
myself, just myself, because this much I do know: I'll only find

the truth inside me. We were glad at first that war had finally broken out. It's bound to bring release from the yoke. A yoke Germany has brought upon itself.

Perhaps this mass murder will go on for a long time. Perhaps the people of Europe are doomed to undergo a profound upheaval. Will we then rise a stage higher?

All our hopes are pinned on this frightful war!

Diary, undated [September/October 1939]

I reread some old letters today. Isn't that the finest form of relaxation, browsing over old love letters in the silence of your room when you come home tired after a long walk?

Ah, no! The old rover-cum-adventurer-cum-lumberjack[48] finds it too heartrending. His eyes smart, the corners of his mouth tremble, his cheeks burn. It assails his soul. He feels like weeping but can't anymore. Ah, restless one, stop delving into times gone by. Leave that till later on, when your feet are firmly planted on the ground.

I'm preoccupied with thoughts about man's relationship to Nature, or rather; is Nature true? I must do a lot more soul-searching and try to explore all the fundamental reasons.

A year ago I remarked to Lisa that forests show off in the fall because they know they'll soon be rearing their bare black branches into the cold winter sky. That's untrue. Vanity is foreign to nature. Human beings merely credit her with it – human beings, who view the world and make inferences from their own standpoint.

In October 1939 Hans Scholl embarked on his second semester, or rather trimester, as a medical student at Munich. All university courses having been shortened because of the war, the academic year was now divided into three terms instead of two.

To his parents, Munich, December 1, 1939

. . . Hectic activity reigns here. Everything's being crammed together because we're nearing the end [of term]. The semester ends on the 22nd of this month. You, too, may have read in the paper that they're going to retain the three-term year in 1940. Aside from being a strain on our health, it'll mean a heavy financial burden on our parents. However, it looks as if we won't be lucky enough to go on studying in the new year. Fresh divisions are now being formed, and they're drafting one student after another. Letters A–K are supposed to be called up on January 1. That would give me more time. . . .

The Christmas vacation won't amount to much because the new term starts on January 8. That being so, I'll probably take my Latin exam beforehand, which means I'll need a few hours' extra coaching from a teacher. Otherwise I won't make it.

I'll be staying in Munich on Sunday. There's so much work to get through.

Fondest love,

Hans

Hans Scholl was able to complete two trimesters before being drafted in March 1940. He was assigned to a Munich-based students' company.

To his parents, Munich, March 19, 1940

Dear Parents,

We heard today that we'll be staying in Munich for the present, but we're still the company on standby. To our universal regret, therefore, we've been reprieved for another two weeks. You can well imagine how disagreeable it is to have to fritter away our time in barracks. Will the war get going later on? Many here are already expressing the hope that it's gradually petering out. I take quite a different view. . . . If peace were suddenly concluded, the war would have lost its point, and every sacrifice would have been in vain.

We'll probably get some time off over the Easter vacation, but we won't be allowed to leave the military district. I shall probably go cycling in the vicinity with my friend. We may "touch" Tölz[49] again on our travels, though I already feel ashamed of always drinking the same people's coffee.[50] I plan to take them a few loaves of army bread to make up for all the cakes I devour. . . .

To his mother, Bad Tölz, March 22, 1940

Dear Mother,

Since your last letter was so full of sage exhortations, I'd better tell you how I spent Good Friday. You urged me to take Communion in some church or other. I couldn't, because that gesture doesn't redeem all a person's sins. It's just an outward rite whose significance I think I understand, and of which I approve because so many people derive a measure of relief from it.

Well, yesterday, the anniversary of Christ's death, I heard the *St. Matthew Passion.* I can't find words to convey the impact this work made on me, and anyway, it's a mistake to talk about profound religious emotions. However, you'll have guessed that the music touched me very deeply. A lot of things inside me were stirred and liberated, at least while I was listening to it. Afterward I went home happy, knowing that although the body may die, the soul will rise again from the dead on the third day.

Tomorrow I shall celebrate Easter here in mountain solitude. . . .

> All my fondest love to you,
> Hans

Hans before his participation in the French campaign, probably early 1940

To his parents, Kempten, April 9, 1940

Dear Parents,

. . . But on Sunday we suddenly had to return to Munich and get ourselves kitted out in full marching order. Now we're back in our beloved Kempten.

April is looking its best today. I have a strong urge to go out, especially as we're really off duty the whole time. We lead a tranquil (too tranquil) life here because the battalion is scheduled to be sent to the front a week from now. Life is permanently tinged with a certain suspense, but it doesn't bother me much.

... But my spell of front-line duty won't last long, as far as I can tell, and afterward we'll most probably return to Munich. . . .

To his sister Elisabeth, Ulm, April 29, 1940

My dear sister Elisabeth,

You must forgive me for not having written to you for so long, but I haven't had any real peace and quiet for days. It isn't that our duties were particularly onerous, but there was so much to see, almost every hour of the day, and one had to absorb and experience it to the full.

After spending some happy April days at Kempten, we made a trip to the Western front, where we were stationed near Zweibrücken. We were soon transported back to Munich, however, and I'm stopping off here today on my way to Kassel. What will become of me then I don't yet know. It doesn't really matter much, because I'm me wherever I go, and the trees are in leaf everywhere, and in the afternoons you can already stretch out on the grass in the shade of a birch tree. Our surroundings aren't all that important. What counts is what we put into them.

The books and your nice letter arrived safely. I'm really delighted you get so much pleasure out of Rilke. I thought him the greatest of poets for a long time, till I got to know Stefan George. . . .

I'll write to you again as soon as I get to Kassel.

Fond love,

Hans

Hans Scholl was redirected from Kassel to Bad Sooden. When term started at the beginning of May 1940, he obtained permission to continue his studies at nearby Göttingen.

To his parents, Bad Sooden, May 2, 1940

. . . I'm really pleased to be able to go on with my studies. There's absolutely nothing to do here but wait, so I'd have been bored stiff. If I can manage to complete this semester, I'll sit my medical prelims at Munich in about ten weeks' time. After that I'll report to the front again.

Sooden is a very neat little town with a lot of colorful half-timbered houses. It stands on an ancient site in the former Electorate of Hesse. A brown river, the Werra, flows through the valley below, and everywhere, for as far as the eye can see, stretches forest and still more forest.

I've been billeted on an aristocratic old lady. I'm very much at home in her house. My room could scarcely be better, and I can work there. Today, Ascension Day, I've volunteered to be duty NCO. Although it's a nuisance being cooped up like a caged lion on such a sunny day, I'm off to Göttingen for the first time tomorrow, and that's enough to dispel any temporary annoyance.

I'll have to work hard in the next few weeks. I'm looking forward to it.

Fond love,
Hans

To his mother, OU,[51] May 4, 1940

Dear Mother,

I well remember the last birthday letter I wrote you. The year seems to have flown by. You can't write your mother a long letter on her birthday. I can only devote a lot of grateful thought to you and pray God to keep you with us for a long time to come.

I'm going to try hard to make strides with my studies in the coming weeks. I don't ever want to be one-sided, though, so hard work mustn't be allowed to parch the soul. It's wonderful, the way I can organize my time here. At nights I sit reading in my room, and before turning in I take an evening stroll down to the Werra. Rivers always attract me. The nights are mild and warm already. Sometimes I chat with the fishermen who stand on the river bank far into the night, smoking pipes and plying their peaceful trade.

This letter will reach you a little late, but you'll have to forgive me. I was too tired to write last night.

All my loving thoughts are with you.

Yours,

Hans

The Western campaign opened on May 10, 1940, when German troops invaded Holland and Belgium. Hans Scholl's unit received its marching orders. Ernst Reden of Cologne, whom Hans mentions in the letter below, had done his military service in 1935. Introduced to the Scholl family by friends in the youth movement, he jointly organized the Ulm branch of the banned dj-1/11 with Hans, was arrested along with the young Scholls in consequence of the campaign against "subversive activities," and spent eight months in prison, latterly at Welzheim concentration camp.

A particularly close friend of Inge's, Reden wielded considerable influence over the young Scholls, primarily because of his enthusiasm for literature and knowledge of poetry. He enhanced their appreciation of Rilke and George, read Wolf von Niebelschütz and Ernst Jünger's Marmorklippen *with them, and interested them in Georg Heym, Georg Trakl, Carossa, Hausmann, and – last but not least – Wiechert. To the best of Inge Aicher-Scholl's recollection, the "thoughts on war" referred to by Hans were embodied in letters that have not survived.[52]*

To his parents, OU, May 11, 1940

Dear Parents,

As I warned you to expect in my modest postcard, we shall probably move out in a day or two. I myself have been assigned to the operating theater. We don't have any nurses.

As far as my studies are concerned, I'll be credited with this fourth semester.[53] I'll then be able to take some furlough and sit my preliminary exam. I must see to it that I make some headway. I want to complete my professional training by the time the war's over.

I've been carefully saving my pay. For a start, I bought myself some textbooks to the value of 30 marks. My student's monthly season ticket cost 15, and I also paid my re-registration fee and other expenses. I've had to meet the cost of my midday meals, too, so I've used up about 80. . . .

I'll be able to take some of my books along. We have a few foreign doctors, so I hope to learn something.

I've had to readjust my ideas somewhat, as you can imagine, because I was already well into my work and feeling very pleased with such progress as I'd made. But the immediate future may bring me closer to my profession than the lecture hall. Then again, maybe it won't.

I had my swim in the Werra yesterday. It must be really lovely here in the summer!

Today I dipped into Ernst Reden's thoughts on war. Jünger[54] said much the same thing, but I'm strongly inclined to doubt it all. Heraclitus[55] didn't say the last word on the subject either, because he didn't live in our day and age.

Tonight, I'm on switchboard duty. A noncom always has to be on call these days.

All my love,

Hans

To his parents, OU, May 14, 1940

. . . We're leaving here tomorrow morning for the west. We don't yet know what awaits us there. Personally, I'm relieved to be moving out. All we've done in the last few days is wait. . . .

On May 15 the unit was transferred from Bad Sooden to the Western front. Hans's next letter was posted from France.

To his parents, OU, May 22, 1940

Dear Parents,

Today is a rest day. We need a rest, too. So you won't worry, I'm sending you a few lines right away. I can't manage a long letter at present. My wrists are swollen and aching from riding [on a motorbike] over bad roads. I've been acting as a dispatch rider during the advance.

The trip though Luxembourg was very pleasant. We were all delighted to see such lovely countryside. Good roads, well-kept houses, nice-looking people. Belgium made a very good impression on me too, but here one sees a certain amount of destruction. The roads are churned up and the villages crowded with refugees. I soon made friends with the farmers and am picking up their language very quickly. I'm the interpreter for the entire unit. I'm well off here.[56] The farmers have plenty of everything. Rare delicacies such as milk and eggs are taken for granted. We're spending two days here (Neufchâteau). Then we move on.

I'll write again soon.

Fond love,
Hans

To his parents, OU, May 29, 1940

Dear Parents,

I got your eagerly awaited letters and parcels yesterday evening. We sat around the table by candlelight and for a few minutes each of us was back home. — We're now at St. Quentin awaiting reassignment. I have to cover around 300 kilometers a day carrying orders on my motorbike, which is tiring.

Rear echelon life doesn't appeal to me. Although we're favored with the occasional air raid, we lead such an idle existence in general that one feels like bolting. There isn't a soul here I can hold an intelligent conversation with, either. I'm half tempted to transfer to the infantry as a medic.

We've commandeered the best available houses. Personally, I felt more at home in the straw. What am I, a thief or a self-respecting human being? You've no idea the looting that goes on.

My French is steadily improving. I'm always on the lookout for additions to my store of books.

We shake our heads at the tactics of the French. They try to bomb the Somme bridge day after day, but without success.

The sun is really hot today, but we aren't allowed to go swimming.

I'll write more often from now on.

Yours,

Hans

To his parents, OU, June 3, 1940

Dear Parents,

I've received several letters and parcels from you in the last few days. It's disgraceful how seldom I write to thank you. I planned a letter to Inge ages ago, but I haven't written it yet. I've enough money and laundry here.

I had my third [motorbike] crash yesterday. Now I have some quiet days ahead. We've pulled back 60 kilometers or so from St.

Quentin. We're billeted in a very quiet village. There are lots of ownerless horses in the fields, and there's no one around to cut the hay, but it's peaceful here. All you can hear is the rumbling in the distance.

I spend most of my time lying in the long grass. I'm translating an excellent book by André Gide. Don't reproach me for doing no other form of work. It's out of the question at this particular juncture. I can't be sufficiently businesslike in the face of so much suffering.

I cracked my tenth rib and compressed a kidney. Otherwise I'm perfectly fit.

I bought Werner a copy of *Le Journal d'un cure dé campagne*,[57] but it got left behind at St. Quentin.

It's a good thing I can always find something to occupy myself with. I don't have any idle hours, only sad ones.

I intend to try, as best I can, to find my way around the French mentality and get to understand the French character.

This isn't too easy because the people are very reserved, but I meet with kind words wherever I go. It's marvelous the way most of the womenfolk behave toward German soldiers.

Every letter from you is a delight. Please give my regards to all our friends. I'll write again really soon.

Yours,
Hans

To his parents, OU, June 6, 1940

Dear Parents,

In spite of my injury I couldn't resist catching a horse today and going for a brief ride. It's so lovely! I guess I'll soon be fit again. Our people think the war will be over by August. I don't believe it, even though the French are behaving like amateurs. The number of prisoners trudging past every day is positively startling. . . .

We're having glorious weather the whole time. You can't swim here. The Somme flows far too slowly and the same goes for the Oisne. Both rivers are muddy and turbid. Oh, for the Iller! The Isar's high too, so I'm told.

Ask Werner to write and tell me if he got the two books I sent him (*Sous le soleil* . . . [58] and *Journal d' un cure dé campagne*). I strongly advise him to learn French. It's a wonderful language.

Fond love,
Hans

To his parents, OU, June 11, 1940

Dear Parents,

Our present assignment is to support a divisional field hospital.

June 12, 1940

We had to move out unexpectedly. There was a tremendous amount to do. The fighting around Soissons inflicted a lot of casualties. Last night we were supposed to set up a field hospital at Rheims, but it seems the French have since recaptured the city. However, it won't be long before they evacuate that city too. I can't understand the French way of making war.

Today I received the parcel containing the underpants. Many thanks.

I don't know how much longer I can bear to watch this butchery of ours. I'm going to try to get myself transferred to the infantry as a medic.

It's always been sunny till now. Last night it rained for the first time. We spent the night in the open.

Fondest love to you both,
Hans

The Franco-German armistice was signed at Compiègne on June 22, 1940, bringing a respite in fighting to Hans's unit. Hans acquired a delightful six-week-old St. Bernard puppy at about this time, intending to give it to Sophie if he came home safe and sound.

To his parents, OU, July 2, 1940

My dear Parents,

I'm still billeted in the country. I can stick it out here till I come home. Today I'm going to put in a request to be released for purposes of study. It's possible that our unit will form part of the occupation force. The sun continues to shine without a break. My dog is getting naughtier every day. Yesterday we caught ourselves another horse. We now have three saddle horses in our riding stable. There are masses of roses blooming in the garden.

Fondest love,

Hans

To his sister Inge, OU, July 2, 1940

Dear Inge,

Many thanks for your letter. You all write to me a great deal, for which I'm grateful. Personally, I find letter writing difficult even though I have time to spare, and the war is temporarily over. We lead a regular trooper's life here. It's a question of piling up experiences so as to keep from thinking. Cowardly?

I can't read a thing. My head is brimming over. You mustn't imagine that war fundamentally changes us. Far from it. It's just that we have to be a bit tougher on the outside. We have to assert ourselves the whole time.

It's wonderfully peaceful here, but we're off tomorrow. What a shame!

We treasure your letters above all else, not being happy in our work. Your letters and the horses we ride through the woods in the evenings.

Fond love,
Hans

To his parents, OU, July 12, 1940

Dear Parents,

Two days ago we took over a hospital with four hundred casualties. Our predecessors were Prussians. They handed over the patients in a pitiful condition. We have some French nurses to assist us, but the bulk of the work we do ourselves, including an average of twenty operations a day. This morning there were two mid-thigh amputations.

I've paid several visits to Paris. In the mornings I play tennis between 6 and 7, which is the only time off I get.

My dog couldn't be nicer now. All the children adore him.

Fond love,
Hans

To his parents, OU, July 21, 1940

Dear Parents,

Just a line to let you know I'm still alive.

I'm having to work extremely hard. I'm always on the go.

I got your letters, Father. I wrote to Göttingen about my course as soon as I received a form from there.

The French are good patriots – every day brings that home to me. I've become good friends with several French nurses. They work with greater devotion than our own Red Cross nurses.

Nursing and military spirit are completely at odds, I realize that daily. I assist at every operation. That teaches me a great deal, of course. There are road accidents every night. We're the only hospital for miles around.

We're suffering almost as many casualties as we did in the war. They all show off like mad in their requisitioned cars and kill each other in the process.

I'm very favorably impressed with Paris and its inhabitants. It won't be long before I'm home again.

Yours,
Hans

[P.S.] I've bought Werner a Voigtländer Brillant,[59] but if he'd sooner have my Löwen,[60] he can swap with Inge.

To his sister Inge, Versailles, August 1, 1940

Dear Inge,

Your latest letters were like stars in my dark sky.

Today is our first rest day. It feels wonderful, having nothing to do. You can't imagine how hard we've had to work in the past few weeks. A lot of patients died in spite of all the care they received. Many of the men wept when we left. I've had some profoundly moving experiences in France, needless to say, but I can't describe them in my letters. I'm incapable of doing so. It would entail an ability to handle words like a woodcarver carving passive wood, and that I can't manage.

You may believe a man should return from the wars wiser and more mature. That applies only in the rarest instance. I think I was more sensitive and receptive before this madness started.

War sets us back a long way. It's unbelievable how absurd human beings have become. We quit the operating theater with someone dying inside and smoke a cigarette.

The day before yesterday I was in the south of France. I had a wonderful swim in the Bay of Biscay.

I hope you're having some sunny days during your vacation. I'm sure you can use some sunshine. It would be nice if Father could get a few days off too. I'll be writing soon to thank him for his kind letter.

Lots of love,
Hans

To his parents, Versailles, August 4, 1940

Dear Parents,

I'm gradually going to start sending some of my vast accumulation of baggage home. The photos date from my happiest time in France, when we were looking after refugees. I steadfastly avoided taking pictures of horrors, unlike my comrades.

Today is Sunday. The sun is wonderfully hot. Versailles doesn't tempt me. I play tennis, listen to good music on the radio. Our respite won't last long, that's for sure.

This evening I plan to immerse myself in Victor Hugo's[61] poems. It's remarkable how chary the French are of discussing André Gide,[62] Bernanos,[63] Jammes.[64] Most of the adults dismiss Gide as a source of intellectual confusion. In many respects he's a French Nietzsche. Lectures are starting at Paris University. If only I could be there. One of the greatest French doctors has committed suicide because he declined to live under German rule. Strange patriots, just when France has need of strong men.

Fond love,
Hans

P.S. If only I could present you with a can or two of my delicious pineapple juice! You'd adore it.

To his sister Inge, Versailles, August 11, 1940

Dear Inge,

I've been to Paris again. I was amazed that the city could have recovered so quickly from the rigors of war. It's incredible how stimulating I find the Parisian way of life. You can't thread your way through such a profusion of thoughts, ideas, and traditions, which bubble over, perform death-defying leaps, and land on their own two feet again.

But there's nothing that moves me to the core. My innermost thoughts are doing battle on another plane.

I'm playing up to four hours' tennis a day. The rest of the time I read French poetry. Now and then I cycle along the vast avenues, through the Trianon's spacious grounds and past the fountains. In my next I'll enclose some snaps of an eleven-year-old girl who reads to me beautifully in French in the evenings. My teacher. She's a scream sometimes.

Do write and tell me if the three parcels I got someone to mail from Cologne have arrived.

Fond love,
Hans

To his mother, Versailles, September 1, 1940

Dear Mother,

Many thanks for your two Sunday letters. I'm in a specially good mood today because I finally managed to go swimming again. Physical exercise is one of my main occupations at present. Inge sent me a parcel of the nut cookies I like so much. My dog was equally delighted to be privileged to sample such goodies. I was also pleased to receive a letter from Lisl.

Recently I've often toyed with the idea of becoming an officer while the war lasts, because I can't endure my subordinate status indefinitely. However, I want to go on furlough before I make any other decisions. We don't have any prospect of continuing our studies. I paid a visit to the medical faculty in Paris yesterday. Lectures haven't started there yet, unfortunately.

The people of France are gradually coming to their senses. They deserved a drubbing.

I bought some wool yesterday. You'll find it useful for the winter. The French are very apprehensive of the coming winter. Next week I plan to see *Carmen* at the Paris opera. I have a season ticket for Paris.

Four more weeks to furlough!

Fond love,
Hans

Sophie Scholl

1939–1940

My dear Fritz,

My hands are all stained with resin from the parcel that's just going off to you, and I won't get them clean in a hurry. As for the way they smell, you'll detect that as soon as you start unwrapping it. I'll bet you haven't remembered which day you're meant to light the little red candles on – and I hope you get a chance to, so that in the evening, the chocolate having probably been eaten already, you get a whiff of the scent we enjoy in the hallway here on evenings in Advent. Our great big Advent wreath, with its four fat candles, is hanging in the middle of the hallway. We also have Christmas carols for flute and piano, and Werner can play *"O du fröhliche, o du selige"* on the violin. All this, plus Christmas chores and other things, will keep us busy on Advent evenings. We all enjoy them so much – better almost than Christmas Eve itself. Prettify things a bit for yourself too, won't you? I only wish I could help you. Maybe you could put the little wreath on your bedside table. Every member of the family helped to polish the apples, and I put in the beeswax candle because it smells so good. Werner

Sophie in Ulm, 1940

actually eats them, but this year we've forbidden him to because candles are almost unobtainable.

All I rather doubt is whether the things will ever reach you. I'm expecting a letter from you any day. Maybe I'll get one tomorrow, seeing how often our letters cross. I hope there isn't any more serious reason for your silence (though it's only ten days old). You always know that I'm all right, but what do I know about you?

While waiting to hear from you, I always think at nights of our walk along that narrow path beside the Danube. The moon has been visible here nearly every night since then. Remember how the moon battled with the clouds? Tonight it's round and hazy, with a huge corona whose outer edge is all the colors of the rainbow. —But I'd sooner get a letter from you! Couldn't you manage that?

> Happy Advent!
> Sofie

To Fritz Hartnagel, Ulm, January 12, 1940

My dear Fritz,

I just got another letter from you today. Many thanks. I'm afraid one has to allow at least a week for a letter to get there and two weeks for a reply. That's a long time, but other letters that aren't just replies can also turn up. – I worry about your leave every day. It might have been better if you'd come at Christmas after all. I probably won't be through till the beginning of March, so the whole thing's vague from your point of view. For some strange reason we won't be told when the school-leaving exam will take place until a few days before (before the exam, I mean). It seems the ministry enjoys torturing us a little. They just don't want to make things too easy for us. Mergenthaler[65] is famous for his antics, as you know. I'll pass all right, but I'll really be relieved when it's over. You know – it's a bit like the feeling you get when you know you've still got the dishes to do.

About your leave again. Why not take it right away? I could come skiing with you over the weekend, and you'd surely find it better than nothing, to say the least, being in the mountains by yourself. I wouldn't want you to miss out on my account. You must know yourself what's best to do.

The weather has been glorious for the past few days. At this moment the sun's above the old roofs we can see from our living room. Its lower edge is just touching the ridge. Then the snow on the roof catches fire, and you can't look without screwing up your eyes. There's about an hour of daylight left now.

While Hans was here, I often went walking in the woods with him. We tested the ice on the Iller backwater, which was frozen in many places. We even made it to the other bank without going through. When we got cold we would run awhile. Once, when it was already getting dark, we followed some deer tracks in the Eselswald. The little plateau looked like a vast plain because you couldn't see far, and dimly at that. The sky, too, is all misty and flat at night. I like that.

Although my hair's dark and I don't have a pale complexion, I'd much rather go north than south. I get a regular craving for it sometimes. Maybe the time will come again when you can go wherever you please without having to rush things.

You tell me so little about yourself: whose company you prefer, what he's like and what he looks like, and what you do when you're off duty. Is that so unimportant? Me you know everything about. Do you know what would be great for you? A piano or some other instrument. Do you have anything of the kind or could you rent one? I've just embarked on some Bach inventions, and now I can hardly imagine life without a piano, even though I don't play well yet.

When your birthday comes around and the mailman doesn't bring you anything, don't be angry, just blame the inefficient army postal service. At least you'll be getting another letter before then.

Write to me often!

Sofie

P.S. You keep forgetting to tell me how much the white wool cost. When are you going to remember!

I wore your dress to the theater recently. I felt quite embarrassed, everyone stared at me so hard. Only one other female there had straight hair, and that was Similde Valet.[66] I pass her every morning on the way to school.

Sofie

Fritz took his leave early in March, and he and Sophie spent it together in the mountains. The Gemstal and the Hochalp Pass, mentioned in the letter below, are south of Pfronten im Allgäu.

To her sister Elisabeth, Ulm, March 8, 1940

. . . The four days we've already spent in the mountains were
fabulous, needless to say. On Sunday we made a long excursion via the Gemstal and the Hochalp pass. It was terribly icy
and rather dangerous, and above all tiring, but the weather
was glorious in the middle of the day. I went up in my swim-
suit. We met only one = 1 person all day long. The scenery is
marvelous. The next day the snow was softened by the sun, but
by five o'clock it had turned so icy that our skis simply whizzed
over it. After zigzagging along the mountainside we headed
straight downhill. The surface undulated gently all the way, and
I took off a little after every hummock. It was my best run to
date. Also, we suddenly noticed that the peaks had turned pink.
It was indescribably beautiful. We followed a splendid track
through the woods on the way back, and even Fritz was amazed
how seldom I fell. By the time we got back we could see all the
constellations quite clearly. I bet I've made your mouth water,
haven't I? Mine's watering too, and I'm looking forward to some
more of the same. . . .

*Sophie Scholl passed her school-leaving examination at Ulm
in mid-March 1940. She had planned to begin studying biology
and philosophy at Munich during the summer semester of
1940. However, the government required prospective students
to furnish proof of six months' satisfactory service in the Arbeitsdienst (short for Reicharbeitsdienst). To get around that
requirement, Sophie applied to join the Fröbel course at Ulm
at the beginning of May 1940. Employment as a kindergarten
teacher counted – or so it was originally stated – as an acceptable
substitute for the Arbeitsdienst.*

    *Sophie spent the interval between school and the Fröbel
course at home, reading, making excursions, and leisurely*

pursuing her interests and hobbies. She also helped out in her father's office, making fair copies of her father's annual accounts.

To Fritz Hartnagel, Ulm, April 3, 1940

... Lisa left yesterday. Before that we went on a two-day cycle tour in really glorious weather. We visited three monasteries: Untermarchtal, Obermarchtal, and Zwiefalten. At Obermarchtal, opposite the fine baroque church (I prefer not to see it from too close up), we spent the night at the castle inn in a double room with dark red plush upholstery, and for supper we got two fried eggs each, plus sausage and butter, all without coupons and not expensive. It was sumptuous. When it got dark, we strolled down to the Danube. You walk through a little gate and down some rough-and-ready steps that lead through the woods to the Danube. There were only two stars in the west at first, but gradually they all appeared, and we picked out a few of the constellations we knew with the aid of Lisa's glasses. If they hadn't had any names, we'd have named them there and then. The Danube resembles a lake at that point, wooded on both banks. One sees so little at night, and all we saw was the beauty of the place. We could make out the reflection of Orion in the water, and plenty more [stars] besides. We headed west along a straight path of some kind, and saw dark forest and the stars above it. It was really lovely. We drank a glass of mulled wine before going up to bed, with all the regular customers grinning at us. We slept in our matrimonial beds till 9 a.m., and the weather the next day was just as fine. To start with, while the sun was melting the hoarfrost, we toured the church and the chapter house, found a few hidden doors, and combed through some forbidden rooms. Then we rode on. (I'll forbear to tell you how sore our backsides were.) We whizzed downhill and promptly got off whenever we came to rising ground. Of course, we were wearing socks and had our sleeves rolled up. Those were the first two really warm spring days. At Zwiefalten,

Sophie on a hiking tour in the Swabian Alps, 1940

which is another nice little place, we lunched for 70 pfennigs (three bowls of soup, a huge mound of potato salad, and ten liver dumplings apiece), bought two tubes of fruit drops, and headed for home. Between 2 and 4 p.m. we snoozed in a little copse, still leafless, just in our shirts and shorts, and sunned our tummies. Then we hurried on because, not that either of us would admit it, we were hungry. At Ehingen we had two coffees and ate ices and cake and stocked up with pretzels. Then we rode leisurely on. Catching sight of an island in the Danube, we dismounted, removed our shoes and socks, and waded hero- ically across. Once there we tried skipping stones, to see if we still could, till the setting sun lost too much of its strength. Then we waded back (the water didn't quite come up to our shorts) and went in search of some violets. I found a lovely shell and stuffed it with damp moss. It made a perfect vase for our bunch of violets. Even after another 20 kilometers, they looked as if they'd just been picked.

The sky is gray today, thank goodness, because I've got to work in the office [her father's]. I'm being incredibly diligent: eight hours' work a day (no exaggeration). My poor little finger is quite numb from writing.

I hope you've found the time and patience to read this long letter. But then, you *are* patient. You've only been impatient with me twice: the first time in the car, when that bus came straight for us. I nearly cried then. The second time was when we were looking for rooms in Kiel, but I couldn't have cared less. And the third time when my ski binding kept coming loose. I almost laughed that time, remember?

I may get a letter from you tomorrow. It certainly won't be as long as this one, but I'll enjoy it just as much. (Is "it" already on the way? I do hope so.)

So now lots of love until I have to answer another one from you.

Sofie

To Fritz Hartnagel, Ulm, April 5, 1940

. . . Are oranges as much of a rarity with you as they are here? Wrapping parcels wouldn't be half as nice if one didn't have to hoard everything so carefully. And if there weren't such masses of wrapping paper and ribbons. . . .

On April 9, while Sophie was waiting to start training as a kindergarten teacher, German troops invaded Denmark and Norway.

To Fritz Hartnagel, Ulm, April 9, 1940

. . . There are times when I dread the war and feel like giving up hope completely. I hate thinking about it, but politics are almost all there is, and as long as they're so confused and nasty, it's cowardly to turn your back on them. You're probably smiling at this and telling yourself, "She's a girl." But I think I'd be far happier if I weren't under pressure all the time – then I could devote myself to other things with a far better conscience. As it is, everything else takes second place. We were politically educated, after all. (Now you're laughing again.) I'd just like to relax in your company again and see and feel nothing but the cloth of your suit.

Is this a poor letter? It won't bring a breath of fresh air into your stuffy room – it may make the air even stuffier. Don't be angry, though. It makes me so nervous, being on edge all the time. On edge everywhere including home, where work goes on till after dark, and where my father's in an irritable mood, and where I never get an hour's peace and quiet. (I'm exaggerating again. I do sometimes, but not often.) . . .

To Fritz Hartnagel, Ulm, April 1940

My dear Fritz,

When you open this parcel, pretend I'm with you. No, then there'd be no need for a parcel. I'd make some tea and sand-wiches, and we'd be really cozy. You'd have to sit opposite me like a good boy, so you wouldn't spill your tea, and afterward we'd sit on your sofa (or don't you have one?) and look at one another, and suddenly the magazine or book would fall to the floor, and we'd let it lie there. Childish, aren't I?

If you weren't so far away,[67] I'd send you some scillas, anem-ones, coltsfoot, butterfly orchids, and violets, but they'd only wither. Pick yourself some. I don't intend to write much today, and I'm not going to write about what everyone's talking about (in very different ways) [that is, the invasion]. I'd sooner tell you some springtime stories. Make some up yourself. About the woods, the fields, the water, and the two of us.

And whatever you do, don't turn into an arrogant, uncaring lieutenant. (Forgive me!) It's so easy to become callous, and I think that would be a shame.

All the best and lots of love,
Sofie

Sophie Scholl's course at the Fröbel Institute in Ulm started at the beginning of May. It was almost like going back to school again, because the preliminary part of the syllabus included no teaching practice, but this phase of Sophie's life was soon overshadowed by the German invasion of Holland, Belgium, and France. Fritz Hartnagel's unit was one of those sent into action, invading the Netherlands on May 10, 1940, when the Blitzkrieg began.

To Fritz Hartnagel, Ulm, May 16, 1940

My dear Fritz,

I was nineteen a week ago today. Remember how we rounded off the day? What's been happening to you since then? Everything went so very quickly, including our good-byes at the station.

I'm on tenterhooks for news of you. Do write as soon as you have the time and the permission, because a letter would be doubly welcome now that everything's so uncertain. Hans and Hanspeter[68] have also been transferred, and we still haven't heard from them. We notice the war, even here, because scarcely a minute passes without the ears being assailed by the sound of airplanes.

Pentecost was really glorious, though, and it's wonderful how nothing throws nature off course. We lay in the grass with the pale-green birch twigs overhead silhouetted against a sky coated with white cobwebs, and the beauty of it scarcely left room for the war and our worries. Campions suffused the grass beside the stream with red, and the dandelions were splendidly big and lush.

But there were hundreds more kinds of flowers and herbs growing in the fields and woods. A bird was singing in the tree above us, and another one answered from the woods with the same lovely melody. I'd been given a harmonica for my birthday, so we were able to play and sing as we walked.

I've another nice thing to tell you. A little bird has nested and is hatching four little off-white eggs in the blackberry hedge in the garden (it caught the frost, unfortunately, and doesn't have a single leaf left). I'm glad the hedge is so prickly, or the joiner's apprentices across the way wouldn't leave it in peace.

Klaus and Peter[69] often went for walks with me during the vacation. Klaus has developed a terrific crush on me and sobs heartrendingly when he has to be put to bed by the nursemaid instead of me. Last night he toddled upstairs in his pajamas and said, "Mummy isn't there." And when I put him back to bed, he said happily, "You'll stay for ages, won't you?"

Your narcissi have withered. I liked them so much I didn't want to throw them away. I've pressed one. Have you seen any nice flowers yet in Holland? It's *the* place for them, after all. I hope the innocent little things haven't all been destroyed. How are you? Are you stationed on the frontier? Do write to me soon.

It's a shame we couldn't look at your birthday present [his to Sophie] together. It's lovely, and far too good for me. There are things I'd have liked to say and tell you that I can't put down on paper. Our ideas are so different, I sometimes wonder if it's really so unimportant, when it ought to be the basis of any relationship. But all this must be shelved for now. It really is unimportant at present, because what you and I need now is love, not friendship and companionship. We'll keep things between us that way till we can be by ourselves again.

Spare a thought for something other than your work some-times. Do you ever get a chance to read? My dearest wish is that you should survive the war and these times without becoming a product of them. All of us have standards inside ourselves, but we don't go looking for them often enough. Maybe it's because they're the toughest standards of all.

Think of me sometimes, but don't dream of me. I'm often with you in spirit, wishing you well and loving you.

Yours,
Sofie

To Fritz Hartnagel, Ulm, May 29, 1940

My dear Fritz,

We're having some really glorious early summer weather. If I had the time, I'd stretch out beside the Iller, swim, laze, and try to think of nothing but the beauty around me. It isn't easy to banish all thoughts of the war. Although I don't know much about politics and have no ambition to do so, I do have some idea of right and wrong, because that has nothing to do with politics and nationality. And I could weep at how mean people are, in high-level politics as well, and how they betray their fellow creatures, perhaps for the sake of personal advantage. Isn't it enough to make a person lose heart sometimes? Often my one desire is to live on a Robinson Crusoe island. I'm sometimes tempted to regard mankind as a terrestrial skin disease. But only sometimes, when I'm very tired, and people who are worse than beasts loom large in my mind's eye. But all that matters fundamentally is whether we come through, whether we manage to hold our own among the majority, whose sole concern is self-interest – those who approve of any means to their own ends. It's so overwhelming, that majority, you have to be bad to survive at all. Only one person has ever managed to go straight to God, probably, but who still looks for him nowadays?

Dear Fritz, this whole letter will probably strike you as odd in the extreme. I expect you've so much to see and do that you never have time to think about yourself anymore. That scares

Sophie, spring 1940

me a little. You do sometimes think of me at night, don't you?
If so, you must sometimes dream of our vacation. Don't just
think of me as I am, though – think of me also as I'd like to
be. We'll only be completely at one if you still like me as much

then. We don't know one another anything like well enough, and I'm a lot to blame. I always felt that, but I was too comfortable to change things. You mustn't think it stands between us, because I try hard to be with you and support you in spirit. But don't think, either, that this is unimportant in wartime. Grave events are no justification for letting oneself go. My dear, don't misunderstand me, just forgive anything in this letter that strikes you as clumsy. If much of what I say seems silly, hurtful, and unnecessary, remember that I judge things from my own standpoint, and that I may be crediting you with many of my own characteristics.

Fondest love,
Sofie

After overrunning Holland, Belgium, and Luxembourg, the German armies defeated the French and at the beginning of June drove the British Expeditionary Force back across the Channel from Dunkirk – the British completing their extraordinary evacuation June 4. Three days after Sophie wrote the following letter, on June 17, 1940, Marshal Pétain's government requested an armistice.

To Fritz Hartnagel, Ulm, June 14, 1940

My dear Fritz,

Forgive me if I only send you a few lines today. I intend to sit down on Sunday and try to write you a long letter. I'm very grateful to you for writing so relatively often. Many thanks for the chocolate, too. I gave some of it to Li, née Hörsch,[70] who has just had a little boy called Hans Jörg. Another share went to Frau Geyer, who may also be expecting. I shall look after her later on. Herr Geyer has been drafted.

Are you still in your tent in the woods? Or have you made a trip to Paris? It looks as if you may all be coming home soon. I won't prophesy. Things may turn out quite differently. To tell the truth, I'm pretty unmoved by each new turn of events. By that I mean I'm prepared for anything in advance. All I sometimes wonder is whether people's ideas and lives were as shallow in previous centuries as they are today, or whether, as an era recedes, its bad aspects gradually recede into the background too, and its good ones take on a special luster.

Anyway, however things turn out, I think individuals should be on their guard, and doubly so when people make it hard for them. I'm sure you believe like me that one can never level upward, however desirable that may seem. If any leveling takes place, it's always in a downward direction. Even here, though, fate has offered us a splendid chance to prove ourselves. Perhaps we shouldn't underrate it.

I often think of you all on active service. I'm always worrying about Hans in particular. He's so vulnerable. Still, I doubt if the war will do *him* much harm.

This letter may leave you completely cold and seem alien to you, but I don't propose to rhapsodize unnecessarily. That would surely be unwholesome. But I assure you I often think of you, and of our times together, and of what we've embarked on, whether rightly or wrongly.

I hope this letter doesn't take as long as its predecessors.

All the best,
Sofie

During her Fröbel course, which had been cut to one year, Sophie had to do four weeks' teaching practice at an Ulm kindergarten between mid-June and mid-July 1940 – an occupation described by one fellow student as "working at all hours, plus nightly cleaning and tidying up." Sophie's stint at the kindergarten not only entailed a lot of unaccustomed hard work but brought her some formative experiences.

To Fritz Hartnagel, Ulm, undated [June/July 1940]

My dear Fritz,

This penciled heading may have been written in September, likewise in bed from the look of it. I must at least get a line off to you after three long days. Thanks so much for your letter. You can't imagine how impatient we are for mail – we haven't heard from Hans for two weeks – so I'm doubly glad when I get something. Mother always calls your mother up as soon as she's asked me how you are. I hope you don't mind.

At the kindergarten today I and the bigger boys played with some Matador.[71] To begin with I thought of making a nice big gun, but I soon abandoned the idea. One shouldn't encourage such baneful tendencies in children. Instead we built a marvelous fire engine complete with a long ladder. That's a more useful gadget.

I always have a great deal to do when I get home – in fact I really ought to work all evening. I'm sorry it leaves me no time for reading and writing. I owe a whole heap of letters. My thoughts still turn to you first of all. I looked up your where-abouts on the map, but to be honest, I couldn't really decipher the name in your letter. Please write place names a bit more clearly.

Next day . . . I'm going to finish off this letter quickly and mail it. So that you get something often, I can continue it in my next. I don't have the time just now. The first bombs fell here last night.

The children give me a lot of pleasure. Working with them is an immensely tiring business, because you have to adjust to them completely. This certainly isn't an egotistical profession, and I doubt if I could stick it indefinitely – I've been brought up too self-centered. – Klaus loves me dearly at present. That delights me too, as you can imagine. Peter also likes coming to me best.

I think of you a lot.

Yours,
Sofie

To Fritz Hartnagel, Ulm, June 17, 1940

My dear Fritz,

I'm in bed early tonight, so there's time for another letter to you before I go to sleep. It's hardly an ideal time to write, one's so preoccupied with political and military develop-ments (we heard today that the French want to lay down their arms). I shrink from writing in general, but that's just weari-ness, laziness, and idleness, which have to be overcome, thank goodness. I sometimes feel like laying down my arms, too. Still, *allen Gewalten zum Trotz!* ["In defiance of all the powers that be . . ."][72] Life is an endless series of ups and downs. All one needs is the ability to wait. I'll try not to be content with dreams, aestheticism, and noble gestures. One mustn't be too softhearted these days.

There are two roses on my bedside table. Strings of tiny beads have formed on the stems and the foliage, which hangs down into the water. What a pure and beautiful sight, and what chill indifference it conveys. To think that it exists. That trees simply go on growing, and grain and flowers, and that hydrogen and oxygen have combined to form such wonderful, tepid summer raindrops. There are times when this comes home to me with such force that I'm absolutely filled with it and have no room left for a single thought. All this exists, although human beings behave so inhumanly, not to say bestially, in the midst of creation. That's a great blessing in itself.

I never tire of talking about myself. I'd be lying if I told you that the children gave me unadulterated pleasure. Almost every little face conveys so clearly what it promises to become, in other words, the kind of people that exist today. But most of them still retain the childish charm we love because we mourn its passing. The satisfying part of the job is that they claim your full attention, and that you're utterly drained afterward. Drained but not empty, that's the good thing.

When you compare my relationship with Klaus to yours with your dog, you're really reproaching me. You may have a point, but I think that although his affection has done me good, I haven't regarded or treated him merely as a little comforter, but also as a person. A little person, perhaps, but a developing one. Have you ever met anyone who derives his or her *sole* pleasure from children and spends more than a few hours at a time in their company? It's terribly tiring, having to think yourself into the world of children but remain detached from it at the same time. It takes patience and love not to become abruptly, abominably grown-up again. I've always done my best with Klaus, too, often with success.

I would have loved to have your dog when the war's over. I'm fond of him already. But in the middle of town? If he can't find a better home than here with me, by all means bring him. But if you can find him more suitable surroundings someplace else, do what's best for him.

I look forward to hearing from you again. Maybe you'll even get some leave soon?

> Lots of love,
> Sofie

Despite Sophie's claim that she never tired of talking about herself, in much of her conversation with Fritz Hartnagel she struggled to clarify and bear witness to her feelings about the war and the regime that sponsored it. Reminiscing to Hermann Vinke years later, Fritz recalled Sophie's crucial contribution to the mental process through which he had to pass before he could acknowledge that "the regime I served as a [professional] soldier was a criminal one."[73]

To Fritz Hartnagel, Ulm, June 22, 1940

My dear Fritz,

How long is it since I last wrote to you? Meantime, another of your letters has turned up. However much I always enjoy answering your latest letter, I find it very difficult because it's hard to say things in writing that can only be resolved by conversational toing and froing. I'm perfectly prepared to believe that you simply argue with me for argument's sake when we get onto ideological and political subjects – the two go hand in hand. It's enjoyable, I appreciate that. Personally, though, I've never argued for argument's sake, as you may secretly believe. On the contrary, I've always unconsciously made certain allowances for the profession you're tied to, in the hope that you'll weigh these things more carefully and perhaps make concessions here and there.

I can't imagine two people living together when they differ on these questions in their views, or at least in their activities.

People shouldn't be ambivalent themselves just because everything else is, yet one constantly meets the view that, because we've been born into a world of contradictions, we must defer to it. Oddly enough, this thoroughly un-Christian attitude is especially common among self-styled Christians.

If it were so, how could one expect fate to make a just cause prevail when so few people unwaveringly sacrifice themselves for a just cause?

I'm reminded of an Old Testament story[74] that tells how Moses raised his arms in prayer every hour of the day and night, asking God for victory. As soon as he let them drop, his people forfeited divine favor in battle.

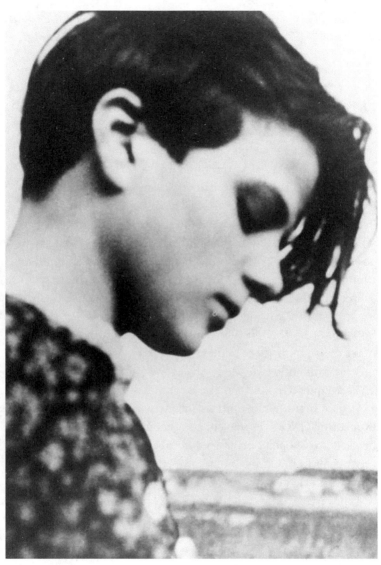

Sophie, 1940

Do people still exist today who never tire of undividedly
focusing all their thoughts and desires on a single objective?

That doesn't mean I would range myself on the side of those who are single-hearted in the true sense. Scarcely an hour passes without one of my thoughts flying off at a tangent, and very few of my actions correspond to what I consider right. I'm so often scared of those actions, which loom over me like dark mountains, that all I want to do is cease to exist, or become a grain of earth, or a fragment of bark. But this often overpowering desire is equally bad because it only stems from weariness.

Weariness is my principal possession. It keeps me silent when I ought to speak out – when I ought to admit to you what concerns us both, I put it off till later. How I wish I could live awhile on an island where I could do and say what I want, instead of having to be patient indefinitely.

I only meant to tell you nice, cheerful things, and now you're getting a letter like this.

Don't think I'm good, that's all I ask, because I'm bad. Don't do it for my sake, so I needn't always be afraid of disillusioning you badly someday. I know what I'm like, and I'm too tired, lazy, and bad to change.

Forgive me if you find this letter puzzling, but I can't always show myself the way I'm not.

Sofie

The following letter was written six days after the French signed the armistice at Compiègne. Mussolini had declared war on France on June 10.

To Fritz Hartnagel, Ulm, June 28, 1940

My dear Fritz,

I received another letter from you the day before yesterday. I'm glad you get some time to yourself occasionally. Your Wolf reminds me a lot of our Lux, who lived in the garden till a year ago. Whenever I was doing something outside, he would suddenly appear beside me with a stick in his mouth. That meant, "Let's see who's the stronger." I never managed to wrest the stick away from him by force, only by trickery (which coincidentally saved his teeth). However, it isn't a good game for training dogs. After that Lux bit anyone he didn't know. For a while he had a companion, a young German shepherd. Whenever anyone appeared, he would slink beneath a woodpile and peer out with an incredibly comical expression. He died, though, and Lux went off on one of his long walks and never returned.

Hans writes that he's busy day and night. He's quite fit again (so he says) and working at a field hospital[75] – near Rheims, I think. He'd been helping to nurse the wounded from Soissons. Most people here take the attitude: Who cares how the war turns out as long as my son or husband soon comes home in one piece?

It looks as if the French were only interested in their home comforts. I'd have been more impressed if they'd defended Paris to the last round, regardless of all the art treasures housed there, even if they'd achieved nothing, or nothing of any immediate value. But expediency is everything these days, and true purpose no longer exists. Nor does honor, I suppose. Saving your own skin is the main thing. —Well, now that France is in the Führer's hands, will home leave cease to be so out of the question?

If I didn't know I'll probably outlive many of my elders, I'd sometimes shudder at the spirit that governs history today. Now that the mighty lion has killed, the jackal and the hyena[76] are venturing forth to claim their share.

I'm sure your attitude to all that's happening today is quite unlike mine. You have plenty to do. I'm doing work that's the same in wartime as in peacetime. Sometimes I do it gladly, often I don't. I'm sure you find it unfeminine, the way I write to you. It must seem absurd for a girl to worry her head about politics. She's supposed to let her feminine emotions rule her thoughts. But I find that thoughts take precedence and that emotions often lead you astray because you can't see big things for the little things that may concern you more directly – personally, perhaps. It's the same with children. You can't provide them with all they need to console them when they cry, not right away, because it's often better for their development if you don't give in to your immediate feelings.

I never come back empty-handed these days when I go out into the garden. It's a grand feeling, picking what you've grown yourself, no matter how little it is.

I went down to the Iller yesterday, but not for a swim. I enjoy being by myself beside a river in the evening. There are no distractions.

You see, I always come back to myself.

I'm working too little rather than too much. I don't do half as much as I could. I've cured myself of something, too: dreaming about things I find pleasant. It makes you torpid.

Fond regards for now. I'll soon sit down and get close to you again, if only by letter.

Sofie

To Fritz Hartnagel, Ulm, July 1, 1940

My dear Fritz,

Just a few lines before I go to sleep. I'm hoping for another letter from you before long. We always wait for the mail on tenterhooks, especially the army mail. We heard from Hans today, and just imagine, Father is going to have to renounce his principle that dogs don't belong in a town apartment without a garden. The fact is, Hans has acquired a three-month-old St. Bernard pup, which he plans to give me if he gets it home safely. Werner and I are absolutely thrilled. Whenever we catch one another's eye, we burst into a delighted laughter at the knowledge that we're both thinking about the same thing. So, Fritz my dear, if you don't need or "like" that dog of yours (these things do happen sometimes), send him to me rather than leave him with someone else. I'd be tremendously pleased. If you went to England,[77] for instance, you could surely find someone to bring him back to Germany. Or you could bring him yourself – that would be best of all.

He'd be well cared for. I feel warm inside already at the thought of having those dogs here with me. It would be lovely, not being all alone.

For the present, though, I expect you two get more out of them and need them more than we do. But if you ever didn't want Wolf, I'd return him to you well trained later on.

I bet I'll dream of puppies all night long.

Yours,
Sofie

To Fritz Hartnagel, Ulm, July 8, 1940

. . . I'm more at home in the kindergarten these days. I've grown very fond of many of the children, and it makes me happy when they're nice to me. It's only now that I see how superficial my attitude to children really is. You need more than the kind of emotion children so readily arouse. I now realize what infinite love for all living things you need to be able to cope with those unpredictable, often spiteful, often heartwarming little childish creatures. Few people possess as much love as that, but one can cultivate it. . . .

To Fritz Hartnagel, Ulm, July 19, 1940

My dear Fritz,

Just a quick line before going to sleep. I can't write a real letter, I'm too tired. I went for a two-hour cycle ride with Inge this afternoon. It was lovely, and I came home rich. It's so grand to be able to take things, just like that, without depriving anyone. It's so good that the fields and forests and clouds never change, unlike us human beings. (We remain the same too, or so it might seem to a giant, but our mutual relationships are constantly changing.) And even when you think that everything's about to end, the moon reappears in the sky the following night, the same as ever. And the birds continue to sing as sweetly and busily without worrying whether there's any point in it. Have you noticed the way they tilt their little heads to the sky and sing with complete abandon, and how their little throats swell? It's good that such things are always with us. You have them too. It's enough to gladden one's heart, isn't it?

Yours,
Sofie

To her brother Hans, Ulm, July 21, 1940

Dear Hans,

I meant to write you a long time ago to tell you how glad I am that you'll be bringing your dog back for me from the war. I've been ill since then, which is why I've put off writing for so long that I can now thank you for the polo shirt at the same time. Instead of my giving you presents, you give them to me and us. Werner is now waiting eagerly for his shirt. He's almost as delighted as I am about the dog. Our eyes meet sometimes, and if we both start laughing, we know we've thought of the dog simultaneously. Let's hope you can keep him while the war lasts.

Inge and I went cycling this afternoon. We meant to head for the Illerwald, but we enjoyed cycling so much, and there was a bit of a wind blowing. We felt like senior officials of the Almighty who'd been sent off to find out if the earth was still good – and we found it very good indeed. (We couldn't think of people at that moment. We were fully preoccupied with the beautiful woods around us, and the people in them looked so friendly, too.) I wish I could paint well and fast so as to capture such fleeting, lovely moments and delight myself and others with them later on, but I'm sure there's another way of achieving both objects if only I take the trouble to think of it. Later, beyond Oberkirchberg, we turned off into the woods. Inge said there was a smell of strawberries, but all I could smell was resin. Inge has a keener sense of smell, that's why. We sat down under some small fir trees with long, bare trunks. The treetops kept crashing into each other overhead, so you never knew if it wasn't some animal stepping on a twig. It was only the wind, though. Then I smelled strawberries too, because I'd sat down in the middle of some. Wherever you brushed the ground with your hand, the berries showed up red. We gathered masses of them on big leaves, but just as we were about to reward ourselves for our trouble it started to rain. We ate all the strawberries up just the same. Then it poured so hard that we hurriedly took refuge under a thick, leafy tree. When the downpour moderated, we cycled off fast to the nearest farmhouse, where the cows and hens gave us a very cordial reception. We soon deserted them because the treacherous rain had stopped, only to take it out on us twice as hard later on. But we were glad it was raining. You taught us that. (If we hadn't been glad. . .)[78] By the time we got back to Ulm, the sun had dried us out again.

I hope I'll also be home when you get your leave, because I'm spending the next four weeks at a children's home in the Monbachtal.[79] I'll write to you once from there if I get the time. I ought to learn a lot there, too. I'll get to read your letters even there, Mother will see to that.

All my love,
Sofie

To her brother Hans, Ulm, July 25, 1940

Mon cher frère,

I won't continue this in French because you've acquired too good an eye for howlers. Just a line before I leave for my vacation practice. You probably won't have the time or inclination to read the little books,[80] but your patients might like to. Are you going to be able to take your prelims?

You'll have already heard from Mother that we received our consignment of coffee, and that it's dwindling rapidly. It's only fair that it should run out before I leave. I'll be seeing Lisa on Sunday.

Mais je fermerai maintenant.

> *Salut à toi*
> *toujours ta soeur*
> Sofie

Before embarking on another spell of teaching practice after vacation, Sophie went off to the mountains for ten days with her friend Lisa Remppis.

To Fritz Hartnagel, Warth, August 1, 1940

Dear Fritz,

Today I saw the ski runs we did together in February and March in their summer finery. I was pleasantly surprised, because the mountains are very beautiful in summer too, though in quite a different way. You need good eyesight to be able to pick out every last little detail. It's a long time since I got as much pleasure out of flowers as I did today. For that matter, it's a long time since I felt as happy in general as I did this morning, when Lisa and I were sitting on a little hill in the Gamstal pass, possibly the one where I came over cold so suddenly. It was mainly the hill itself that delighted me so much. It was covered all over with daphne and campanulas, one clump of which, sprouting from between some stones, must have had a hundred little bells on it. There were all kinds of herbs, too, and forget-me-nots and arnica and a hundred other flowers whose names I don't know, each of them a marvel, exceptionally delicate in color and shape. – Now we've both landed up at a Catholic rectory, and we're delighted. We'll live on black bread and butter and cheese, because this time we don't have any Fritz with us to order meals fit for a king. But that's only secondary. At least we've got whole milk. I intend to relax here for ten days before going off to a children's sanitarium [The Kinderheim Kohlerman] at Bad Dürrheim. . . .

To Fritz Hartnagel, Steeg, Tyrol, August 8, 1940

. . . I'll be back home again tomorrow, just when we've found somewhere perfect to stay here in Steeg. It's raining, but that makes our room all the cozier. You must know those big, low-tiled stoves with comfortable, upholstered benches around them. It's the ideal place for lazing around. I'm growing fonder and fonder of the mountains, and also of the local inhabitants. We've seldom had as warm and hospitable a reception as we got from the people here, and if we're ever in a bad way, we'll know where to come. Besides, the wind blows wonderfully free here, from every point of view. What a tonic simple folk can be. —We left Warth yesterday, after Inge had joined us. Earlier we were invited up the Hochkrumbacher Alpe, where Lisa and I had previously stopped for a snack on our walks and, most notably, drunk some milk. The cowherds are very nice and hospitable, and if I'd had more time to spare, we'd definitely have stayed on up there. We did our own milking, and I'm sure I'd have become a good milkmaid with a bit more practice. I can't tell you how kind the people were. One local inhabitant, who'd climbed the hardest face of the Warther Hörner with us, kept rooting around in his rucksack for things for us to eat. He also offered us jobs on the spot, so we could have worked nearby during vacation. The people where we're staying now are just as sweet and kind, too.

It's only very rarely that any mental picture or idea from the time immediately beforehand has come into my head, for instance of my parents, or the war, or you, or anything else. Who would have thought it possible that a tiny little flower could preoccupy a person so completely that there simply wasn't room for any other thought, or that I could have turned into earth, I liked it so much, or thrown my arms around the first person I met, I was so happy. What I enjoyed most was lying on the ground, where I was close to all the little creatures and a part of everything. The ants and beetles regarded me simply as a piece of wood, which was why I quite liked it when they crawled over me. Everything was so very lovely.

I got your letter. Many thanks. I'm glad you're well. Perhaps there'll be another one waiting for me at Ulm.

Sofie

On August 10, immediately after her return from the mountains, Sophie started work at a children's sanitarium in Bad Dürrheim.

To Fritz Hartnagel, Bad Dürrheim, August 11, 1940

. . . I can't tell you anything about this place yet; I've only been here since yesterday. The children range in age from four to seventeen, boys and girls. They're from better-class families, unfortunately, and spend most of their time kicking up a frightful din. I'm anxious to see how I get along with them. To be honest, I look forward to the end of my time here. The place is run by a major and his wife. Their cousins, sons, fathers, and the rest of their relations seem to be officers as well.

I found it very hard to bid the mountains farewell, as you can imagine, even after so short a time. I did spend a summer up there three years ago, but these last few days have made a far stronger and deeper impression on me. If I had the money, I'd move there later on, lock, stock, and barrel. Not to the very bottom of a valley, but halfway up. I'm sure I'd get ill far less often there. All the little flowers, all the friendly little things that rob the mountains of their overwhelming grandeur when seen at close quarters, are a pure delight. That's why, provided they haven't been spoiled by some outside influence, mountain folk can't be compared with townsfolk or the farmers in our own part of the world. I've never met peasants who take such pleasure in plants or treat animals so kindly. I've no doubt they also brandish a milking stool if they can't get a cow to its preordained place any other way, but how sweetly they talk to the little calves afterward. "The full life" still exists here in its most pristine form. (I'm sure there are others.) That, too, did us so much good. . . .

To her parents, Bad Dürrheim, August 12, 1940

Dear Parents,

I was already given the afternoon off today (probably so that the transition wouldn't be too abrupt). I bought myself some fruit and headed for the woods. I didn't go far because the unaccustomed work and the change of air had made me pretty tired. The surrounding woods are quite "civilized," I regret to say, meaning there isn't a single spot without a path leading to it for anyone to take. However, I sat down somewhere or other and started reading. Before long I was slowly and warily approached by a squirrel, which spent a long time vainly sniffing, scrabbling, and chewing my briefcase. I kept absolutely still, so it was bold enough to clamber up me. As soon as it reached my bare neck, it darted back to the ground and up the nearest fir tree. It didn't reappear, unfortunately.

There are around forty-five children here – quite enough to kick up an awful, incessant din. The youngest boy is two and a half, the eldest, seventeen and a half. Most of them come from the north. All the other "aunties" are North Germans too, which isn't making it any easier for me to settle in. The dialect alone is slightly inhibiting. It's easiest to get along with the big boys, who butter the aunties up and are on very friendly terms with them. The permanent auntie is disagreeably Prussian, I'm afraid, but I'll get along with her just the same. We have to feed the children, wash them, replenish the washing water twice a day (there's no running water, worse luck), take the children for walks, get them up, and put them to bed. Washing them in the evenings is the devil of a job, because they have to be washed from head to foot in little basins. We start at seven in the morning, and everything is more or less over by nine thirty at night. The lunch break varies between half an hour and an hour. I get two afternoons off a week. I also get time to read or write while the children are having their compulsory rest, unless I have some darning to do, so I'd be grateful if you could send me some books.

It's quite dark already, and I don't want to do the blackout, so fond love for now.

Yours,
Sofie

To her sister Elisabeth, Bad Dürrheim, August 15, 1940

Dear Lisel,

Today you're getting a short preliminary report from my children's home, written in the hope that it will coax a letter out of you. There have been four of us aunties up to now, but two are leaving tomorrow. That'll mean more work, but never mind, it'll make the time pass quicker. You can picture what this brine spa is like from your knowledge of Hall. Almost the only difference, I suppose, is the children. Only so-called better-class children come here, because the home is pretty expensive, but there are very few that appeal to me particularly. On the contrary, I'm surprised how conceited and spoiled some of them already are. The bigger boys especially. There's no nice community spirit, either, so one can't do anything sensible with them. I've nothing to do but attend to their physical needs and yell for silence. We have a number of eight-year-old boys who are genuinely amusing and give me pleasure, also a two-year-old, Klaus, who's a scream but immensely spoiled. I'm always tired out in the evenings. We work till nine thirty. In my spare time I read, and that means a lot to me here. – I keep wishing the four weeks were up, especially when I climb into bed and my roommate starts snoring. She's got the brain of a hen and 130 pounds of unappealing flesh to go with it. On top of that, she never washes, and considers herself a beauty. The rest you can imagine. I had a spat with her right away, so as to be left in peace.

Nothing much has happened here, nor will it until some younger children arrive at the beginning of September, or so we're told. I'm tickled pink at the thought that I'll have completed a quarter of my time here tomorrow. How is Gottfried?[81] And how are you? Are you going to Tübingen?[82] I hope you write really soon.

I have to go shopping now.

Fond love from
your sister Sofie

To Fritz Hartnagel, Bad Dürrheim, August 16, 1940

My dear Fritz,

I bet you didn't think I'd write you so often from Bad Dürrheim. This makes three times already. The thing is, when I get half an hour off I'm all alone (or often not) in my dreary little room. I can't do much in that time. I do have the *Stunden-buch* [by Rilke][83] with me, and it's just what I need because these half hours are what lend character to my day. I'm often tempted to pick up one of my roommate's frivolous paperback romances. Can you understand that? Anything for a change, like a movie. So I'd sooner dash off a letter, even if it's the dullest recital of facts. That way I suppress the temptation, which, though absurd, is strong. Do you find that incomprehensible?

Today I bought myself some fruit in the village. I feel such an urge to have something on my bedside table at nights. It makes my bed seem much cozier if I come in and know: now you can enjoy something of your own, all to yourself. It's a feeling that erects four walls around me. Inge felt the same at Lesum. Funny, isn't it? . . .

To Fritz Hartnagel, Bad Dürrheim, August 19, 1940

. . . I got a letter from you this morning. I'm always waiting eagerly for letters at present. Very many thanks. – Because I'm on afternoon rest duty (i.e., have to make sure that none of the twenty children who've been sleeping on the terrace for two hours speaks or does anything else), I can reply right away.

I sometimes think of last summer too, but I don't brood about it. I don't have the time.

I think you misunderstand my views on your profession. Or rather, I think that the soldier's profession today is different from what you described. A soldier has to swear an oath, after all, so his job is to carry out his government's orders. Tomorrow he may have to comply with a view diametrically opposed to yesterday's. His profession is obedience. So the soldierly attitude isn't really a profession. In your ideal conception of it, it really accords with the moral demands made on every individual. I can well appreciate that you regard your profession as an educative one, but I think that's only a part of it. How can a soldier have an honest attitude, as you put it, when he's compelled to lie? Or isn't it lying when you have to swear one oath to the government one day and another the next? You have to allow for that situation, and it's already arisen before now. You weren't so very much in favor of a war, to the best of my knowledge, yet you spend all your time training people for it.

You surely don't believe it's the job of the armed forces to teach people an honest, modest, sincere attitude. And as for your comparing this to Christianity, I believe a person can be a Christian without belonging to a church. Besides, a Christian isn't compelled to be anything other than what his principal commandments require of him. If a soldier's commandment is to be loyal, sincere, modest, and honest, he certainly can't obey it, because if he receives an order, he has to carry it out, whether he considers it right or wrong. If he doesn't carry it out, he's dismissed, isn't he?

Forgive me if I've been vague or incoherent in what I've written. The little rascals are such a handful. All one can do is scold them the whole time. But most of the pranks they play to make themselves look big are so childishly silly I'm tempted to laugh behind my hand.

I'll definitely be writing to you again before long. You're being inundated with letters from me at present. The afternoon rest is over now. I must sign off.

Affectionately yours,
Sofie

To her sister Inge, Bad Dürrheim, August 22, 1940

Dear Inge,

First of all, many thanks indeed for your lovely letter and the much appreciated parcel of goodies. I've already made a big hole in it. Your letter came at an ideal moment. I felt cheerful all day afterward. I keep rereading it (letters from home are my favorites, I don't know why), but not just to wallow in memories. On the contrary, they restore my spirits every time. Whenever I'm in a relatively pleasant situation, I feel it'll soon be over, and if only you dear people knew how many hidden resources I have. It often surprises me how little I mind about things, compared to Auntie Inge and her everlasting blues. The major's wife is very nice and great fun, but we "aunties" mean nothing to her except in relation to the children. Mild reprimands are frequent (one always takes them too much to heart), pats on the back very few and far between. I'm often too scatter-brained, and I'm learning here to keep my eye on lots of things at once. While working, I used to forget to do something else of equal importance. There was too much to remember, especially as we had so many sick children (there are only five left, thank God). I'm still not good, but I'm genuinely proud that I'm at least doing a bit better than I was. Not one of our children is completely fit. That, of course, is why we have a sanitarium here. Most of them suffer from asthma or something similar. They have attacks now and then, but only rarely.

I can tell that I'm still not relaxed or patient enough to cope with children. I'm always having to make an effort when it's time to tell them off, and I'm too tired or lazy to take all their stupidities in my stride. Some of the worst little devils have left, thank goodness, and more will be leaving on the 31st. The home's favorite hit of the moment is *"Kann denn Liebe Sünde sein?"* ["Can love be a sin?"].[84] Whenever I start to give one of the bigger boys a telling-off, he grins and says, "Is it a sin to love?" The twelve-year-olds are as bad as the older ones. I'm gradually coaxing them into displaying their better nature, but their philistinism is well developed and remains as unappealing as ever.

I get on better with the girls, or at least the older ones, who've already taken me to their hearts. They often prevail on me to stay and chat with them at night, which is all the more enjoyable for being against the rules. The little girls of six and seven spend the entire day squabbling, and it's often an effort to see beyond their stupidity. The boys do likewise in their own way. They persist in hitting each other, and you can imagine how good I feel when I'm out of earshot of their yelling. Unfortunately, my roommate makes up for that by chattering incessantly. The worst of it is, she's a hysteric. I often feel quite uncomfortable at night when she bursts out laughing, usually for no reason at all. She's the talk of the entire home. I'm still not immune to the almost physical pain inflicted on me by her proximity and her noisy ways (she's never still for a moment, even in her sleep). Perhaps it's doing me good to sleep near her, so I acquire a certain immunity to such trivia.

Did you go away with Ernst [Reden]? I'm so glad you saw the alpine flowers that only grow very high up. As Lisa will have told you, we felt the same on every mountain as you did on the Bienig.[85] My happiest discovery was that big mountains bring forth such little things, such little flowers and grasses.

I hope I'll be there when Hans comes. I'm only here for another seventeen days. If you send me an "APO parcel," put in a small unbreakable bowl for me to keep my little bits and pieces in.

My roommate has just been reading *Lerke* (I couldn't stop her). When she finished the last page, she said, "Six men died for her sake."

I've run out of spare time and paper.

Fondest love to all from
your sister Sofie

P.S. Please send some writing paper and stamps.

To Fritz Hartnagel, Bad Dürrheim, September 3, 1940

. . . I'm deriving greater pleasure from the little children, more and more of whom are arriving, because my impulse to help the helpless little things is gradually overcoming my personal antipathies. (I wish I could say as much of my attitude to everyone or almost everyone else.) The little people are a lot of work. On average, I have to wash five children from top to toe every evening, get them dressed and everything (one wet bed a night, if not more), and then inspect and/or clean the ears and nails of another ten, replenish the washing water, and so on. I wasn't completely through till ten o'clock last night. Now, although I've already brushed my teeth, I'm eating another of your candies. I couldn't decline with thanks if you sent me some more, because these little treats (i.e., much-prized rarities) can prove useful in a lot of ways. . . .

To Fritz Hartnagel, Ulm, September 12, 1940

. . . I stayed on at Bad Dürrheim till yesterday, because they couldn't spare me before, and I was only able to leave then because my sister Elisabeth turned up to act as a stand-in until a children's nurse arrives. So I was released at lunchtime yesterday, after getting the brine baths ready and attending to the children for the last time that morning. It's nice to know you've endeared yourself to them, and that they notice when you leave. I always did my best to make them like me. I had to promise one little boy to come back right away. He used to cry whenever I went down to the station (usually to meet someone). I found it harder to say good-bye than I'd have thought possible, partly because I had to leave my sister behind. I was amply rewarded in the end. The major's wife was very cordial (I slowly but steadily gained their affection, which they promptly extended to Liesel, thank goodness) and gave me 50 marks – the first money I've ever earned. . . .

To Fritz Hartnagel, In school [the Fröbel Institute], September 23, 1940

My dear Fritz,

I don't know for sure if my letters will be less frequent from now on, but it's in the cards. There's always so much to do when I get home from school, and I always have a lot more distractions there. (That's the wrong way of putting it, actually, because are drawing, piano playing, etc.,[86] – which I seldom get around to in spite of everything – distractions?)

Even now I'm sitting in college and should really be doing some practical work, but I'm going to put it off for half an hour. I can't answer your last letter in detail, because it's at home, but many thanks indeed for your latest parcel. The stockings, which I shared with my sisters, were especially welcome.

We're expecting Hans home any day. He was counting on some leave around now, but in wartime you never can tell. I'd sooner your leave didn't coincide with his, if you know what I mean. Then I could devote myself exclusively to each of you. But I mustn't expect too much. I'll be content if you both come at all.

You asked me to write you my views on nationhood. I won't have the time right now, but my notion of the concept, though not clearly defined, is pretty straightforward.

As I see it, a soldier's position vis-à-vis his nation is rather like that of a son who vows to stand up for his father and family come what may. If his father does another family an injustice and gets into trouble as a result, the son has to back his father regardless. Personally, I can't raise that much family feeling. To me, justice takes precedence over all other attachments, many of which are purely sentimental.

And it would surely be better if people engaged in a conflict could take the side they consider right.

I've always thought it wrong for a father to take his child's side on principle, for instance when a teacher punishes him or her. However much he may love the child, or for that very reason. I think it's just as wrong for a German or a Frenchman, or whatever else a person may be, to defend his nation doggedly just because it's his. Emotions can often be misleading. I, too, am moved when I see soldiers on the street, possibly marching to a band, and I used to have to fight back my tears at the sound of military marches. But those are old wives' sentiments. It's absurd to let them get the better of you.

We were taught in school that a German's attitude is deliberately subjective. Unless it's objective as well, I can't accept it. But this subjective approach has caught on with a lot of people, and many who were looking for a pattern to fit their conflicting emotions have adopted it with a sigh of relief.

I'm sure you're bewildered by my often clumsy metaphors and wild effusions. I hope you can thread your way through them. The next time I'll try to be clearer and more deliberate. It's too late today.

Are your travels in Holland[87] over? I hope you had a lot of good times there. Maybe I'll hear from you again now. (Not that I can complain.)

> Fond love for now,
> Sofie

P.S. I'll reply to your last letter and tell you what nationhood means to me later on.

Please forgive the exercise-book paper!

Hans also had to shoot the dog I was going to get because it got sick, so you're both in the same boat, and all my happy expectations have come to nothing.

Hans Scholl

1940–1941

Hans Scholl returned from France to Germany at the end of September, 1940. On October 15, after two weeks' furlough at Ulm, he was reassigned to a students' company and released to continue studying medicine up to preliminary examination level at Munich University.

To his parents, Munich, October 25, 1940

Dear Parents,

    After a long and laborious search I've finally found a nice little room near the Perlacher Forest, outside Munich. What I enjoy there most of all is the wonderful peace and quiet and the good forest air. The family I'm lodging with are very friendly.

    I'm due to take my prelims a few days after Christmas. This means a great deal of work, naturally, but I think everything will go all right.

    I'll be needing some more money by the first of next month because I have to pay my admission fee right away. Please send me my skull[88] and some tea (there wasn't any in my bag) and the light-colored stockings. I also have to get my clothing coupons at my parents' place of residence.

Having spent days filling out sternly worded forms and shut-
tling back and forth, I hope to be able to plunge headlong into
my work at the beginning of next week.

My fondest love to you,
Hans

To his parents, Munich, November 7, 1940

Dear Parents,

I was so pleased to find your nice parcel waiting for me
when I got back. I'm sure I owe my acquisition of the nut
cookies to Inge.

I can't tell you much because my head is stuffed with
anatomy, physiology, and other ologies. "Stick it out," we keep
telling each other, "never say die!" If only these ten weeks were
over, though! I'd give anything to be two months older, but
pipe dreams like that are no help. I would only add that it isn't
pleasant, studying the way we are now. The strongest among us
would definitely lose their love [of medicine] in the long run.
Still, never say die!

Fondest love,
Hans

To his parents, Munich, November 21, 1940

Dear Parents,

Your nice parcel reached me yesterday afternoon. We've
already polished off the apples. Two can get rid of them far
quicker than one. Hellmut [Hartert][89] hasn't found himself a
room yet and is still staying with me. The light-colored sports
jacket looks fine again.

I'm up to my eyes in work but the material I have to absorb
gets more and more instead of less. Once I'm on my own again,
I hope to be able to study even harder. My exams begin on
January 13th and end on the 15th.

I don't yet know whether I can come home at Advent, or if it wouldn't be better to stay put. Sundays are particularly valuable to us at this stage.

I'm well looked after by the Orthlieb family[90] and feel at ease with them.

Fondest regards,

Hans

To his parents, Munich, December 4, 1940

Dear Parents,

I received the parcel of butter and almonds. Many thanks. It's been even colder here since yesterday. I definitely need a scarf and a sleeveless sweater.

The chairman of the examination board has requested us to withdraw from the preliminary exam and postpone taking it till after next semester because the examiners are particularly tough in wartime. It's quite out of the question, of course. Some nerve those bureaucrats have, posting notices like that four weeks before the exam. So we're to be additionally penalized for having served in the war. Unlike us, the lawyers can sit their first public examination after only six semesters.

I'll probably be home on the 22nd.

Fond love,

Hans

To his sister Inge, Munich, December 6, 1940

. . . Please tell Father and Mother I badly need some more money. I have to buy some books. Also, I owed Fräulein Gerstenberger[91] another 20. I'd forgotten that, and I still haven't quite finished paying for a refresher course. We have to shell out fees for every last little thing. You can't imagine what it's like. Life is very expensive now, and I don't have the time to

Hans as a student at Munich University, 1941

economize on food. I live really frugally. I'll be coming home as early as possibly on the 22nd and staying till the 25th.

All his complaints notwithstanding, Hans Scholl passed the preliminary examination in medicine in mid-January 1941. He was now under threat of being recalled for military service.

To his parents, Munich, January 28, 1941

. . . I'm writing to you again because it's been snowing magnif-
icently since yesterday, and I'd love to go skiing in the
mountains, more especially because yesterday I got a letter from
my unit, couched in rather weird German, requesting me to
forward official confirmation that I've passed my preliminary
examination as soon as possible after sitting it. They obviously
intend to recall me, damn them!

It's awful that every road should be closed to us at our age,
just when the world should be our oyster! One feels more and
more like a prisoner. Let's hope this war will soon be over. It's
already getting me down, seeing the same old mostly stupid
faces of my fellow students at lectures. It's time I switched
universities.

On the other hand, living in Harlaching is very pleasant at
the moment. You can go for lovely walks in the afternoons.

I shall have to acquire the clinical textbooks bit by bit. Clinical work naturally holds a particularly strong interest for me. . . .

My time here is very fully occupied. I have thirty hours of
lectures a week. The rest of the time we have to work on our
own, which is almost more important.

I badly need a briefcase, my white coats (two are here), and
my wristwatch.

Is there some regulation under which we're declared exempt
from military service until our finals? Would my unit release
me, though? Our CO is a dour regular. I reported the loss of my
paybook yesterday. I hope the new one turns up soon, so I can
buy rail tickets cheap.

Best of luck to Werner and Sophie in their exams.

All my love,
Hans

P.S. There's a dearth of envelopes in Munich. Better stock up!

The following letter is part of a series that shows Hans's developing relationship with Rose Nägele. She was the daughter of a Stuttgart doctor whose five children were closely associated with the five young Scholls in a variety of ways. The eldest son, Hanspeter, whose work Sophie illustrated, belonged to the illegal dj-1/11 like Hans and Werner Scholl. Hans and Sophie were very fond of the youngest daughter, Eve, then a girl of thirteen, and frequently mention her in their letters.

To Rose Nägele, Munich, February 3, 1941

Dear Rose,

It's snowing like fun today. There's nothing to do but stew in your cozy room, light your pipe, and ponder on your sins! If you'd received all the letters I've written you in my head, you'd be buried beneath a mountain of verbiage.

First, though, the truth. I'm anything but an energetic youngster with both feet planted firmly on the ground. There's a kind of mad melancholy underlying everything, and that's why I'm disinclined to write. Don't get me wrong, though. I'm not talking about weakness on the outside, but an internal, private insecurity that really has no connection at all with weariness. Nor [with] instability. One feels a bit world-weary at times, and all one's best efforts seem futile and superfluous. Perhaps these are symptoms of the age we live in. If so, we ought to be able to overcome them.

You've got a girlfriend in Munich, don't forget. Couldn't you pay her an occasional visit, and me as well? You haven't been skiing yet this year.

I'll write again soon.

Lots of love,
Hans

To his parents, Munich, February 8, 1941

Dear Parents,

I set off for Lenggries on Friday and spent the night up there. On Saturday the sun shone, and the snow was first-class. I had several very enjoyable runs. The visibility was very good that evening, so I guessed a thaw was on the way.

Meantime, I've invested all the money you sent me in books. Our textbooks are still being printed on decent paper, so it pays to buy them now. . . .

If only this godforsaken war would soon be over. I'd like to get out of Germany.

I haven't yet managed to see any of my nicer fellow students. They all seem to have retired into their shells. They've lost their enthusiasm, which is understandable enough. It's the same old story in every profession.

> Fondest love to you both,
> Hans

To his parents, Munich, February 10, 1941

Dear Parents,

I received your big parcel today. The two smaller ones have also turned up. I can't thank you enough.

Everyone's pleased about the first spring day. Droves of people are flocking into the open air. I'm pleased too, but my own instinct is to go where there's no one else around.

I hope Inge and Father are also enjoying the warm spring breeze a little, while the fine weather lasts. The garden will soon be tempting Mother to start work again.

I heard today that we've no hope left of obtaining exemption. This was only to be expected. It means I've got another two months of so-called freedom. I feel like losing my temper sometimes, but today I don't mind too much about these things, especially as the sun is shining on the just and the unjust alike. That, at least, will shine forever. I shall manage to preserve my inner freedom, even in the army. Werner will find it harder to begin with.

I'm now starting to learn English properly. If there's any way of arranging it, I plan to spend six months or a whole year aboard ship after passing my finals, so as to get to know the world.

I'd love to come home at the end of this week. If I do, I'll certainly come on Friday. I've organized my schedule so that all my important lectures fall early in the week.

We toured the wards for the first time today.

Fond love,

Hans

To Rose Nägele, Munich, February 24, 1941

Dear Rose,

It won't be long before my little taste of freedom comes to an end. I'm always on the move these days. It's too tempting to drop everything and play hooky. I've regained my perception of what freedom is. I trudge the highroads once more and leave all else to the Almighty, or my sudden whim, or I set myself a destination and get there if I'm so inclined.

I got back from the mountains yesterday. I must definitely pay them one more visit, it's so incredibly beautiful there. If only you could come with me, and if only I could hear your tinkling voice beside me – but, no, I mustn't think of that. I often do, though, damn it.

The sun's shining. The snowdrops are out, and white clouds are sailing across the sky. Dark earth and bright sky. I feel like saying yes to everything. I feel like saying, yes, I love you, yes, I know the way, oh, yes, it's bliss to be a human being.

And then someone slams the door on me. It's dark again – night. A little human being, huddled up, crushed by his own misery, cowers in the darkness, thinking, brooding, realizing that it's futile, that he'll never make it. . . .

What you say in your letters is right: we lack humility. I lack it above all else. I can't weep, so I curse. A lot of it may be imagination, of course. The war may have distorted a lot of things in my brain.

These bold effusions aren't the product of a nocturnal whim. On the contrary, I'm striving to make an accurate assessment of my experiences in recent months, a process impossible over there because I still lacked the requisite detachment.

Write to me again soon.

Lots of love,

Hans

To his sister Inge, Munich, March 10, 1941

Dear Inge,

I've simply got to touch you for some cash!

Disgraceful. But if I did it to anyone else, it would be even more so. The thing is, I've arranged to go skiing with Rose Nägele. Rose is currently at Montafon (Arlberg). It's awfully sweet of her to come all this way on my account, and I can't let her subsidize me into the bargain. I do have a smidgen of self-respect left, so please send me 20 marks by return. Pay you back as soon as I can.

I quite understand why you received an adverse response about [James Joyce's] *Ulysses*[92] from Ernst Reden. I've now read the second volume and couldn't make head or tail of it.

I was invited to Tölz yesterday. My first visit for four weeks and probably my last. I'm on very cordial terms with Frau Borchers, and reason tells me, contrary to all my emotions, that I must let little Ute[93] retain her childlike innocence. (Which certainly isn't dispelled by the odd cigarette.)

I was absolutely delighted that the lost paybook turned up again. Now I can afford to lose one again with total impunity.

I bumped into Olga[94] at the station today. She went skiing too.

I hope I'll soon be able to help you with the books[95] again.

Lots of love,

Hans

In the following letter Hans passes along a bit of advice to Werner Scholl. On April 1, 1941, after graduating from secondary school, Werner, the youngest of the Scholl children, was conscripted into the Arbeitsdienst. He spent some time at a camp near Biberach and was then assigned to construction work on the Atlantic Wall in Brittany.

To his parents, Munich, March 13, 1941

Dear Parents,

Many thanks for Mother's letters and parcels. I'd love to sneak off to the mountains with Werner for a day or two before he joins the Prussians. Anyway, I'd strongly advise him to put his freedom in the right perspective by doing such a thing, because man lives by memories as well as ideas. I probably won't spend more than a couple of days with Rose. I think I'll have to be back by Monday or Tuesday.

I wrote to my unit to inquire when I have to report again. Several fellow students have been deferred until their finals, so I'm putting in another request for exemption anyway. It would be wonderful to complete the course by Christmas '42.

On my way back from Tölz the day before yesterday, I watched a fantastic display of lightning lasting about an hour, the most magnificent I've ever seen. Perhaps you heard something of the storm. It was far away to the west.

I'm currently reading a book by Lily Abegg[96] (you may know the name, Father): *Chinas Erneurung,* subtitled *Der Raum als Waffe!* Societäts-Verlag 1940.

Remarkable how many sun-tanned faces there are to be seen among my fellow students, more than ever before. Since we're groping our way so uncertainly into the future, the general tendency is: live while you can!

I don't mean to bewail the lot of our generation, but it really is in a pretty poor way. . . .

Hans Scholl had to spend his university vacation doing a student internship at a hospital in Miesbach, from which the following letter was sent. Miesbach was a small town some thirty miles southeast of Munich.

To Rose Nägele, Miesbach, April 15, 1941

Dear Rose,

You'll already have had my other letter. There's nothing special about my being here, but my theories are proving correct again. What I said about man in the mass is absolutely right. Innumerable things confirm it.

It's awful to have to see my fellow students' boring faces again. If only they were new ones, but they're still the same old mugs. Frightful.

We're told of the straight and narrow path which the wise man has to tread, but I see that this one is a thousand times better, and that the shadows it skirts turn to diamonds in our soul once we're through them.

I'm living in seclusion as a matter of course, without any fuss. I've taken a hotel room to avoid communal quarters, so I can read in peace at nights. I shall restrict my friends to a minimum.

In spite of all that, I'm a socialist to the core. But more of that another time.

My mind goes back to our Easter together. How happy I am! However many storms rage over our souls, we'll always regain the equilibrium of our existence. However much we worship the young and lovely god Eros, too, the basis of our friendship is purely spiritual in the all-embracing sense. This will matter in the future, I know. There are things that far transcend the sexes when two clear-minded people, who aren't man and wife, confront one another and say "Yes."

I realize how much my hand is trembling, and that all my thoughts are ruled by confusion, turmoil, youthful turbulence, and agitation, but there's a force that's showing me the way, an invisible force born of the fire of love, pure and fresh.

Write to me soon!

Yours,
Hans

In April 1941 Hans Scholl was ordered to rejoin his students' company. In mid-April he requested exempt status until his finals, but he was turned down. He was, however, granted a few days' leave before the beginning of term.

To Rose Nägele, Ulm, April 18, 1941

Dear Röselein,

I'm back in Ulm. Our leave has been extended to April 22nd. Then I have to continue studying at Munich, worse luck. On what basis, whether in barracks or private lodgings, uniform or civvies, hasn't been decided yet. Nor does it really matter. . . .

To Rose Nägele, Ulm, April 19, 1941

Dear Röselein,

What I want to tell you today is a dream I had early this morning, just before waking up.

I saw myself on a subway train in Paris, bound for a tour of the city with you and a crowd of acquaintances and my brother and sisters and friends. The train went racing along. We found it great fun and were in high spirits. The train emerged from the dark tunnel and soared up an elevated track between houses and towers, up hill and down dale. It sped on, groaning, hissing,

Hans Scholl, 1941

screeching, occasionally passing over trains that raced off in the opposite direction. Subway, elevated, roller coaster – a fantastic mixture of permutations, and always the same breakneck, aimless speed. It struck me that there probably wasn't anything grander anywhere else in the world. We focused our attention on the vistas that flashed past our eyes in quick succession, now a sea of gray buildings, now a lush green field bright with flowers. Finally we reached a suburb and got out. Enchanted by the gabled houses overlooking us, I told you that this suburb was medieval and rural in character, and thus in complete contrast to the incredible product of ultramodern technology that had brought us there. We liked it there, too. Everything made a snug, homey impression: the sunlight, the marketplace with its fountain, the wind rustling in the ancient trees.

On impulse I entered one of the houses. I groped my way in semidarkness along a yawning passage, caught a whiff of empty wine barrels, felt a door that creaked open at my touch. And lo, oh horrors of hell, oh crazy inferno of all that's dreadful, I found myself, as I instantly realized, in a very, very old infirmary with cracked gray walls, a rough uneven floor, and a soot-stained ceiling. Beds knocked together out of rough-hewn planks were scattered at random around the room, an incalculable number of them, one above the other, and over everything hung a bestial stench. It didn't deter me from exploring, though. I was overcome with feverish curiosity. I knew that this was virgin territory, that I was the conqueror of a totally unknown land, the first man to set foot there. I boldly walked up to the beds. The strange thing was, what then met my eye no longer appalled me in the least. I was completely transformed and sobered by the sight of that infinitely bleak and cheerless room. I was a professional, accepting what met my gaze as a matter of course, rather like someone unsurprised by the fact that people should sometimes start praying aloud in church. —Röselein, you may think I'm trying to keep you in suspense with long-winded sentences, but oh, you must fill your nostrils with that scent of unwashed bodies, that effluvium of hell, so read on and don't be annoyed with me. The patients were terribly mutilated creatures, monstrosities of the most dreadful kind, deformities such as only the Devil's imagination could have devised. There were girls with harelips, cleft palates, crooked facial clefts, men whose lower extremities were entirely missing, and old crones whose breasts were so enlarged that they hung down to the ground. They scarcely noticed me. One of the men, all of whom were legless but sitting up in bed, eventually inquired what I was doing there. "I'm a doctor," I told him. "A doctor, eh?" the cripple replied with a mocking grin, and all the others grinned too. The women and girls twisted their facial clefts into a ghastly grin that seemed to communicate itself to the beds, rafters, and floor. The very air contorted itself into an indefinable, repulsive, horrible semblance of a grin. "A doctor, eh?" said the patient, and went on, "So what's this place got to do with doctoring?" The floor gave way, the sky caved in, I retched, felt the cold breath of death. I took to my heels. I ran, I stumbled, but not the way one usually does in dreams. Everything seemed terribly real. I ran on until someone stopped me and ordered me to assist at an operation that had to be performed at once. Just then I thought of you and recalled that you were waiting for me outside. "Damnation," I thought, "what am I to do?" Love and duty are a favorite problem in classical drama, but I wasn't thinking in dramatic terms. I dashed outside to tell you that I had to assist at an operation, and that it would take two hours. You didn't say a word. If only you'd said something. I knew that you were gradually succumbing to pangs of conscience, but still you said nothing – weren't even sad. I just stood there, gazing into your infinitely dear face. Then I woke up.

Only one of many dreams, but it was so remarkable I had to tell you about it. Maybe you can sense how I feel when I wake up.

So you had a visit from Hanspeter [Nägele]. It's never a dull moment with you. If only I could pay you another visit soon. I'm off to Munich again tomorrow, and then the new semester starts, the seventh.

If the sun shines tomorrow, you're sure to stretch out on the grass somewhere and gently doze off.

Sleep well!

Yours,
Hans

To his parents, Munich, April 23, 1941

Dear Parents,

There's only one word to describe our present existence: bleak. We're housed in an old school, eighteen men to one room. Our duties consist in reporting for duty and waiting. As far as I can assess the situation, these arrangements are quite impossible because they're impractical, and the requisite reforms will soon be introduced. I'm looking for a nice room, turning out obediently for musters, sleeping in barracks most nights, and in other respects leading a life that suits my taste, insofar as I can.

Anyway, I'll be home for Mother's birthday [May 5] come what may.

Fond love,
Hans

To his sister Sophie, Munich, April 24, 1941

Dear little sister,

I've as little to tell you as you have me, but I did promise to write to you. Just wait, before long you'll have so many long-winded, awful, occasionally amusing letters to decipher, it may scare you.

The thing is, since today I've had a new room,[97] a bigger and better one than before, even though a lot of junk – vases, bronze busts, carvings, African trophies – has still to be brutally dumped outside my landlady's door. It won't be long before I can welcome you to it, because one's time in the Arbeitsdienst passes very quickly, take it from me. I'll also keep you supplied with books to the best of my ability.

Our barracks are frightful. Still, I'm going to buy some flowers today and put them in the room. Flowers and bright eyes can brighten the most squalid place on earth.

Lots of love,
Hans

To Rose Nägele, Munich, April 25, 1941

My dear Röselein,

This is my first evening in my new room. I'm staying in although it's cold and the room still leaves a lot to be desired. But I'm smoking my pipe and sitting by the window while writing to you. I feel at ease in my new home. It's a big room with a high ceiling and one huge bay window. There's no bed in it because I have to be back in barracks by 1 a.m. I shall take the pictures down by degrees and hang others in their place. All I'll really need here then is an occasional visit from you.

In front of me lie the pictures of you I took during my visit to Lake Constance. I'll send you them in one of my next letters. Not that my memories of those wonderful days require any pictures. I feed on them like daily bread.

I wish us all some sunshine from the bottom of my heart. Are the days really as cold and gray with you as they are here? You're a true child of the South, with your yearning for the sun.

How did you enjoy my dream story? I expect I wrote it down rather superficially, but my highly critical approach to our literature doesn't stop short of my own dream visions at level-headed moments. That's why I don't dare write as I'd sometimes like to. Anyway, my repetitions are superfluous. Hasn't it all been said before?

Röselein, from now on, you won't be alone when you're working. I aim to compete with you. When I get up, I think, ah, Röselein has been awake for ages. I'm not allowed to get up before 7 a.m., but at night – remind yourself at night that Hans will be awake for a long time yet. All the same, I won't miss an occasional chance to salute the dew-fresh morning as you do every day. There'll be times when I don't have to sleep in barracks, and then I'll sally forth at crack of dawn just like you. . . .

Don't think me a dreamer, Rose, because I plan to visit you again soon. Is that odd? Anything but. It would be odd if I thought differently, so write me where and which Saturday night I can find you. Tell me in your very next letter!

> All my love,
> Hans

To his sister Inge, Munich, April 25, 1941

Dear Inge,

Thanks for sending the photos and the deckle-edged paper so promptly. It's almost like a gift from the gods, having at last found a reasonably nice room. I feel so much more at ease on my own territory than I do in the eternal drabness of the military environment, so you must pay me a visit here soon.

My room is big, with a high ceiling. There's only one window, but it's very large and projects slightly to form a small bay with a table and some old-fashioned chairs in it. That's where I write my letters and read my beloved books in the afternoons. At night I generally sit at a solid oak desk bathed in warm light by a table lamp. Although the room still suffers from the presence of a lot of old junk, I hope to get rid of it by degrees until the place gradually takes on an appearance not too utterly unlike my own room at home.

Could you sometime send me the Franz Marc picture Fritz gave us? I'd like to get it framed and hang it in my room for the time being.

You'll soon be getting a better letter from me. Everything's still under construction here!

Yours,

Hans

P.S. I also received Father's 20 marks. Thanks a lot!

To Rose Nägele, Munich, April 27, 1941

. . . This is the right time for reading. I have Rilke's early poems[98] in front of me again, though my perception of them is different from what it was five years ago. Rilke meant everything to me in those days. I've only now discovered the real Rilke, that's why I'm starting all over again.

On top of that I'm still a long way from the end of Grimm's *Michelangelo*.[99] Then there's Guardini on Hölderlin[100] waiting for me, and on May 2 lectures begin at last. I'm a regular glutton for knowledge. (I wasn't for a long time.) . . .

Hans Scholl took time off from his studies to visit Weyarn, the former Augustinian Canons' Collegiate Church at Weyarn, Upper Bavaria, some twenty miles south of Munich. It was an elaborate baroque church with a sacristy decorated by the eighteenth-century German sculptor Ignaz Günther. Later (see his May 11 letter), he cycled to Kloster Schäftlarn, a former Premonstratensian monastery rebuilt in the eighteenth century with some notable stucco and fresco work (1754–1756) by Johann Baptist Zimmerman.

News from home, meanwhile, included Sophie's induction into the Arbeitsdienst April 6, despite her hopes that she would be exempted from these duties. She experienced some difficulty fitting in at the camp to which she was assigned.

To his brother Werner, Munich, May 1, 1941

Be not forgetful of those that never write to us. The heavens have compelled me to stay at home. I meant to cycle to Weyarn today to look at the baroque works of the Günther school,[101] but it's drizzling incessantly, so I'm smoking my pipe and writing letters instead. I'm alive and breathing through my pipe and finding this rainy day far from unpleasant.

I urge you to come home after all for Mother's sixtieth birthday. It's a [legitimate] ground for leave of absence. It would be so nice to be all together again for a short time, because who knows where the coming months will take you?

Geyer[102] [the Ulm painter] is engaged on some church windows here. I often go to see him. He gets through an incredible amount of work. I hear that Sophie doesn't much care for the whole Arbeitsdienst to-do. I trust you don't either. . . .

Lots of love,

Hans

To Rose Nägele, Munich, May 2, 1941

My dainty, doughty little Rose,

Even though May came in accompanied by rain, all the fields were bright with the loveliest green imaginable. A sunbeam pierced a little gap in the dark sea of cloud, and the world laughed and glittered in the light of heaven. I stood there marveling and thought, Does God take us for fools, that he should light up the world for us with such consummate beauty in the radiance of his glory, in his honor? And nothing, on the other hand, but rapine and murder? Where does the truth lie? Should one go off and build a little house with flowers outside the windows and a garden outside the door and extol and thank God and turn one's back on the world and its filth? Isn't seclusion a form of treachery – of desertion? Things are tolerable in succession – the youthful spirit emerges from the ruins and soars toward the light – but simultaneities are antithetical, ruins and light at the same time. I'm weak and puny, but I want to do what is right.

Goethe says that if a miracle occurs in the world, it does so through the medium of pure, loving hearts. That consolation has been mine since you loved me.

Are the cherry trees in blossom with you?

I now get up almost as early as you do, but I can't see the sun yet at that time of day, the houses are too tall.

Tomorrow I'm going home for my mother's birthday. The others may also be there. Sophie, Lisl, Werner. Eve [Rose's younger sister] wrote me a nice letter. She seems to enjoy writing.

Me, I only enjoy writing to you!

Yours,

Hans

P.S. Please write per APO to my home address!

To his mother, Munich, May 8, 1941

Dear Mother,

As you gathered from my last letter, I'm in good spirits as regards my work despite the difficult conditions. I was delighted to receive your two parcels. The weather today is really spring-like, but it doesn't prevent me from attending my lectures. I'm now at a stage when I'd like to devote myself entirely to the natural sciences. I'm reading a lot and don't regard my work as work, just a Sunday stroll in my own special meaning of the term. . . .

I'm still sleeping in my room. No one has spotted it yet. I doubt if more than a third of us are sleeping in barracks. If the sergeant knew, he wouldn't sleep soundly at nights.

I wish you all a halcyon May. In particular, I hope Father gets plenty of much-needed opportunities to relax outdoors.

All my love,

Hans

P.S. Like Father, I spent the air raid in bed.

To Rose Nägele, Munich, May 9, 1941

. . . I'm working with gusto. I'm most anxious to gain a thorough understanding of the sciences with a view to someday solving the problems that currently plague us. To put it very roughly, the method I ultimately favor is as follows. Truth is discoverable in two ways: first by means of logic, and secondly through the precise investigation of things. The object is to combine these two schools of thought, which engage in futile competition, on a single plane. Philosophy and science must conduce to the same end. Let the findings of the one, if incontestable, serve as proof of the other. . . .

To his sister Inge, Munich, May 11, 1941

Dear Inge,

One of my friends, whom I told you about, is in the hospital, having developed acute appendicitis but not, thank God, died of it. His vermiform appendix was perforated and his abdominal cavity awash with a turbid body of fluid, *pus bonum et laudabile* [good and wholesome pus].[103] However, he's now doomed to a long spell in bed, which is not only depriving him of precious lectures but preventing him, as you'll readily appreciate, from concentrating on his work. He's asked me to get him some modern French literature, and I think the best bet would be Bernanos, because apart from their superb language, which is the mark of the true writer, his books are thoroughly exciting in content. Please would you send me *Sous le soleil de satan.*

I've resumed my study of the Latin tongue (with no outside assistance). I find the work genuinely enjoyable.

I'm spending most of Sunday in my room. It's cold and rainy outside, and there's so much to read and "tinker with." Yesterday, when the sun was shining, I cycled up the Isar to Kloster Schäftlarn.

I hope Father's thermometer has risen a degree or two.

Cordiale poignée de mains.[104]

Votre Hans

The "thermometer" Hans mentions in the preceding letter (also called his "barometer of opinion") is a reference to Robert Scholl's views on political developments.[105]

To his sister Sophie, Munich, May 14, 1941

Dear Sophia,

I've got a bit of time to write to you tonight. I'm very fully occupied during the week, with lectures till 7 p.m. as a rule, and pointless musters are held in our spare time. I steer clear as far as possible and haven't slept in barracks for ages, but just wearing army boots makes me tired, especially in this fantastically beautiful spring weather.

So spring has come after all! People must have been thinking that every year for thousands of years, and it's true: However much our spirits may rise and fall, we see the light above us in the vale of despair, and when we're up again after untold trials and tribulations, we breathe a sigh of relief and tell ourselves: It had to be this way — everything's bound to come right again.

Everyone must have been delighted that you managed to get home. I'm sure Inge feels lonely without you sometimes. But how lovely it would be if you came here!

Don't you have any free time over Pentecost? Perhaps I could visit you. It's only two weeks off.

The Mozart festival ended today with a big orchestral concert at the Tonhalle. You should have been there! Art like that is as essential to us as our daily bread. Definitely! What would life be without it?

Yes, and next week comes the Bach festival. The six Brandenburgs.

By and large, these are peripheral occurrences in my day. The rest of my day is extremely important, and never routine, but to tell you about it would take too long. You'll find it all out for yourself.

Lots of love for now,

Hans

To Rose Nägele, Munich, May 14, 1941

. . . Another evening which I couldn't have borne to spend in my room in the old days, but I'd sooner stay at home with my books. I'm just reading Pascal's *Pensées*[106] and I've also got a philosophy of religion by Dempf.[107] Sometimes I read one of Rilke's letters from Muzot,[108] but more in order to justify or solace the yearning nature of my own innermost desires. Pascal is incredibly tough. Essential reading, though.

Apart from that, of course, work claims much of my time. I've enrolled for around forty hours [of lectures] a week. . . .

To Rose Nägele, Munich, May 22, 1941

. . . I'm still working at the same old pace. I'm childishly pleased with every bit of progress I make, but I sometimes peer into the dark pit of our ignorance and long for a complete, well-rounded view of life. . . .

Both Sophie and Werner were now serving in the Arbeitsdienst. Werner was shipped off to France to do construction work on the German coastal defenses in Brittany, and Sophie, still at the camp, was assigned daytime duties at a nearby farm, though she hoped to join Hans soon at Munich University.

To his brother Werner, Munich, June 6, 1941

Dear Werner,

You're getting a few lines from me today because I've at last discovered your address. It's strange, and it sometimes strikes me as rather incredible, that I should now be writing to you in France, the same France where I myself underwent such a variety of experiences a year ago. The signs of devastation must still tell their own story, but the rumbling has stopped, and the people who were then so completely divorced from their outer shell, i.e., convention, self-respect, work, must now be clutching the charred and tattered remnants of their attire to them and doggedly surviving. Or isn't it like that? The children play like ours, no doubt, but don't the faces of the men and women bear traces? Perhaps things are different, as they are here – superficial, vague, futile.

I hope you open-mindedly cling to everything good that comes your way, but that you firmly shun everything sordid and go your own way without worrying too much about the others. They'll only take your finest pearls and cast them before swine.

Don't be annoyed with me if what I've said was unnecessary, and write soon. I'm keen to hear your impressions. . . .

Yours,
Hans

To Rose Nägele, Munich, June 15, 1941

My Röselein,

A brief account of the past week: it went by only too quickly. One ought to spend more time on oneself, not just go hunting for novelties. Our impressions are worth nothing until they've gradually permeated us and roam on through our innermost selves in the form of purified images. That takes time – a great deal of time – and people complain of boredom. There's no more appalling term than self-distraction. Far from distracting ourselves, we should do the opposite. We shouldn't grouse about the rain either. I've found that the best time for walking is evenings in the rain. This afternoon I walked a good way along the edge of the woods with my coat collar turned up, smoking my pipe, through a steady downpour. . . .

To his sister Sophie, Munich, July 1, 1941

Dear Sophie,

Is it all right if I pay you a visit next weekend, i.e., Saturday–Sunday? If so, please write and tell me where to meet you. What I'd like best is to visit you at your farm.

Here at the Brunnenhof last night they played the Haydn Serenade and several other wonderful string quartets. I can't wait for you to share in all these experiences. If they don't let me study next semester, I've already commandeered you a nice room.

Lots of love,

Hans

To Rose Nägele, Munich, July 17, 1941

What are doubts, if not doubts about ourselves? Uncertainty seldom resides in others or in our relationship with them, but usually in our own hearts, and we strive to generalize it. Nothing, I know, is more understandable than our environment, which precisely obeys the laws that govern it, provided we explore the nature of things. Man in the midst of his world resembles a fire that flickers relentlessly, inflames us with apparent unpredictability, burns, and dies. Should we blind ourselves to these dangers? Isn't it preferable to die of ever-gnawing pain than to roam the world freely and easily, but falsely? Is there no consolation?

Love is the only consolation, because love requires no proof. It exists like God himself, whose existence could doubtless be proved but was sensed by mankind long before any evidence could be produced.

Yes, there's such a thing as love for its own sake. It's unconstrained and exempt from human jurisdiction.

Sophie Scholl

1940–1941

After France fell, Fritz Hartnagel and his signals unit were stationed near Wissant, south of Calais, in a château enclosed by spacious grounds. Sophie was still studying at the Fröbel Institute.

To Fritz Hartnagel, Ulm, November 4, 1940

Dear Fritz,

I'm writing to you in bed. I shall mail this letter and the little parcel on the off chance that they reach you. You've been so silent, I've absolutely no idea how or where you are. If only I could get a line from you. Do write me however things are with you, good or bad. Is anything wrong?

Not having heard from you, I've been rereading your old letters. They're equally incapable of telling me how you are at present.

You once wrote: "I intend to be quiet and self-effacing." And another time: "I can sense new ground beneath my feet." I've correlated those two statements, and although they're different, I think they spring from the same sentiment. And it made me very happy, because a person who senses the ground you mention doesn't fumble his way aimlessly along anymore. And

I think you'll know from now on what to do when you hear that voice. This new state of affairs means a lot to us both as well. To me, at least, it has meant the greatest (and finest) change in our friendship to date. And if I understand you correctly, it must mean the same to you, for the threads of our relationship no longer run between you and me, but between us and something higher. And that's a better state of affairs.

Or have I completely misunderstood you? I don't think so.

Yesterday Inge and I went for a walk in the Klosterwald. The fall wind was blowing so briskly that the tops of the fir trees kept crashing together, and one of them, not being supple enough, had to pay the supreme penalty. The larches still have their needles, though they're quite yellow now. It was a marvelous sight when the wind tore into them and bent their twigs and branches sideways. We leaned against the wind, tousle-headed as witches, and the leaves whirled past overhead as though obliquely hurled from above by some mighty hand. And the little leaves on the ground went tumbling along too, whole hordes of them, as if they had to go faster still. How we laughed at them!

Is there a wind blowing in your park, too? Tell me if you can. It's so infuriating, waiting in ignorance. If only I could will you to write, but all I can do is wait.

I hope this reaches you. And please, put an end to my needless suspense.

Sofie

To Fritz Hartnagel, Ulm, November 7, 1940

. . . I'm just about to give a talk on *Vorsommer.*[109] I've still got half an hour to prepare it in. If you have the time, look up the passage in Psalms where it says: "Lighten mine eyes,[110] lest I sleep the sleep of death; lest mine enemy say, I have prevailed against him. . . ."

To Fritz Hartnagel, Ulm, November 10, 1940

. . . I've been debating whether to dispense with your letters, because the motive that prompts me to go on writing to you is a selfish one. I think it's unnecessary, though. It may even be bad, because my assumption (which needn't coincide with yours) is that you're all alone in an atmosphere that has nothing in common with the one I'd like to win you over to. And at bottom you're already half on my side, and you'll never feel entirely at ease there again.

The battle I wage with myself will be yours as well: not to subside into a state of well-being, into the warmth of the herd, into philistinism. Isn't it a prop and a consolation, knowing that one isn't all alone? Or rather, feeling it.

Although you sound as if you're very lonely, I can't help you. I mustn't, however much it hurts me not to. You know that yourself.

I can only advise you to brace up (how absurd that sounds). You say yourself that you're getting nowhere. If only you'd read some books, however much of an effort you found it. If only you had some minor task that demanded concentration.

I've no need to wish that on myself because I'm up to my eyes in unwelcome work.

Dear Fritz, please don't think me inconsiderate. Being hard is far more difficult than turning soft.

If only I could do something for you that would help us both.

Do you still enjoy writing to me?

Affectionate regards,
Sofie

To Fritz Hartnagel, Ulm, November 12, 1940

Dear Fritz,

Just a line before I go back to work. Here on Münsterplatz the wind plays such funny tricks it would be silly not to laugh.

When I go outside it completely ruins my hairdo (which is no great shakes anyway). One feels a regular urge to prance around and join in. A shame I can't spare the time.

I hope it visits you too, the wind, and takes you out of yourself a bit, so that you can't help rejoicing in the wind and yourself, because you're the person in whom the wind is unleashing such wonderful emotions. It really can, you'll see.

This is only one of the many good things I wish you. If they happen, the credit will be partly yours.

And don't waste time on unproductive things. That's something to be calmly (and not always gently) thrust aside.

Affectionate regards,
Sofie

P.S. If you're angry with me, be angry by all means, but vent your anger on the wind or on me, don't bottle it up inside you so much.

To Fritz Hartnagel, Ulm, November 23, 1940

. . . I sent you a little Advent parcel today. Let's hope it arrives in time. You'll have to straighten the candles a bit. I'll send you some more before long, because they'll burn up too soon. I hope you won't have any gloomy thoughts by their light. You've always got the Advent story to read.

Tonight's letter won't be a long one, I'm too tired. You won't be annoyed with me, will you?

The sprigs of fir on top you must burn the night you set fire to the wreath. But make sure you're alone at the time. (A child or an animal can keep you company, but that's all.) You wouldn't believe what a good atmosphere the scent of burning fir sprigs can conjure into being. . . .

To Fritz Hartnagel, Ulm, December 11, 1940

. . . Your latest letter was written sixteen days ago. Now I'm permanently on tenterhooks for another. It isn't that I'm urging you to write more often. I don't mean to influence you anymore from that point of view, because I know you're aware of what you're doing, but I'd like to be able to have a far bigger share in you. It's worrying, hearing so little about other people's doings. I know absolutely nothing about your professional life proper, but I don't think that's your most important side. As for the other side, I do share a little in that. I don't want to be a part of that other life, you understand, but I'd like to share in it, that's to say, look on at it so as not to fail you in any way. But this is probably an unfair request, and an impossible one as well. . . .

To Fritz Hartnagel, Ulm, January 13, 1941

Dear Fritz,

I received yet another letter from you this morning. We're really spoiling one another in that respect, at least for now. It sounds silly when I write it down, but I'm sorry that you should have to waste your spare time, which you probably need more than ever, on such trivial and tedious things.

You asked me to tell you about the skiing trip, so here goes. The party consisted of Inge, Werner, Lisa, me, Otl Aicher, and Grogo (a newly fledged biology student, in case you don't know him). We stayed above Elbigenalp in the Lech Valley at a well-nigh luxurious skiing lodge (we'd have liked a rough-and-ready one better), at around 1,800 meters. But the main thing was, we had it to ourselves. We lived on tea and bread, went to bed late, and got up late as well. In the evenings we read together, a book by Bernanos. I wish you could get something by him where you are. He isn't published in Germany anymore, being a living French author. The title of the book was *Diary of a Country*

Priest. If only you could get hold of it. I'd like to acquire a copy sometime.

It was often amusing and serious by turns. The atmosphere was enlivened by a little cuckoo clock that cuckooed every quarter-hour. Grogo's real name is Willy, a nice enough name, but we poked fun at it one night. I said I found it unsuitable, at least for Grogo, and vowed to call him Grogo for the rest of his days, and said, "Your wife will call you . . ." And while I was thinking up a really silly pet name, the cuckoo clock sang out "Grogo!" loud and clear. We laughed our heads off. From then on it was "Grogo, your wife's calling!" whenever the clock went cuckoo. Poor old Grogo. Still, the cuckoo clock managed to Grogo us out of many a bad mood after that.

We practiced telemarks like mad while skiing, mainly because of the deep snow. We didn't get around to any longish excursions, as you and I did last year. The surrounding area wasn't too suitable.

I returned home two days before the boys (Inge and Lisa stayed on). That was when I noticed the difference between our set and the others. I longed so much during the train journey to see a face that bore comparison with those of my brothers and sisters or friends. Know what I mean? It wasn't nostalgia, just the recognition of a difference. Even the hordes of young people I saw on the train weren't young anymore – they were simply exploiting their youth for pleasure's sake. But my brother and sisters and friends, though often more gauche and unsophisticated, were brimming with goodwill. Or filled with good intentions.

Coal vacations[111] have started here again. They don't apply to our college, worse luck. I hope at least that our exams won't be postponed as a result.

I'll be dying to know if this letter reaches you at your old quarters or if you've been transferred, heaven knows where to. The possibilities are legion.

Fondest regards for now. I promise to step up my letter-writing rate again, because I can well imagine how disagreeable it must be to be marooned somewhere in enforced idleness.

Affectionate regards from my mother as well. You ought to have received her letter by now.

Sofie

Fritz was able to spend some leave at Ulm during February 1941.

To Fritz Hartnagel, Ulm, February 21, 1941

Dear Fritz,

It's only nine o'clock, so you can't be all that far from Ulm yet. I was fifteen minutes late getting to the college on account of us, and had to dash back home on my bike because I'd forgotten a host of other important things. Sometimes, though, other things are even more important.

In college I was sort of bubbling over with high spirits. I was surprised at myself – I and my classmates could hardly stop laughing. (Ask a psychologist what overcompensation means, and you'll get a rough idea of my state of mind.) It didn't occur to me that you'd gone, irrevocably gone, till I was free to go home. All the preceding days I could look forward after school to an evening with you, but not anymore – a funny feeling. I'd grown too accustomed to your warmth and affection. That's a danger, too. At home I just looked at the magazines you bought so recently, and was foolish enough to hope that I'd find something from you meant specially for me. I'd have liked a note from you – something I could carry around unseen by the others. However, such are the first intense emotions born of parting, and I can't even approve of them all myself. . . .

To Fritz Hartnagel, Ulm, February 28, 1941

. . . I'm thinking of you, too, more often than usual. Perhaps it's because, in my state of slight exhaustion (which sets in quickly with me), I'm looking for a prop. I know I can depend on you, and that you love me. That's why we needn't tie one another down. I can tell I'm growing fond of you all over again, in a different way. I'm fond of you because of the good that's in you – because of what makes you a human being. That can form a special bond. . . .

Sophie passed her kindergarten teacher's examination at the beginning of March. Only a few days later, on March 17, she started work at an Ulm day nursery in the hope that this would exempt her, once and for all, from having to join the Arbeitsdienst. Her hopes were soon dashed.

To Fritz Hartnagel, Ulm, March 22, 1941

. . . I received some unwelcome news today: I've got to go into the Arbeitsdienst. However, I've already come to terms with my immediate future. I always try to acclimatize myself as quickly as possible (mentally, too, and to new ideas). It's an aid to maximum independence from all outward circumstances, pleasant or unpleasant. I've become so expert in self-adjustment that I got over my annoyance at the RAD in five minutes flat, and when I left school, Fräulein Kretschmer[112] defined my most salient characteristic as imperturbability. Perhaps it'll compensate a little for my moodiness during your leave if I quote two lines from a graduation day poem: "She (S. Scholl) always was a cheerful sort, and nothing ever put her out." I'm rather dumbfounded myself at the impression I make on such people.

I'll probably be joining up in the next 10–14 days. . . .

Sophie began her RAD service on April 6, 1941, at Krauchenwies Camp near Sigmaringen, on the same day that Germany invaded Greece. After desperate resistance the Greek army, despite assistance from the British, was forced to surrender. When Sophie refers below to the surrender of Greece, she probably means the fall of Salonika on April 9, which forced the surrender of Greek troops defending the Metaxas line in Thrace. She also refers to her father's "barometer of opinion."

Diary, Krauchenwies, April 10, 1941

I arrived here four days ago.

I'm sharing a dormitory with ten other girls. I often have to close my ears to their chatter in the evenings. Every time I join in, it seems like a concession, and I regret it. I've managed to stay pretty much in the background so far, thanks to my shyness. I wish I could keep it up, but I'm forever catching myself showing off in little ways. It's awful, my craving for recognition. Even as I write that, I'm wondering how it will look on paper. It's destructive of mental harmony.

At nights, while the others are cracking jokes (I haven't entirely steered clear of those, I'm afraid), I read St. Augustine.[113] I have to read slowly, it's so hard to concentrate, but read I do, even when I don't feel like it. I also read some of Thomas Mann's *Zauberberg*[114] in the lunch break today. I don't think it's quite as reprehensible, or rather, put-downable, as Otl finds it. It's very precisely conceited and, above all, *thought out*. I don't think Otl grasps that.

I'm trying hard to remain as impervious as possible to current influences. Not the ideological and political kind, which have ceased to have the slightest effect on me, but atmospheric influences. *Il faut avoir un esprit dûr et coeur tendre.*[115]

Everyone grumbles like mad about our supervisor. I've no personal grounds for complaint. She handles me with kid gloves, so much so that it puzzles me at times. (Yet again I have to repress a little thrill of triumph at this.) Although she forbids the others to have books, she lets me have them (why, I've no idea). But she's as chary of patting me on the back as she is of telling me off. I had to draw some Easter cards. I only gathered that she liked them when she gave me some more to do. But this state of affairs will change too, and so will my present relations with the other girls. I know this only too well from experience, much as I'd prefer to avoid it.

It's strange, but as soon as I'm away from Inge, I feel far closer to her. Then she becomes a real sister to me – more of a friend. I'm already looking forward a lot to her letters. The fact that I get much closer to Lisa when we're together is probably attributable to our workaday way of looking at things. We sometimes see them in a horribly down-to-earth light. Inge takes a childish, sometimes rhapsodic view of everything, with far too much self-involvement. She responds to everything with an outpouring of emotion, so she finds life far harder in one way than we do. But far easier in another! I don't think she would find it possible, in addition to the emotions or thoughts that claim her entirely, to have the kind of awful little demon that watches you and your potential effect on other people. I shall find that hard to get rid of. Will I succeed? That conflict, or rather ambivalence, spoils a lot of things for me and makes me mean and nasty.

Greece surrendered yesterday. It made a depressing impression on me at the time. (Depressing impression is repetitive.) The effect has now worn off completely. It'll return this evening when I listen to the news with the other eighty, but after that the mail will be given out, thank God.

I'm wondering if I'm really so dependent on mail. I hope not, after all my lectures to Fritz on self-sufficiency. No, one shouldn't call it that, one should call it "independence of people and things." I genuinely meant that at the time, I suppose, but I so often fail to act on it myself. . . .

To her parents and her sister Inge, Krauchenwies, April 10, 1941

Dear Parents, dear Inge,

This is the first really free quarter-hour I've had. Now I can tell you some more about the camp. The most noticeable thing is the cold. If I didn't know it simply must turn warmer soon, I'd ask you to send me a heating pad. I take ages to get off to sleep because it's just too cold. Lots of dear little mice are the other noticeable feature. I'm getting to know them really well during my hours of insomnia, and can only congratulate myself on being upstairs (in the upper bunk). They're also careful to keep us slim here, and I don't understand how people can say you have to eat a lot in the RAD. The food runs out long before you can stuff yourself. That has its good side, too.

In spite of the negative aspects I've just listed, I'm feeling pretty good here. That's because of my couldn't-care-less attitude, which I'm cultivating even more here. I haven't done much work yet. We waste a lot of time standing around waiting for our supervisor, etc. I often regret this when I think what else I could do with the time. Everyone grumbles incessantly at the supervisor, but it's more of a vogue than a justified complaint. I don't think she's particularly competent either. She's sarcastic to everyone at all times, never friendly, and doesn't have any of the pleasant characteristics that would help to create a congenial atmosphere. I often feel sorry for her, she's so crotchety. I think she'd make life far easier for herself if she was less acerbic.

I hope I'll get a letter from Father or another of you, telling me how high the barometer of opinion stands as a result of Greece's surrender. Here it's immensely high.

I'm looking forward eagerly to your next batch of mail, which I hope will turn out to be big at Easter. We're very dependent on mail here, and I always count the hours between one delivery and the next. If my own letters are delayed, don't blame me. We have to hand them in, here in camp, and I've no idea how long it is before they're forwarded to the station.

I'll be quite content with one extra Easter-cum-birthday letter. Inge, don't forget Uncle's box and Auntie's little basket.

All my love,
Sofie

P.S. Eve wrote to me too: "To the Arbeitsdienst Girl."

Many thanks for Mother's card.

Please type out the declarations overleaf on two separate sheets and return them signed as soon as possible (Wednesday latest). In theory we get leave of absence every six weeks, in practice less often. Shall I come home on my first Sunday out, or will Inge come here? Then we could go to Lake Constance together. There are visiting Sundays too, but that's still a long way off. Please be quick and send me some writing paper too. I don't have a single sheet left.

Declaration

I hereby permit my daughter Sofie Scholl to use the outdoor and indoor swimming pools.

Father's signature

I hereby authorize my daughter S. Sch. to make free use of her Sunday leaves of absence, and to spend the night with friends or relations or at a youth hostel, inn, or hotel.

Father's signature

To her sister Elisabeth, Krauchenwies, April 10, 1941

. . . Our billet (an old manor house, not terribly grand) stands on the edge of a big, handsome park, which I plan to explore as soon as the snow has melted a bit (it's still snowing at present). It'll take some exploring, it's so big, and they say there are deer in it, too.

Diary, Krauchenwies, April 11, 1941

This evening, as I glanced quickly out of the window of our cheerful, bustling room, I saw the yellow skyline through the bare trees. It suddenly struck me then that it was Good Friday. I was saddened by the strangely remote and detached sky. Or by all the laughing people who were so divorced from the sky. I felt excluded, both from the cheerful company around me and from the indifferent sky.

I would like very much to go to church. Not the Protestant one, where I listen critically to what the parson says, but the other one, where I tolerate everything and have only to be open and receptive. But is that the right one?

I'm afraid I showed off again for a moment this evening. I didn't lie or exaggerate, but it occurred to me while speaking that I was eager to impress.

I'm gradually becoming acclimatized, I'm afraid. I shall take myself in hand. Reading at nights will be a help.

To Lisa Remppis, Krauchenwies, April 13, 1941

Dear Lisa,

This won't be much of a letter, not with sixty-odd girls sitting around me, but I had to thank you right away for your nice parcel. I've grown particularly susceptible to that sort of thing here, as you can imagine. Honestly, almost every letter and parcel is a cause for celebration. Little things mean a lot here. I'm always rather horrified to think that I'm going to be here for six months, and I always think it's something that doesn't concern me. I don't worry about it, though. I firmly suppress any silly feelings that come over me and treat what is fundamentally unimportant (which wastes the bulk of our time here) as unimportant in the extreme – in other words, I dismiss it altogether. I read a little every night with grim determination (I've finished the second volume of Thomas Mann's *Zauberberg*, and I also have *Augustinus, Gestalt als Gefüge* with me), which not unnaturally attracts a lot of snide comments from my new roommates, who prefer to indulge in risqué stories. You mustn't infer from this that they're exceptionally vulgar. They're quite ordinary, decent girls, and this poor topic of conversation is probably what matters most to them. (It's true, if you think about it. Some girls are discreet, others less restrained.) If only for that reason, I'm grateful to my books for keeping me out of their conversations, though they naturally put it down in part to haughtiness.

As I think I already wrote, I'm glad I'm finding it so hard to fit in and wouldn't wish myself into that condition (the routine one). On the contrary, it blunts your mind too quickly.

I hope you're having some real spring weather at Langenburg, and that you'll let me share in it a little by courtesy of the mail. We're confined to camp, poor things, and won't be allowed out till April 20.

Repay me in kind for being such a good correspondent.

Affectionate regards,
Sofie

P.S. I got a very nice letter from Hans. I think it would be grand if we could study together, because I wouldn't slack in front of Hans. (I wouldn't want to in front of anyone, for that matter, not anymore.) The same goes for him, and that's the best educational incentive of all. I'd sooner talk about him than write about him, incidentally, because he's a rather tricky subject. I really need to talk about him, too, especially with you.[116] Ah, well.

Diary, Krauchenwies, April 13, 1941

Today is Easter Day, but how have I celebrated it so far? If only I could be alone. I'm going to do some reading now. The whole of the Easter story, and then some St. Augustine. Someone's playing an accordion beside me. The girls are dancing to it.

Diary, Krauchenwies, April 14, 1941

Earlier on, while I was walking past a girl from the Saar, I drew a pencil line across her cheek for fun, without thinking. She came after me, shouting, "You may be a year older than me, but I won't put up with it!" Being in a flippant mood, I thought she was half joking. "You poor thing," I said, all prepared to make it up with her. "Keep your sympathy," she said. "Very well," I said, "I take it back." To which she angrily retorted, "I want your sympathy as little as you have mine. . . ." She followed that up with a whole torrent of words, but I walked off. I was defeated in a flash. It's the unwarranted little meannesses that wound me most and leave me defenseless. I'd never spoken to the girl before and don't know what made her so spiteful. She's universally popular because of her brazen impudence and the infectious laugh she often lets out quite uninhibitedly, at the top of her voice. I can never help joining in, though I always feel faintly repelled by the sight of her. She's big and fat, and her personal appearance would make her look thoroughly at home in a waterfront tavern. What lies behind it I've no idea. I wouldn't want to do her an injustice, but I suspect she's incredibly crude (like a lot of men). I've always sensed that and been startled by it when she laughs and cracks jokes.

The following diary entry remarks upon the beginning of Sophie's correspondence with Otto Aicher, familiarly known as Otl, a school friend of Werner Scholl's. Otl first came into close contact with Werner's brother and sisters in the fall of 1939, as the result of an essay he had written on Michelangelo's sonnets. Otl had refused to join the Hitler Youth, and the growth of his friendship with Hans, whose membership in the Hitler Youth at first put the two in opposing camps, was a gradual process. He and Hans discovered common ground after the Gestapo detained them both for "subversive [youth movement] activities," and thereafter Otl assumed an increasingly important role in the Ulm circle.

Diary, Krauchenwies, April 17, 1941

I got a letter from Otl today (prompted by Inge, I secretly surmise). I'll do my best to answer it, but first I'll get in touch with Fräulein Fries. She may be able to tell me something.

Diary: Draft of a letter addressed to Fritz Hartnagel but probably never sent, Krauchenwies, April 18, 1941

I received another note from you today, for which many thanks. I think it's really infuriating of them to take up your evenings. Can't you refuse? They'll soon deprive a person of any chance to preserve his poor soul from their uniforms with that grim and ubiquitous martial spirit of theirs. What a chapter in the history of the German nation! What will people find to put in it later on, apart from the dates of battles and suchlike?

Diary: Draft of a letter addressed to Fritz Hartnagel but probably never sent, Krauchenwies, April 20, 1941

My dear Fritz,

Let me call you that this time. I spent half an hour in the park this evening, and just as you were able to pick snowdrops in yours some months back, so I now find innumerable cowslips in mine. And in my park the clumps of trees looked so lovely in the evening light that I walked home backward so as to prolong the sight of them. Clouds were floating high above like the slender white feathers of some strange bird, and the spring sky and the lower-lying clouds were tinged all over with orange by the setting sun. I would so much have liked to walk with you awhile, so very much. Do you remember the time we watched the alpenglow in the mountains? I couldn't help thinking of that this evening, and of our trip to the North Sea, and the way we lay and frolicked in the sand. I also thought of our walk beside the Danube in the fall, and it only dawned on me then how mean I was and what an impression of me you were obliged to take away with you. How nasty I can be at times. Yet I'm so glad you were with me in February, and that we went skiing together. Even though a lot of things would have been better left undone, they led to the mutual understanding I'd craved for so long. My dear Fritz, I'm glad now when I think of you and me, and I'm often filled with hope.

I must go to sleep now. I've been writing under the covers, hence my handwriting.

Fondest love,
Sofie

Diary, Krauchenwies, April 20, 1941

This evening I paid a brief visit to the park. It was a wonderful evening, the first time I've ever felt at home here. I'd have liked to perch on a stone somewhere and write to Fritz, but there was another girl with me. She means well, though I'm sure she finds me a bit eccentric.

To her parents and her sister Inge, Krauchenwies, April 25, 1941

Dear Parents and Inge,

First I want to thank you for the lovely, elaborate, and capacious parcel. As usual, it made my day. Although our supervisor has forbidden us to receive parcels, I hope you won't comply.

She's afraid we'll write home for extra food, that's all, but there's no need. The food is getting better and more plentiful as time goes by. Besides, I have some good friends in the kitchen who slip me things occasionally.

I'm afraid I won't be assigned to outside duties as soon as all that (only in three to four weeks' time), but I'm fine as I am. For some unknown reason, and not because of any effort on my part, the camp commandant is being very nice to me. She lets me sit in the office (where it's warm!) and write and sketch there. Today I drew a nice map of Greece, but that was all. Yesterday I was allowed to go to Sigmaringen to buy some cardboard (Arbeitsdienst girls aren't allowed out of camp unac-companied, as a rule). That meant I was free once more between 8 a.m. and noon. They gave me a sausage sandwich thickly spread with butter from the staff canteen, so I sat down some-where in the woods for a snack and enjoyed myself thoroughly. It was my nicest day here to date. The road to Sigmaringen runs through woods nearly all the way. It's a really lovely walk.

I'm very grateful for the books. We're forbidden to have any of our own (even Bibles had to be sent home), but the supervisor merely told me to put them away in my locker.

As you can imagine, being in her good books feels rather like being in a greenhouse (which can smash any moment).

I haven't made any special friends here, though I'm on fairly good terms with everyone. I'm quite glad, not having to fritter away my time with this person or that.

I may get a Sunday pass at the middle or end of May, but I don't know for sure. We haven't been allowed out of camp once so far.

I'll be sending you a parcel of civilian clothes in the near future. Give Winfried [117] my love and thank her very much for the cookies and candies.

Fondest love to you all. Will the office work be finished soon? Write to me again before long.

Sofie

P.S. What news of Werner?

To Lisa Remppis, Krauchenwies, April 27, 1941

Dear Lisa,

I'm really only writing to you because I don't have anything else to do at present. Where a lot of my books are concerned, I'm shy of reading them in front of the others. Today is my third Sunday here, and I'm feeling thoroughly miserable. However objectively I view this place, I'm bound to say that it isn't pleasant. Thank goodness it won't be long before I get out of camp, at least for a few hours. It almost horrifies me to find that not one of the eighty-odd girls here is even remotely cultured. They include some high school graduates who keep copies of *Faust* for form's sake and put on refined airs, but it's all so transparent, rather like a hair style worn for purposes of self-adornment. The sole, favorite, and most frequent topic of conversation is men. I get sick of it sometimes, like now, so please don't keep this letter any longer than a day, all right? I'm depending on you.

It's very educational for me, all the same.

I look forward to getting a few lines from you soon.

Fondest love,
Sophie

To her sister Inge, Krauchenwies, April 27, 1941

Dear Inge,

We've been given time off to write letters, so I'm doing like everyone else. If it wouldn't be so conspicuous, I'd go for a stroll or do some painting – after all, I can't read all the time. If you'd send me a *dictionnaire* I could translate an occasional passage from *Ma fille Bernadette* [118] – there are such lovely little bits in it. Unless you've got some specific little chores to do here, you become submerged in the general hubbub. Till now, these little mainstays of mine have been – and will, of course, continue to be – my nightly cold shower and my nightly read. (I must confess I'm only up to section 32 in St. Augustine, but that's as much as I've been able to manage.) . . .

To Lisa Remppis, Krauchenwies, May 1, 1941

. . . In answer to your question about my companions, I find them (suppressing any dangerous emotions) very average in a way that precludes both one extreme and the other. Not a particularly good average. You have to be wary of people in the mass. They exert a tremendous attraction in many respects. On the other hand, it's often difficult to avoid being unfair. . . .

Diary, Krauchenwies, May 1, 1941

I've received a card from Fräulein Fries, written just after she'd read my letter. I'm delighted (I don't think anything I've received here has delighted me more) that she should have given it such prompt and serious consideration. If only they all knew how much I depend on letters and the minor chore of answering them.

I've only had two letters from Fritz in the whole of the four weeks I've been here.

I've found a number of passages in St. Augustine that can serve as a reply to Otl's letter. Although I still skim over a lot of things or forget them as soon as I've taken them in, many of them seem to supply an answer, and I'm immensely pleased about it.

Diary, Krauchenwies, May 4, 1941

Otl has sent me his essay on the philosophers.[119] I read it yesterday and today.

To her brother Hans, Krauchenwies, May 18, 1941

Dear Hans,

Many thanks for your letters. They're like a breath of fresh air from another, faraway world which I long to enter soon.

Here, where they forcibly deprive us of the means of entertainment (actually, I'm grateful to them), I'm very much more receptive to, and eager for, things that are important to me, and I don't think I'd often be tempted to fritter my time away, for instance on a movie. I started the James Jeans[120] book yesterday. —I only hope Inge sends me a flashlight battery soon, to help prolong such time as I get to myself. I now have some idea of your attitude to army life. Me, I blithely ignore it as far as possible.

It's a glorious May morning. With a sky like this and the birds singing so loudly, I can't feel anything but happy, nor do I try to resist the feeling.

Yours cheerfully,
Sofie

From the beginning of June 1941 onward, Sophie enjoyed a certain measure of relief from camp routine. She and her RAD companions were assigned to outside duties during the day. This

Sophie (*bottom right*) celebrating her twentieth birthday in the RAD camp at Krauchenwies, May 1941

exempted them, if only for limited periods, from personal supervision by the women in command of them.

To Lisa Remppis, Krauchenwies, June 5, 1941

Dear Lisa,

. . . I've been doing outside work for a farmer since the beginning of the week. It's odd, but the Arbeitsdienst has taken on an entirely different complexion. Perhaps it's because of the glorious sunshine we've had since Pentecost, which has made the whole countryside blossom out wonderfully. My route to work is simply lovely – 8 kilometers up hill and down dale through open woodland. I've a genuine feeling of happiness, and once more find myself wanting someone to share it with. My work on the farm, which is earthy and strenuous (I've been weeding poppies and hoeing turnips for days), leaves me pleasantly weary in the evenings, though the temptation to take things easy is far stronger (I haven't succumbed to it so far). I read a chapter every night, and I've supplemented my evening shower with a morning one.

I think I've grown a bit slower mentally. I often have to read words out loud to grasp their meaning, and even then they just lie there inside me, inert, without my being able to absorb them. I'll have to keep plugging on, that's all. I think I'll thaw out a bit as soon as I can talk with someone sensible – and I'm to be allowed home the day after tomorrow!

I've never looked forward so much to going home. And especially to seeing Inge.

Will you write to me soon? I'm completely in the dark about you. Happy birthday. You won't be getting a parcel till Saturday.

Fondest love,
Sofie

To her brother Hans, Krauchenwies, June 13, 1941

Dear Hans,

It seems unlikely that I'll ever feel like writing letters in the Arbeitsdienst, but I don't want to keep you waiting for one too long. You'll already have heard about the most important event in my last few weeks. I spent last Sunday at Ulm, which fortified me a lot – and that's one's main requirement in the Arbeitsdienst. . . .

I've now been on the farm for two weeks, praise be. I'm out of camp for eight hours a day, and enjoying the work. It puzzles me sometimes, because weeding for an entire morning is neither interesting nor unstrenuous. I feel quite happy and at home in the stables and the filth of the farmyard, and I spoon up my lunch from the communal bowl without a qualm. It would be silly, and it would only spoil my appetite, if I had any inhibitions about it. – As for the rest of my time, you know what it's like, so there's no point in enlarging on it. . . .

Doggerel on the back of a letter from Eve Nägele, Krauchenwies,
undated [June 1941]

Dear Inge,

Today I sing
of you alone.
Willin's crocheting,
Trude's lounging;
me, I'm thinking of you.
You're going away.
One night left till you depart
for Stuttgart, light of heart.
Alas, if only you could stay!
When your sweet voice
is heard abroad,
we all rejoice
that such a sound
should strike a chord
in every heart around.
To man and beast
you give pleasure,
my treasure.
In my next parcel you'll get a candy,
if there's one handy.

To Lisa Remppis, Krauchenwies, June 21, 1941

Dear Lisa,

I'm sitting on the edge of a fountain, and the naughty wind keeps blowing spray onto my paper. That's why this looks such a mess, but now you know the reason, you won't blame me. I've got a nice, enjoyable hour ahead of me. I've already cleaned my shoes, long ago, and tidied my chaotic locker. When the hour has passed, I shall get up off the fountain and hurry down to the station to escort Inge and Otl back to camp. See what I mean by a nice, enjoyable hour in the middle of it all? It's high time I thanked you for your letter, which arrived yesterday. I must tell you what occurred to me while I was weeding. You dream up all kinds of ideas when you're weeding, voluntarily and involuntarily. Anyway, I debated among other things how to construct a machine that would do my hard work for me, simply and effectively. It also occurred to me that fields should be treated before they're sown and planted, so weeds won't grow there. And then I looked up from my cogitations and realized that this was pure theory, and that practice is quite another matter. Weeds always grow everywhere. You just have to be patient and pull them up. So I bent my head again and tried to go on weeding placidly, without thinking of doing it any other way – and lo and behold, it worked, and I actually enjoyed it. So much for weeding.

I often feel the way you do when I'm out among the trees and fields. I wish I was just like them, with no responsibilities. (Once upon a time even a plant was too much for me, and there were occasions when I simply yearned to be a piece of tree bark – an odd notion, but it haunted me for years.) But we mustn't forget that, although we're living creatures, we aren't plants and animals, however much less trouble we might find it. The unchanging rhythm of agricultural labor is much the same, it's just occurred to me, and there's certainly a grain of truth in the ideal. The farmer does his work year after year in compliance with laws he's almost unaware of, they're so immensely ancient and his work is as innocent and soothing as the invariable blossoming and ripening of an apple tree every year – or am I wrong?

Fondest love,
Sophie

To her brother Hans, Krauchenwies, June 23, 1941

Dear Hans,

This is to acknowledge the three snaps you sent me via
Inge. I was delighted to get them. I've now (though only since
yesterday) joined the universal and much maligned vogue for
pinning snaps to the inside of my locker door. For a long time
now, the only picture there was a photo of the cathedral spire
[at Ulm] taken over the top of the two rear towers. It's very fine.
Otl took it – maybe you know the one I mean. Anyway, I've
now pinned up the ones of Werner, Inge, and you. Nobody sees
them but me, and it gives me such a homey feeling to open the
locker door and see you all hanging there – a tiny little place
that belongs to me alone. Talking of photos, couldn't you send
me a postcard print of the one of Father taken in profile? I think
it's really first-class, photographically and as regards every
other quality a portrait photo ought to possess. Then I'd only be
missing Mother and Lisl. There aren't any snaps that do them
justice, are there?

I'm also leaving the postcard of the sheep on my locker door,
at least until the three weeks are up and you finally redeem your
promise to pay me a visit. If you caught the same train as Inge,
I'd have time to pick some strawberries in the deer park beforehand, and if the warm weather persists, there'd be enough for
a whole meal of strawberries. Doesn't that sound tempting?
Besides, there are so many lovely things to show you in our park
that I needn't be ashamed of having visitors.

Today I feel as if it were time to bid the Arbeitsdienst farewell. What does the immediate future hold in store for you, I
wonder? We live in interesting times. I, too, get to hear what's
been happening now and then.

I spent the whole of today loading hay. I'm dog-tired, as you
can imagine, but we aren't to be left in peace yet, worse luck.
They attend to our spiritual welfare here too. As a visible (not

too visible) token of my abiding opposition I shall smoke one of Anneliese's excellent cigarettes before the night's out (she gave me a whole pack yesterday – nice of her, wasn't it?) because that's against the rules as well. The gong has just sounded.

Love,
Sofie

Sophie Scholl would normally have completed her spell in the Arbeitsdienst at the beginning of October. Early in August, however, the girls were informed that their term of service had been extended.

To her brother Hans, Krauchenwies, August 2, 1941

Dear Hans,

Many thanks for the book[121] – I'd like to read it myself before sending it on – and your letter. I'm still reeling under the impact of the latest, appalling piece of news: we're to do another six months' compulsory war work in camps under the auspices of the RAD, which intends to organize our leisure time as well. I'm ready to contract any reasonably tolerable disease or do anything else that would spare me this fate. You must try to think of something too.

So much for all my rosy prospects! Instead, it's another dose of this ridiculous boarding school.[122]

Thank goodness I can go home next Sunday and maybe set some wheels in motion. Will you be home too?

Did you get my card from Beuron? That was a lovely Sunday.

Lots of love for now from
your sorely afflicted sister

To her brother Werner, Krauchenwies, August 4, 1941

Dear Werner,

I just received your letter, for which many thanks. Getting mail from you is a rarity, rather like whipped cream. —I also heard this evening that all Arbeitsdienst girls are to do an extra six months' war work after leaving the RAD, but I'm still too attached to all my fine plans and prospects to drop them just like that. Anyway, I propose to try everything – even study medicine without a second thought, if that's any use. Perhaps all three of us will be lucky.

I'll be home next Sunday and back here after that for another six weeks – how long, I still don't know, but at least I'll be free again.

I've managed to do some reading in recent weeks. I've had more time to spare and, above all, more heart for it. There are lots of other ways of filling the days here, too – plenty of them, in fact. One mustn't simply fritter the time away.

I look forward to your next letter. Write and tell me what you're up to.

Much love,
Sofie

By the beginning of 1941 German troops were being shifted to the Eastern front, and on June 22 Hitler's armies invaded Russia. By mid-July they had taken Minsk and by July 19 Smolensk, taking nearly 400,000 prisoners and proceeding at a terrific pace through most of the summer. Fritz Hartnagel was among the German troops in the invasion force.

To Lisa Remppis, Krauchenwies, August 11, 1941

Dear Lisa,

You see? I've only just received a letter from you, and here I am already, sitting down to answer it.

Yesterday I made a brief trip home – too brief. These visits are all rather snatched and hurried, and I wind up realizing how many important things I've forgotten. —Anyway, the little time I spent there sufficed to repaint the camp in glaring colors, reinforce my individuality (don't be too quick to equate that with arrogance), and redefine my position here more clearly. It really hurts, the sense of alienation that dominates me after such days away, but still.

Hans was also home yesterday. I'd been so looking forward to our studying together, but it's no use clinging to one's personal desires when every surrounding circumstance conspires against them. Hans is doing an internship at München-Harlaching and Werner is in France, near Brest. Fritz is in Russia. He's operating with an armored formation, so he's always pretty far forward. Postal communications are very poor. None of our letters get there at all, and theirs take three weeks to reach here.

I think the war is starting to have powerful repercussions in every respect. Sometimes, and especially of late, I've felt that it's grossly unfair to have to live in an age so filled with momentous events. But that's nonsense, of course. Perhaps we're really being presented with scope for direct outside action, though it seems as if our sole function is to wait. That's hard, and one's patience often wears thin, and one longs to set oneself another, more promising and easily attainable goal.

What are you reading at present? Will you write again soon?

Fond love for now from

Sofie

To her brother Hans, Krauchenwies, undated, postmarked August 16, 1941

Dear Hans,

I just wanted to ask you quickly if you've already received a book for me[123] (via Grogo), so I can give it to Inge next Sunday. I suppose you'll also be coming to her birthday party?

I doubt if my fury at the accursed new decree re Arbeitsdienst girls will have subsided by Saturday. I'll be an old crone before I can start university. —But I won't abandon the struggle in a hurry. I'd sooner take poison. Our supervisor says we ought to feel honored! I can't get the subject out of my mind. To think you had to do two years of it.

I'm going to stop grouching, though. After all, what's the use? If you have the book already, don't forget it. I can pay you right away (20 marks).

See you soon,
Sofie

To Lisa Remppis, Krauchenwies, August 23, 1941

Dear Lisa,

. . . I'm going on outside duty in fifteen minutes, looking after the baby while the others are working in the fields. I should really have had the afternoon off, but I'm quite content to spend it on outside duty. I'll be all on my own there with the baby, and I feel quite at home in the tiny household under my care (though my longing for total independence is as fierce and strong as ever). The work is often pleasant and extremely enjoyable, but the camp remains its ever present basis and background. You get so used to the pressure, you soon become unconscious of it as long as you don't know or see anything else. On a far smaller scale, it's rather like the war, which we're already so inured to that we can still take pleasure in the woods and the sky. Except that now the war is weighing more heavily on us than ever before (it's funny, but that applies to everyone). I think we at last have a chance to prove ourselves – and preserve our integrity. I often get such a glorious feeling, like the one you get before doing something athletic – an exultant awareness that you're in full command of all your muscles. I feel strong inside. Not always, but willpower is what counts, and I'm getting to know my own moods well enough to assess them accurately.

If it can be arranged, I'm going to Krauchenwies church this evening with an RAD girl from Thuringia.[124] (I'm often glad of her company and feel that our friendship, if that fairly casual and unemotional relationship can be described as such, will outlast the RAD.) There are some four-handed pieces by Handel and Bach we want to play on the organ. We've more than once begged the key from the parson, not without success.

Those are red-letter occasions[125] for me, as you can imagine, especially as they provide such a wonderful contrast to the rest of our doings. How lovely it is to play and sing in the church (which I'm gradually coming to understand).

We've already been told that we won't be getting any leave before our second six months. I still haven't devoted much thought to these objectionable matters. I'll come to terms with them when the time comes, I'm sure, but I still haven't abandoned all hope (only 90 percent of it, and the remaining 10 percent will do me for the time being). I've filled up the page, dear Lisa. Fond love. What are you up to these days?

Write to me soon.

Yours,
Sofie

In the following letter Sophie writes to Werner who, having completed his spell in the Arbeitsdienst, was now faced with the prospect of military service.

To her brother Werner, Krauchenwies, August 27, 1941

Dear Werner,

Many thanks for your letter. It's nice to get some firsthand news of you now and then. The second six months are bound to be far more awful for you than for me, because I at least enjoy a measure of freedom in my work. I've applied for a kindergarten, making it clear that I want to run it on my own, and that it must be in a town. That would have many advantages: (a) shorter working hours, and (b) during the few leisure hours one does get, a town has more to offer in the way of mental sustenance (if one still doesn't have enough within oneself). The RAD will be organizing our spare time as well, worse luck, but I'll get my rights all the same (as a kindergarten teacher I'll need some spare time for preparation).

Later on I'm going to Krauchenwies church to play the organ with a friend. It always makes such a lovely change from unbroken camp routine. I only made friends with the girl recently, less from affection (though I took to her at once) than because of one or two talks we've had, and that strikes me as a pretty good reason. I can talk more freely with her than I'd ever have thought it possible to talk with anyone during these six months, and I doubt if our friendship will be restricted to the RAD. It does me good, and I often feel glad to have such a person around, even though she's younger than me in many ways. It's only here that I can realize how much another person can mean. —Heavens, if she could see this letter! Our relationship is very matter-of-fact and unemotional, and that's the way it must stay. Otherwise it might lose its value.

Won't you be getting some leave sometime? I hope the RAD isn't wearing you down more than me.

I've got a really nice job at present. I'm working for a small family of simple folk, and we get along extremely well. I look after their little home, and I feel as if it's my own. I'm changing jobs next week, unfortunately, but there are only five more weeks to go now (till it starts all over again).

I think we're both equally glad to get letters. What are you reading?

Fond love for now,
Sofie

To her sister Inge, Krauchenwies, August 27, 1941

. . . I'm sure your idea of my role at harvest time is quite wrong. Herr Krele (that's the name of the family I'm with) works at a munitions factory, and his wife has usually gone off to look after their little farm by the time I get there in the mornings. First I have to bathe the baby, feed it, and wash its diapers (it gets changed innumerable times, and is thoroughly pampered in general). Then I do the housework and get the lunch ready. Then the woman and her ten-year-old daughter come home to eat. After that come the usual household chores, washing up, darning, etc., plus looking after the baby. The woman is always very nice to me. She puts aside one or two liters of milk for me every day (the only thing they've got plenty of aside from bread and jam – they're badly off in other respects), and she's generally sweet and kind. It's a pity I'm changing jobs so soon. I could happily have stuck it out there for the remaining five weeks. . . .

The extension of compulsory national service for female university students-to-be was confirmed at the end of August. Sophie still hoped, nonetheless, that her parents would obtain her recall to Ulm to help with all the work arising at home and in her father's office.

To her brother Hans, Krauchenwies, September 7, 1941

Dear Hans,

Thank you for your letter. So now I'm to spend another six months in the straitjacket. Actually, my time here to date would have been quite enough to develop my loathing and contempt for it to the full. That's not just a figure of speech, but a feeling I get only too often.

Strangely enough, though, it's only now that I really feel proof against any form of compulsion. I have a marvelous sense of strength sometimes, and it gives me immense pleasure[126] to bamboozle my superiors and enjoy my freedom in secret.

The fall is beautiful. There's a blue haze already hovering over the distant woods and hoarfrost coating the fields in the mornings, though it can still get really hot.

There's a great deal of beauty here – enough and to spare – and because I have far more important things to think about and do, I'm not too bothered by the camp and everything connected with it.

I hope the army isn't impinging on you too much. Maybe I'll manage a trip to Munich sometime.

Much love,

Sofie

To Lisa Remppis, Krauchenwies, September 13, 1941

Dear Lisa,

Thank you for the letter from school. It seems funny to me that I used to do that once upon a time – write letters in school, I mean. It's so long ago now. By next spring, you'll probably be in much the same position as I am.

My parents are still doing their level best to get me out of my compulsory war work, and my father has already fired off some splendidly heartening letters to the local authorities. The first request was denied. The fate of the second is still unknown.

I'm just off to Ulm, incidentally, on a Sunday pass. I think Fritz will be there – I asked him to come, anyway. He's at Weimar at present, and will be leaving for Africa* in a few days' time.

I'm rather dreading this Sunday outing. I'd have liked to have a word with Otl before he's drafted (in October). So much is happening all at once!

How are you in other respects, discounting the tribulations of school and everyday life? What are you reading at present? I hope you'll soon get another free period to write to me in. . . . *Die Sonette einer Griechin:*[127] The ending isn't like an ending at all, is it? It should have resolved itself into a major key.

Fond love for now,
Sophie

Early in September 1941 Fritz Hartnagel was transferred from Russia to Weimar to raise a signals company for the German Afrika Korps in Libya. Though soon up to strength and operational, the company received no marching orders. It later transpired that the new unit had simply been forgotten. That was how Oberleutnant Hartnagel came to spend the period between September 1941 and April 1942 at Weimar – "in relative idleness," as he himself puts it.

Hans Scholl

Summer–Fall 1941

As the summer semester of 1941 drew to a close, Hans was able to apply for his first student internship at a hospital of his own choosing.

To his parents, Munich, July 17, 1941

Dear Parents,

You'll be interested to know that we're now at liberty to gain hospital experience, the one condition being that we don't leave this military district. I've contacted the hospital at Kochel, and if nothing comes of that, I'll try my luck at Murnau. I've been offered a place at Nymphenburg Hospital, the finest in Munich, but I'd sooner work at a country hospital where you get to know everything and everyone. In any case, I won't be performing any intricate brain surgery to start with. . . .

Hans ended up applying for an internship at the municipal hospital in Harlaching, a town just south of Munich, because his friend Alexander Schmorell had obtained an internship there. Alexander Schmorell would eventually become part of the inner circle of the White Rose. Schmorell had joined the Munich students' company at the end of 1940. When he and Hans first met, they had both gone through the French campaign as medical orderlies, and were preparing for their preliminary examination in medicine. The initial bond between them stemmed from their common field of study and similar political outlook.

Usually known to his friends as Schurik, Schmorell was born in 1917 to a German father and a Russian mother, baptized a Greek Orthodox, and, after his mother's early death, brought up at Munich with his father's new family. The person mainly responsible for his upbringing was a Russian nursemaid who hardly spoke a word of German. Schmorell grew up bilingual, but Russian remained his true mother tongue and Russian culture his spiritual home.

Nonetheless, being a German national, he was obliged to do Arbeitsdienst and military service after graduating from secondary school. As keen a horseman as Hans, he joined a cavalry unit and took part in the occupation of Austria and the Sudetenland. When ordered to swear the oath of personal allegiance to Adolf Hitler, however, he asked to be exempted and discharged from the army. His request was denied. An artistically gifted and sensitive young man whose extreme desire for freedom and independence was incompatible with the discipline and uniformity of military life, he became an undisguised opponent of the Nazi regime.[128] Early in 1941, Schmorell began inviting Hans home to literary soirees at which his father, an equally committed opponent of the regime, regularly assembled like-minded individuals for readings from theological, philosophical, and literary works – "spiritual relaxation," as Schmorell once termed it. One of his guests was Christoph Probst, a former school friend of Schmorell's who also became a part of the White Rose movement.

Hans began work at the hospital in Harlaching on August 1, 1941.

To his parents, Munich, August 3, 1941

Dear Parents,

I've been living in my new, old room[129] since yesterday. I now find it far pleasanter outside town than in. Shows you how a person's views can change. I've fixed up my attic very nicely.

I received your letter enclosing the money, Mother, also the parcel. We're having to provide our own meals again. We can't eat at the hospital.

I'm happy in my work at the sanitarium so far. We have a good personal relationship with the doctors, which is worth a lot. We work till 2 p.m. every day, then we're free. Our pay is [RM]1.20 a day. At present I'm in the surgical unit. They only perform lung operations there, mostly thoracoplasties and pneumothoraxes.

I'm on duty in the barracks today (officer of the day). We also have eight musters a week.

Elly Ney[130] played the "Wanderer-Phantasie"[131] at the Brunnenhof the night before last. This afternoon we're off to Schleissheim, where they're giving some Beethoven piano quartets at the schloss.

I'll pay you another visit soon.

Fondest love,
Hans

To Rose Nägele, Munich, August 8, 1941

Dear Rose,

Many thanks for your letter. Your dear messages made me profoundly happy, so the sun seemed to shine more brilliantly that day and the gold of the grain fields looked brighter than usual, because I know you're out in the midst of that light every day. You know how dearly I'd love to be a farmer, but it wouldn't work. I must go my own way, and I do so gladly. I'm not anxious to avoid a host of dangers and temptations. My sole ambition must be to perceive things *clearly* and calmly. Until I do, many more storms will buffet and shake the roof of my house. But I'll light my lamp even so, and however much it flickers and threatens to go out, its warm red glow will serve as a beacon to many a lonely traveler.

It's essential that I see you again. We know too little about each other, my love. It's not enough for people to love like a pair of flowers leaning toward one another. It takes a great deal of mutual experience and knowledge. No lamentations, though! You know me well enough to know that one day I'll turn up at your home unannounced.

My present employment at Harlaching (TB) hospital leaves me ample time to myself. We work in the mornings, and the work is relatively satisfying.

Are you in the middle of harvesting? The barley must be in by now, surely?

You'll have heard about my youngest sister's dismal fate.[132] She's got to do another six months' service. She's inconsolable, and so am I, because I'd so looked forward to her coming [for the winter semester at Munich University]. Is Hanspeter in the East? I owe him a letter.

Most of all, I wish you and your family God's blessing in the weeks to come.

Yours,
Hans

To Rose Nägele, Munich, August 12, 1941

My dear Rose,

If all my letters convey is restlessness, the fault must lie with the writing, so I'll mend my ways from now on. It's too tempting when writing letters, especially love letters, to let your mind, thoughts, and desires emerge at random from the darkness and scatter them on paper in ill-considered words. I'm not dejected and distracted at heart, truly not. On the contrary, I can see positive values in the midst of a world of brutal negation. It certainly isn't productive of restlessness to recognize suffering as the true and supreme value of the European man. Individuals are lonely in many respects, but when was this ever not so? As for a world of illusion, I don't give a damn for it. None of this implies a morose attitude toward others. Far from it. I try to see them as they are and make an equable impression on them, and I don't shrink from the vilest stench or the muddiest color. They exist. Shadows exist for the sake of light, but light takes precedence.

But enough of that. We're too far apart, that's our trouble. It's impossible to cram long weeks of living into the narrow confines of a letter. How wonderful it'll be when I'm with you again. I'll marvel at your face, your hair, your fragrance. . . . But what a person realizes when he's alone is forgotten at such moments.

And if I don't come to see you, it isn't because there's a war on, and I'm a pseudo-soldier, but for very, very, different reasons.

I was born on September 22, 1918, under the sign of Virgo, and to revert to myself yet again: I don't know myself whether my arrival in the world was a good thing or a bad one. It was a necessity, anyway, and the fact that I'm alive is a reality, and reality is the sole truth. My reflections on self haven't progressed far beyond their starting point, but I do have a star that shines even on the darkest night.

I expect you're tired out at nights after all your work. How do you feel about *labor improbus* [133] and "in the sweat of thy face"? [134] It's true, isn't it? If you'll let me give you a piece of good advice, read one of the Psalms at night. They're among the finest literature in the world and more than that besides.

Yours in love,

Hans

To his mother, Munich, August 13, 1941

Dear Mother,

I've been rather worried about you ever since I left Ulm. I hope you'll soon be better. That's more important than Sophie's Arbeitsdienst [extension]. Please write me soon how you are and what the doctors say.

I'm really well off here. The food . . . is excellent, so you've absolutely no need to worry on that score. As for my work, I'm tackling it with great enthusiasm but not overdoing things in spite of that. I've proved myself useful to my medical supervisor by mastering a number of minor practical procedures such as taking blood, intravenous injections, aspirations, and so on, and am not only learning from him but relieving him of a lot of work.

At present I'm reading Hans Carossa's latest book[135] about his student days at Munich. I detect a great many parallels, although he studied here before the Great War and, thanks to a wide variety of developments, we "moderns" are less preoccupied than his generation with superficial and unprofitable matters. We were presented early on with the choice between genuine and false, and our better selves opted for the genuine and true. It may also be that we're more receptive to what is true, or more impervious to what is false, than the generations before us and to come.

I received a parcel of two books from Werner (*Pensées* by Pascal and *Les fleurs du mal*). I was very pleased, because I venerate those two great Frenchmen, Pascal and Baudelaire.

I received a letter from a girl student[136] who's been drafted into a munitions factory. She says it's unbearable, and her health is bound to suffer. We must save Sophie from that dire fate at all costs.

I close for today with very best wishes for your recovery.

Yours,

Hans

My dear Rose,

If there isn't a letter from you tomorrow morning, I'll know I won't get one this week. Did you have to work last Sunday? You haven't had such a bad harvest after all, have you, or am I wrong? I know how it is though. A farmer's work is never done, even when the harvest is in, and you really ought to relax and enjoy doing nothing.

I won't tell you much about myself, or you'll only say, It's easy for him to talk. The fact is, I almost feel as if I'm on vacation. I've at last got some time to myself, and I'm immensely thankful. Leisure matters a lot to the likes of us. One doesn't let it lie fallow, one fills it. One doesn't dream, either (that I do at night, a great deal), one "contemplates," meditates, reads, learns.

These past few weeks have been more important to my inner self than many of the foregoing months. I realize I'm gradually getting a grip on myself, and that *one* road is materializing out of many illusions and false trails. Am I telling the whole truth? Not everything will be as I would have wished, I'm afraid.

I mean well, anyway, and I also know something I didn't know before. But more of that when I'm with you (in two or three weeks' time. It's very difficult to get away at present because the army does its utmost to keep us in Munich – as if it derived any benefit from our presence!).

Inge is paying me a visit next Sunday. Couldn't you come here one Sunday too? Eve wrote us a charming letter from Alsace. If she keeps it up, she'll make a good writer.

The fall will be upon us before long. The roses are already fading, but every garden is still heavy with the scent of summer, and if there were only one dainty rose in all the world, the scent would be strong enough to guide me to it. Everything fades, but not you.

Yours,
Hans

To his sister Sophie, Munich, September 3, 1941

Dear Sophie,

It's ages since we wrote to one another. How many days left before your happy ending?[137] If all goes well, it can't be more than twenty-seven.

If only I could expect you here then. I'm going home next Sunday. Can't you fix it so we meet up there? —Yesterday I bought myself a lovely Russian samovar. We christened it last night. The way it hummed and sang! The tea was twice as good, too. It's the kind of samovar you heat with charcoal. My little room is going to be nice and warm in the winter!

Do you ever do any drawing or painting these days? You could at least do some drawing. You could always find time for that, so don't let your initiative wane. Not that I'm in favor of drudgery. It's a good thing to conserve one's energy.

The fall and the third year of the war descended on us accompanied by morning mist and chill winds, but the late summer flowers are still wonderfully colorful. The sunflowers are blooming now! The predominant color in the Orthliebs' [his landlord's] garden is yellow.

How much longer before the branches stand out bare and black against a gray sky? That time of year is beautiful too, though – in fact it possesses a charm of its own: faces flushed with the cold, dry air, mouths steaming, pale skies, and evenings indoors around the samovar.

You've simply got to pay me a visit when you're released.
Lots of love,

Hans

To his brother Werner, Munich, September 16, 1941

Dear Werner,

Herewith the Retina.[138] Thanks for your nice letter, which reached me several weeks ago.

Mother is quite ill, as you probably know. We've now tried every means of prying Sophie loose from her stupid Arbeitsdienst service. Everything would be fine if we could, from the short-term point of view, because Mother has been confined to bed and needs careful nursing.

Do you need any books? I've got one on St. Augustine by Étienne Gilson[139] which I'm sure would interest you a lot. I'll gladly send it to you when I'm through with it. Or something else? Would you feel like tackling the *Divine Comedy*? I have a good edition here on thin paper (Insel [-Verlag]).[140]

If only you could be here in Munich this winter. We've got so many things planned. Inge's paying me a visit next Sunday, and I hope Sophie's affairs will also have sorted themselves out by November.

Grogo[141] has been assigned to the antiaircraft artillery at Stettin. Hans Rogner[142] has been badly wounded.

I'm still working at the hospital here.

Lots of love,
Hans

P.S. Films will follow as soon as more become available.

Hans completed his internship early in October. Before term began, students were granted two weeks' vacation.

To Rose Nägele, Munich, October 7, 1941

Dear Rose,

I've been unexpectedly granted some free time. Tomorrow I leave on a trip down the Danube to Vienna with my friend Alex [Schmorell]. Our decision was so instantaneous and instinctive, I doubt if all the best medical brains in Germany and the world at large would be capable of fathoming it. But we're going anyway, and taking nothing, absolutely nothing with us except our toothbrushes. . . .

To his sister Sophie, Linz, October 15, 1941

Best regards from us on our Danube trip. We've paddled as far as Linz, and today we take a local puffer train on from here to Melk.[143] Our trip will then be over, worse luck!

Love,

Hans

Lectures resumed at Munich at the beginning of November. Even though they could communicate only by letter, Hans remained in close touch with Otl Aicher, maintaining the friendship that began when they were both detained by the Gestapo for their youth-movement activities. Although membership in the National Socialist organization was required of anyone wishing to graduate from secondary school, Otl had nevertheless refused to join, and from the fall of 1939 on, he joined Hans and other youth movement friends as an active member of a circle restricted to avowed opponents of National Socialism. Before being drafted in September of 1941, Otl, Hans, and their friends debated the right of resistance under a dictatorial regime, not merely from a topical point of view, but with reference to Thomas Aquinas' theses on just systems of government and forms of rebellion. It was Otl who introduced Hans Scholl – and later Sophie – to Hans's most influential mentor: Carl Muth, a septuagenarian Roman Catholic journalist and editor of the (recently banned) monthly Hochland (Highland).

Hans offered to catalog Muth's library for him, and spent many hours at Muth's house. With the older man's paternal and affectionate encouragement, he found scope for wide-ranging discussions with theologians, philosophers, and writers opposed to the regime – men like Theodor Haecker, Alfred von Martin, Werner Bergengruen, Sigismund von Radecki, and Muth himself, all of whom helped to heighten his awareness of National

Socialism's wholesale threat to individual morality and perver-
sion of human values.

But for Otl Aicher and the young Scholls, Carl Muth repre-
sented more than just the center of a circle in which opponents
of National Socialism could, without fear of denunciation,
discuss political issues and current events as well as aspects of
theology, literature, and philosophy. On a very personal level,
his function was that of an older, more experienced friend and
Socratic mentor who opened up new worlds for them by sugges-
tion and example, and whose stringent though unorthodox
faith provided them with stability. Under Carl Muth's influ-
ence, Hans and Sophie's religious perceptions – as their letters
bear witness – acquired greater intensity and firmer definition:
the Christian gospel became the criterion of their thoughts and
actions.

To Otl Aicher, Munich, October 24, 1941

Dear Otl,

My samovar is humming cozily. My room often feels cozy
now that the winds are blowing colder outside. —Thank you
for your letter. I received it almost by the same mail as Tet and
Oluf's[144] first few lines from their new surroundings – three
very different letters, but they all gave me equal pleasure.

I concede your claim on behalf of dialectics. On the one
hand, it really does offer a useful means of eliminating personal
errors and, not least, of being answerable to others as far as
one can. (I sorely miss the latter here because, although I have
a nice social circle, I'm the one that asks all the questions and
am never asked for a definite answer myself – I'm on the verge
of coaxing a few people into it.) In the second place, dialectics is
probably the only feasible form of communication between the
two of us, for what other recourse do we have?

Because you're so familiar with Bloy's book, *Das Blut des Armen*,[145] a word or two on the mystery of poverty, which has preoccupied me more than anything else for quite a while, and which cried out for solution until I came to Bloy by way of Dostoyevsky. And here's the tragic part of it. Although those books confirmed my belief in the need for absolute poverty and removed the (last) obstacles to my perception of that mystery, they've utterly confused that part of my brain which thinks in political terms.

The basis of this poverty, which leads to "absolute" Christianity, must be primarily spiritual and only secondarily material. But the paradox recurs here too: material poverty becomes the route to spiritual. The poverty I refer to is more serene than that of Bloy the novelist. It lays no claim to the property of the rich, but despises it because it *knows* about real values. Or does Bloy aspire to help the poor gain their right of existence? If so, he should become a politician.

I, who am one of the "haves" and want for nothing, am trying to comprehend the meaning of poverty. That poverty and the poverty of Léon Bloy the novelist are essentially similar, for all that. The phrase "pilgrim of the absolute"[146] has made a deep impression on me.

Best regards,

Hans

P.S. I could get you two books by the Russian writer Berdyaev: *Das neue Mittelalter* and *Die menschliche Persönlichkeit und die überpersönlichen Werte*.[147] Both are small paperbacks. Shall I send them to you?

To Rose Nägele, Munich, October 28, 1941

Dear Rose,

Your letter made me glad but not happy. I'm glad you've safely reached your native land,[148] and just as glad that the truth matters more to you than anything else, and that's why you put it at the beginning of your letter.

I'm in a spiritual crisis, the most important in my life, so it's understandable that I'm taking it very seriously and can't find consolation in mundane things. Nor do I need any, fortunately. My state of mind is such that nothing at all from outside can help me because I've already overcome, perceived, and found happiness in my innermost self. What a paradox! My head aches even though I'm happy. Mine is the happiness of the victor who foresees the end of the battle.

This war (like all major wars) is fundamentally spiritual. I sometimes feel as if my puny brain is the battleground for all these battles. I can't remain aloof because there's no happiness for me in so doing, because there's no happiness without truth – and this war is essentially a war about truth. Every false throne must first crack and splinter, that's the distressing thing, before the genuine can appear in unadulterated form. I mean that personally and spiritually, not politically. I've been presented with the choice.—

You might understand me better if you were with me more often. Reading these words, you may well form an entirely false impression of me.

Perhaps I'll contrive to come and see you at Christmas. It would be lovely.

Affectionately yours,
Hans

Windlicht *(Hurricane Lamp) was a kind of vehicle for discussion and medium of communication between members of the Ulm circle, launched, according to Inge Aicher-Scholl, sometime in the summer of 1941 at the suggestion of Otl Aicher. It included "essays (original wherever possible!), poems, personal reflections, and drawings . . . compiled at regular intervals and circulated in a homemade cover among our friends, the object being to maintain personal contacts precluded by the war. . . ."*[149] *The following essay by Hans Scholl was written for* Windlicht.

"On Poverty," an essay in Windlicht, *undated [November 1941]*

We all aspire to reach the other bank, but none of us is taken there. All we can do is look for the ferry, a quest that often leads us to slip, fall, and pick ourselves up again. The river is low-lying, fast-flowing, dark; nighttime, and not a star in the sky, no path or bridge. Just a faint light on the far bank, shielded from the wind, and only *one* ferry that makes the crossing.

But the ferry's name is poverty. Those that see the light must become poor before they can dwell in the light that has illumined the hungry for two thousand years. Ah, vain fools that prefer to consign yourselves to the waves and perish in them! You see the light and cannot reach it. You see the road and decline to take it. Love impels me to wish many a man hardship and affliction so that he can know poverty! Poverty is stronger than wealth. Poverty enables a person to cast former affluence to the winds without regret, to prize spiritual values more highly than any possession. Poverty confronts a person with the ultimate choice.

The war will render us all very poor. We must abandon all hope of a happy outcome. Hunger and hardship will at first dog our every step, while people from devastated cities, devastated countries, devastated and half-exterminated nations go looking for diamonds indestructibly buried in the ruins.

Yet we do not wish the cup to pass from us, even so. It shall be drained to the dregs. Our enemies will not be slain by falling bricks, nor will they vanish from the face of the earth. Instead, they will be utterly undone by their own incompetence and drowned in their own morass.

That alone will preclude any false glorification of history in the time to come.

The war will subject Europe to dire poverty. Never forget, my friends, that poverty is the road to light.

The fall of 1941 had seen the proclamation of the Police Ordinance for the Identification of Jews in Public, which came into force on September 19, 1941, prescribing that all Jews should wear a palm-size yellow star inscribed "Jude" on the left breast of their outer clothing. This decree was yet another measure undertaken in line with the persecution, arrest, and deportation of Jews in Germany and German-occupied territory. Nazi Gauleiter Albert Forster had pronounced West Prussia "Jew-free" as early as October 1940, and 350,000 Jews were walled up in the Warsaw Ghetto a month later. Between the spring and fall of 1941, the Nazi occupation authorities stepped up their persecution of the Jews in Holland and France. Growing resistance was crushed, and orders were issued at Paris on October 3 to blow up six synagogues. Two weeks later, on October 16, renewed mass deportations began in the East and in Germany proper, last-minute attempts to escape being blocked by an emigration ban imposed on October 23. The death of the actor Joachim Gottschalk, who committed suicide with his Jewish wife and their son on November 6, 1941, symbolized the wave of self-destruction that succeeded the enactment of this law. Himmler responded in the same month by ordering the construction of the Theresienstadt ghetto as a preliminary to "the final solution to the Jewish question."[150]

To Otl Aicher, Munich, November 23, 1941

Dear Otl,

I'd like nothing better than to have your comments on the little essay[151] I contributed to the first issue of *Windlicht*. Its ideas were the product of a lengthy cerebral process, and it was

Léon Bloy, more than anyone else, who prompted me to say something. The language is immature. I would start it differently now. Nothing really changes, though, does it?

The cover design strikes me as amateurish. It bears no comparison with the outstanding workmanship of your woodcut, which adorns one wall of my room. Symbolic themes always call for supreme ability.

As to the content of your short story,[152] "Über ein Wunder," I wouldn't add or subtract a thing. Linguistically I feel bound to draw your attention to one or two little shades of difference between the perfect and imperfect. (The perfect expresses a completed action; the imperfect lies in the past but is still incomplete in its given context. To put it another way, it expresses continuance. The present and imperfect subjunctive are harder to use.) Don't be annoyed with me for being pedantic.

Professor Muth[153] has asked after you several times. I think he's very much looking forward to a letter from you. He's ill at present – bronchitis, though I suspect that the real cause of his illness is psychological. The anti-Jewish measures in Germany and the occupied territories are preying on his mind.

I'm glad to be near him every day. My work in his library[154] will take me several months. I'm temporarily forsaking medicine this winter and focusing my main attention on certain aspects of philology and, not least, philosophy.

If only you could get some leave at Christmas. A party of us are planning to spend the days after the festival of Christ's birth at a skiing lodge.[155]

I'm enclosing a book by Berdyaev.

> All the best,
> Hans

To Otl Aicher, Munich, December 3, 1941

Dear Otl,

To answer you right away and without more ado: the two of us have been talking at cross-purposes. I appreciated every point in your general exposition – in fact many sentences delighted me so much that I almost forgot the origin of your attack: "amateurish." I didn't say that your drawing was bad, or not good, or that it failed to capture the content, but that I found it amateurish, an ill-chosen term because it's employed in various ways. I'd have done better to call it an apprentice piece, i.e., the depiction of a wonderful idea but one that still suffers too much from lack of expression, is too inhibited, not relaxed enough. Even that is open to argument, of course, but thank you very much for your lucid remarks. In my opinion, their validity extends far beyond the realm of art.

I'm afraid I can't get you anything more by Berdyaev. I myself am currently reading his excellent *Philosophie der Freiheit*,[156] which I borrowed from Karl Muth. I'll gladly send you *Das neue Mittelalter* again.

Berdyaev must be in Paris. If you ever get a chance to go there, simply call on him. (Simply give him Muth's regards.)

I can't fulfill your other request either, at present. Having spent my last pfennig on books yesterday, I've become a beggar again overnight. I'd advise you to drop the idea of those presents. My sisters enjoy getting letters from you far more. The best thing of all would be if you yourself. . . . Is it wrong to cling to such hopes?

I've been very preoccupied in the last few days with an important phenomenon: the Turin Shroud.[157] Have you heard of it? Dare I write about it in *Windlicht*?

Affectionate regards,
Hans

Night had to be, that this lamp might appear. —*Claudel.*

Is it necessary to write about this picture, and did this face have
to emerge from the shadows of the unexplored into the harsh
light of day so as to kindle fresh doubts in mankind? Did we
need this questionable evidence, we who have anyway acknowl-
edged Christ as our Lord? Why, then, am I speaking to you?
Because I have seen it. Because my way has been paved by nights
of pondering, by a yearning for light and for knowledge of what
exists. Because my skepticism subsided in a flash and only rein-
sinuated itself into my brain by slow degrees. And because
my reawakened doubts, too, found no grounds for existence;
because I was now prepared for acceptance. I realize how pitiful
my words are and how far they fall short of the impression this
picture has left in my soul. I shall lift up my voice nonetheless,
with no great claim to greatness, but in joy and sincerity.

Medieval crusaders brought the shroud from the Holy Land
to Turin, where it has since been preserved as a precious relic.
It has survived centuries of disasters, and its scorched edges
show how close to destruction it came. The church was burned
down, but the cloth survived. When an Italian, Commendatore
Pis, first photographed the sacred shroud at the end of the nineteenth century, he must have been more than a little surprised
to find a positive in his hand instead of a negative – and what
a positive! His hands shook, his heart was filled with awe and
rejoicing. He had embarked on his work without an inkling
of what lay in store. And now, for the first time in almost two
thousand years, a human eye was seeing that body, that inef-
fable countenance with the closed eyes, asleep yet awesomely
awake, dead yet preserving vivid signs of superhuman suffering,
traces of cruel anguish, just as it is written: a spear thrust in the

left side, countless twin weals inflicted by a Roman scourge, nail marks in the wrists and ankles. The martyrdom of the world in all its actuality, there before our waking eyes! Who would not tremble and call on God anew from the depths!

Scholars, notably the French biologist Alfred de Vignon, photographed the shroud innumerable times thereafter, from every angle and by every possible means, because grave doubts about its authenticity were soon voiced on all sides. I shall not recapitulate the long chain of evidence, but it definitely extends thus far: as seen by the optical lens of a camera, a negative imprint has been left on the cloth by a human cadaver. Provided the body was not kept wrapped up in it for longer than a certain period – three days or so – the physiological and chemical changes occurring after death would have imprinted a photographic negative on the myrrh- and aloes-impregnated fabric. The cloth itself has been identified as woven material dating from the time of Christ's death. The method of burial conforms to the description given in the New Testament. The corpse that left the imprint had not been washed. The Jews have never buried their dead unwashed – a strict rule with them – but it was Friday "and the Sabbath drew on." Unable to violate the law of the Sabbath under any circumstances, Christ's faithful followers had to defer the washing of his corpse.

But that is not all. Evidence other than the purely scientific exists – evidence of the heart. I have seen reproductions of the Roman portrayal of Christ. How did I know, without a moment's hesitation, that Christ did not look like that? When I look at a Christ by Dürer, or Giotto, or Theotocopuli the Greek [El Greco], on the other hand, do I not know just as immediately that they came far closer to the real Christ? And now for the remarkable thing: all these portrayals by the great masters are similar in their essential features, and all resemble the negative image in question. In the imprint on the Turin Shroud, however, the quality that strikes this mysterious chord in our hearts, and which we find consistent with the true nature of Jesus in each separate picture, reaches the greatest possible pitch of perfection that anyone desirous of looking upon Christ can guess at but never quite attain.

"To think that it had to be technology, of all things . . ." So said a recent letter to me from someone just as startled and overjoyed by this phenomenon as I was myself. Yes, to think that it had to be technology that revealed this image – the technology that has also mechanized the weapons of war and is even now celebrating its triumphs over mankind. Has that technology been vindicated thereby? —Claudel speaks of "the second resurrection," Christ's resurrection for the twentieth century. The likeness of the Son of God existed unseen, slumbered, and waited for nearly two thousand years, but our own era was privileged to lift the spell and see the reality.

Sophie Scholl

Fall 1941

*The "Sunday outing" to Ulm that Sophie anticipated in her letter
of September 13 unexpectedly turned into two weeks' special
leave. On returning to Krauchenwies Camp, Sophie received her
next assignment. Starting in October, she was to work at an NSV
[National Socialist Public Welfare]*[158] *kindergarten in Blumberg,
a small town southwest of Donaueschingen, only a few miles
from the Swiss frontier.*

To Lisa Remppis, Blumberg, October 11, 1941

Dear Lisa,

Just a card to let you know my new address. I can hardly
write because a tiny kitten sitting in front of me keeps biting my
pen, so you'll have to blame any inkblots on its little paws.

Write to me soon,

Sofie

*Sophie Scholl had kept a diary throughout her early weeks in
the Arbeitsdienst. She resumed this practice during her months
at Blumberg. Her diary takes the form of a spiritual journal
centered on religious meditations: appeals to God in the manner*

of St. Augustine and Pascal, invocations ranging from inquiry, doubt, and self-reproach to ecstatic professions of faith. Lyrical musings verging on prayer are found alongside dialogues with herself and tactful character sketches of her friends; spontaneous, rapidly composed entries rub shoulders with the precise, artistically formulated litany of her communings with God.

The following passages from Sophie's diary are not cited en bloc but chronologically interspersed with her letters. They clearly illustrate her capacity for supplementing the letters' concrete, realistic, addressee-related content with dialogues conducted on a second, metaphysical plane. Overt and covert dialogue, direct speech and secret statement of accounts, correspondence and spiritual journal – all these, as the following alternation of both modes of expression demonstrates, are inseparably conjoined.

Diary, Blumberg, Fall of 1941

. . . The heart loses its way amid these petty commotions and forgets its great homeward route. Unprepared and given over to futile, abject trifles, it may be caught unawares when the time comes, having squandered the one great joy for the sake of little ones.

I realize that but my heart does not. It dreams on incorrigibly, lulled to sleep by forces that trouble me, torn between desire and melancholy. All that I'm left with is melancholy, incapacity, impotence, and a slender hope.

However stubbornly my heart may cling to its treasures, be it only out of love for the sweetness of life, wrest me away against my will, because I'm too weak to do so myself; turn all my pleasures sour, make me wretched, make me suffer before I dream my salvation away.

Diary, Blumberg, November 1, 1941

I came back yesterday to find a letter and a little book from Professor Muth[159] awaiting me. Yesterday I was delighted, but today I can't summon up the energy to be delighted anymore. I'm so tired, I'd like nothing better than to go to bed right now and sleep forever.

Now I'm back at the Schüles' again. I really came so that I could play the organ in the chapel afterward, or simply be in the chapel. I'd so much like to believe in miracles. I'd so much like to believe that I can acquire strength through prayer. I can't achieve anything by myself.

Muth wrote that we must pray for Otl. I'd never thought of praying for him – he never seemed to need it at all. Who doesn't, though? Even a saint does. . . .

I'm so terribly tired, and I'm always prone to such futile, ridiculous mental digressions.

Thou hast created us in Thine image.

I should like, as that Prophet did, to ask for visible evidence of himself. Or has that ceased to be necessary? I should like to spread myself out like a cloth for him to collect his dew in.

I'm all mixed up, I can tell. That's because I'm tired.

I feel so homesick.

Diary: Draft letters addressed to Professor Carl Muth but probably never sent, undated [October/November 1941]

Dear Professor,

Many thanks for your letter, which was waiting for me when I got back to camp. I've forwarded it to my sister [Inge] right away, because it was meant as much or even more for her as for me. She was the one that came to see you[160] with my brother some time ago, and I was the one that sent you the apples at her suggestion. You thought the recipient of your letter would be my sister.

Sophie Scholl | 187

. . . Because you took it that the recipient of the letter I found here on my return to camp, for which many thanks, would be my sister, I've forwarded it to her right away. I think it's more her place to acknowledge it and lay claim to the promised book. She'll be delighted, I'm sure.

I also got the apples at my sister's suggestion. If you like, I could send you some more.

Otl Aicher's address is: Officer Candidate 20 597 D.

Perhaps you've received it from Otto himself in the meantime.

Yours sincerely,

S.S.

Dear Professor,

I should so much have liked to get the apples off to you sooner, but the ban on mailing fruit has made it all far more difficult, especially as I don't get back to camp till late and my time there isn't my own. Please accept my apologies.

I was so pleased to receive your letter and the little book. No, getting you the fruit wasn't enough of a job to merit such a recompense. I could send you more in small batches. . . .

But is there anything else I could send you?

Diary, Blumberg, November 4, 1941

I visited the church on Saturday afternoon, ostensibly to play the organ. It was absolutely empty. It's a colorful little chapel. I tried to pray. I kneeled down and tried to pray, but even as I did so I thought: better hurry, so you can get up before someone comes. I wasn't afraid of strangers seeing me on my knees, but I was afraid Hildegard[161] might walk in, so I couldn't disclose my innermost thoughts. That's probably wrong, probably a false sense of shame. And that's why I hurried through my prayer and got up just the same as I'd kneeled down. I wasn't ready – I was simply trying to rush things. —And now I'm generally in such a mundane frame of mind, without the urge. I'm homesick the whole time, that's all.

Being reminded by chance of Muth's letter, I'm surprised he found the time and love to turn to me as well, when he had no need. He must have a very kindly heart, to find room in it for lesser people whose connection with him is quite superficial. I couldn't appreciate it more. That in itself puts me under an obligation to better myself. . . .

Diary, Blumberg, November 5, 1941

A letter from Otl today. Like Muth, I pray he remains safe and sound. As for me, whose presence can I enter? Only that of him who knows all the bad there is inside me. I'm too much of a coward to confess everything. Give me time to prove myself.

Diary, Blumberg, November 6, 1941

I'm expected to paint [a cover for] the Christmas issue of *Windlicht*. If only Otl knew how drained I am and how meaningless such a picture would be. Even if God won't help me, I'll have faith just the same. I'll write and tell Otl I'll do the cover.

Now I'm moving on again.[162] It's nerve-racking, this perpetual shoving around, this uncertainty. . . .

To Otl Aicher, Blumberg, November 6, 1941

Dear Otl,

I've just got time for the barest essentials of a reply to your letter before my bucket of water gets hot. I'll gladly paint something for the Christmas number. I'll find the time somehow. Myself, I'm feeling absolutely arid and haven't done much lately except fill my schedule. —The only thing is, I won't be up to anything more than illustrating. If I can't manage anything else, I may resort to doing Dieterle's head[163] on the cover.

At present, I'm all alone in my kindergarten (I sleep in camp). Although I can't do as I pleased or as I'd imagined, I'm well-off here. I take a long walk every morning and evening, to and from work, all by myself amid the snowy, twilit fields and hills. That's nice, and it keeps any unpleasant thoughts at bay.

I'll write to you again in due course. My time's up now, and I want you to get this as soon as possible.

Affectionate regards,
Sofie

Diary, Blumberg, November 10, 1941

. . . I've made up my mind to write to Otl sometime. If it were only my own affair, everything would be much easier. Sometimes I feel I can forge a path to God in an instant, purely by yearning to do so – by yielding up my soul entirely. If I beseech him, if I love him far above all else, if my heart aches so badly because I'm apart from him, he ought to take me unto himself. But that entails many steps, many tiny little steps, and the road is a very long one. One mustn't lose heart. Once, when I'd lost heart because I kept backsliding, I didn't dare pray anymore. I decided not to ask anything more of God until I could enter his presence again. That in itself was a fundamental yearning for God. But I can always ask him, I know that now.

Diary, Blumberg, November 11, 1941

I wrote to Otl but I didn't send it.

To Otl Aicher, Blumberg, November 18, 1941

Dear Otl,

Inge sent me the covers, and I'm forwarding the one with Dieter's head on it right away. His little head doesn't look very Christmassy. If it doesn't go with the contents, discard it. Actually, the head of some small animal would do just as well. There

wouldn't be much difference in expression, or would there? I
don't know how the colors look by daylight. I've no time to paint
during the day.

Will you send me Grogo's essay[164] if you have it. I'll close for
now, so this goes off right away.

Affectionate regards,
Sofie

To her brother Hans, Blumberg, November 20, 1941

Dear Hans,

A few days ago Otl sent me the cover for December's
Windlicht (plus a reply[165] to your "On Poverty" essay) and told
me in passing that you also intend to contribute something to
the Christmas number. He asked me to remind you, so now I
have.

I think *I'm* the one that owes *you* a letter. Lord, it's been such
ages. The last time I saw and wrote to you I was an Arbeitsdienst
girl; now I'm a wartime auxiliary. That designation is quite as
awful as everything else around here, but there's no point in
wasting much ink on it. I'm working in the local day nursery.
Sixty percent of the children's parents have criminal records, but
they're far too good to merit comparison with my bosses.

So now my university course will have to wait till spring (if
they let me go then).

We'll probably see one another at Christmas. Only five more
weeks. —If I don't go home on my Sundays off, I spend them at
Freiburg.[166] It's a really enchanting town.

Fondest love,
Your sister Sofie

Diary: Draft of a letter intended for her sister Inge but never sent, Blumberg, undated [November/December 1941]

I've received four batches of mail from you since Saturday. Very many thanks. The card repeating my requests wasn't a mark of impatience. Not being able to recall what I had or hadn't already said, I simply sent off another list to be on the safe side. So please forgive the bad impression it made. I realize how busy you are. That's why I hate asking you for anything at all.

The photo of Hofu[167] looks very nice with a candle burning in front of it. I'll bring it back in two weeks' time.

About your letter on prayer (I haven't read Deutinger's little book yet – I'll be able to answer your letter properly, if need be, when I have). This much in brief, though: I think I expressed myself incorrectly or inadequately. I think you misunderstood my reference to trust. All I meant was that we should simply entrust God with the worries we so arrogantly cling to and allow to depress us or drive us to despair. I don't find that easy, because when I try to pray and reflect on whom I'm praying to, I almost go crazy, I feel so infinitely small. I get really scared, so the only emotion that can surface is fear. I feel so powerless in general, and doubtless I am. I can't pray for anything except the ability to pray.

Do you know, whenever I think of God, it's as if I'm struck blind. I can't do a thing. I have absolutely no conception of God and no affinity with him aside from my awareness of the fact. And the only remedy for that is prayer.

Prayer.

To Otl Aicher, Blumberg, December 10, 1941

Dear Otl,

I just received your parcel containing the candles. I was thrilled with them and still am, not least because they got here safe and sound. I find them really lovely, especially the shape. Many thanks!

Is there no hope of your coming home for Christmas? It'll be a different skiing camp from last year. I'll probably stay with Lisa, who can't go because of her sciatica. Is Epinal in Alsace? I don't think so. If not, it shouldn't be too hard to get there from here.

You wrote in the first (or last) number of *Windlicht*[168] that Nature is a stool mankind climbs on to reach up to God, and that it will relapse into nothingness once it has served its purpose. I recall that now, as I look through the window at the mountain opposite, the fields sprinkled with snow, and the wintry sky beyond the leafless woods. I find it sad that all these things should someday cease to exist – sad and inconceivable. If they're beautiful and good, why should they someday cease to exist? I delight every morning in the pure air and the sky, with the moon and stars still floating in it, and even though it's initially an unfair pleasure because I may sometimes become intoxicated with the sight, it's good in the long run because it restores things to their proper perspective (which I again find sad, but I'm nonetheless glad because otherwise I might easily overlook the essential point). —I think it's awful to create something, only to consign it to limbo afterward. Trees and flowers and animals were created too, after all, and possess a hint of spirituality.

"Nothingness was created by God." Do you find that statement in *Der verborgene Gott*[169] logical? Anything that exists and was created must be *something*. I don't think we should try to visualize nothingness. Its name and meaning make that impossible. As someone who likes to visualize everything, I find that very hard. But that's only by the by. Who *was* Nikolaus von Kues,[170] anyway?

I realize that one can wallow in the mind (or intellect) while one's soul starves to death. That wouldn't have occurred to me once upon a time.

Affectionate regards,
Sofie

Diary, Blumberg, December 12, 1941

"Lighten my eyes, lest I sleep the sleep of death; lest mine enemy say, I have prevailed against him."[171]

I shall cling to him, and when all else falls away, he alone will remain. How terrible to be remote from him. I can't record my thoughts dispassionately. Everything I once possessed, all my critical discernment, has deserted me. But my soul is hungry, and, oh, no book can assuage that hunger. I remain barred from access to the living world of books. My sole sustenance is Nature, the sky and the stars and the silent earth.

Today's letter from Lisa[172] almost reduced me to tears. I'm utterly at a loss. Letters on their own don't bring her close to me, because she only sends me isolated snippets, little aesthetic descriptions, disjointed little trains of thought, and it would surely be wrong to construe the small expanse they illuminate as the whole of her. I tend to do this, though, and it depresses me. I must think of her with all the love I can muster.

I realize that when I love people very much, I can't do better than include them in my prayers. If I love people in all sincerity, I love them for God's sake. What better thing can I do than take that love to God?

God grant that I come to love Fritz, too, in His name.

To Lisa Remppis, Blumberg, December 12, 1941

Dear Lisa,

As far as I could gather from your letter, we won't be seeing each other at Christmas. There are more important things, I quite understand, though seeing one another doesn't strike me as unimportant, and it's something very close to my heart. How far apart we've grown, thanks to all the things that have intervened. It would be worth examining these things under the light sometime, to see if it's really so essential for them to come between us. (I'm certainly not referring to Gust Schlehe [Lisa's fiancé]. I mean absolutely everything: your vacations, your parties – everything and anything.) When you come down to it, all that has united us to date is a friendship we've clung to for its own sake (there are far worse things), rather than ideas or a common aim, which form a peculiar bond between people even when they seldom write or see each other. I don't know if you're as determined as I am to cling to our friendship.

Maybe we'll manage to meet up after all in the next few months. If not, at least when I'm free again, which is three months from now. Nothing will stop me then.

I still find life so rich and good, in spite of everything, but people fail to make good use of it. Perhaps it would do us good to become really poor, so as to be better prepared for less ephemeral riches. Don't people look for compensation when they're deprived of so much, and don't they then realize that they let themselves be distracted by affluence and set their hearts on unworthy things? Perhaps they first have to discover that they possess a heart.

How fortunate that, even in the army and much as it makes them suffer, there are people who retain their inner independence because they don't rely on things that others can deprive them of, and that we're privileged to number such people among our friends.

Sophie Scholl | 195

Freiburg Cathedral, which I've often visited in recent months, is really beautiful, and it makes me feel warm inside to be there. I'll be there again the day after tomorrow. I'll write and tell you about it.

I've never given any thought to purgatory and the intermediate states, nor to eternal bliss, so there's absolutely nothing I can say about them. For me, there's only "in God" and "outside God" after death. But I don't think it's negated by "today shalt thou be with me in paradise," because not everyone has to fare as the thief on the cross did.

I've read a passage on purgatory in *Kristin Lavranstochter* [by Sigrid Undset][173] in which Kristin expresses the hope that the fire will completely purify her stubborn and impure soul. If so, it would simply be another form of divine mercy. But, as I say, I myself have yet to form an opinion on the subject, and metaphorical concepts like these are beyond my ken. Fondest regards, and drop me a line now and then.

Yours,
Sofie

To Lisa Remppis, Blumberg, December 22, 1941

Dear Lisa,

We'll wake up twice more and – hey, presto – it'll be Christmas Day. I've already done some pre-Christmas celebrating at every conceivable kindergarten and day nursery, and tonight the mayor's entertaining us at the Adler. I look forward to the calm that must eventually follow this storm. How marvelous that I can go home, because being here is a drain on one's nervous energy.

After Christmas come the less agreeable three months, because we're getting a 150 percent [ardent Nazi] woman commandant. Alas for my Sundays! However, I think like Götz von Berlichingen. When the twelve weeks are up, I'd like to meet them all again.

I really meant this to be a Christmas letter, but it's beyond me. This morning I washed 150 chairs and twenty tables, and the cleaning continues this afternoon. Write a Christmas letter in the midst of that? Still, at least this'll demonstrate the desire and intention, and you'll get your joint present from Inge and me. Spare me a loving thought or two. I'm very susceptible to them.

Affectionate regards for now,
Sophie

Diary, Blumberg, undated [1941/1942]

On poverty
Reply to Hans's essay.

Ephesians 4[:18] Having the understanding darkened, being alienated from the life of God through the ignorance that is in them, because of the blindness of their heart.

Colossians 3[:10] And having put on the new man, which is renewed in knowledge after the image of him that created him.

Colossians 2[:2] That their hearts might be comforted, being knit together in love, and unto all riches of the full assurance of understanding, to the acknowledgment of the mystery of God, and of the Father, and of Christ; in whom are hid all the treasures of wisdom and knowledge.

Hans Scholl

Winter 1941–1942

To his mother, Munich, December 6, 1941

Dear Mother,

Another sign of life after barely a week. First I want to thank you for the two parcels, which I was delighted to receive yesterday. The few days since I left Ulm have simply sped by. Now Saturday has come around again, and tomorrow is the 2nd Sunday in Advent! I got an unexpected telegram from Boby[174] warning me to expect him. I'm to pick him up at the station this evening. He plans to spend Sunday with me.

12/7/41. Boby didn't turn up after all. I waited at the station for two fruitless hours. Instead, I went for a tremendous walk along the Isar and lighted the samovar when I got home. Besides, I intend to go to bed early anyway.

There's another pointless muster at 7 a.m. tomorrow. Then comes my first Russian lesson. Just so we don't even feel reasonably content with our lot, strict rules have now been imposed about sleeping in barracks. The latest check revealed that eighty students were missing, me included, of course. Personally, I wouldn't dream of changing my sleeping quarters.

I've now stuck out army life for four years, with comparative equanimity in view of its approaching end, but I'm now in such a state that it's making me ill. Every little thing proves too much of a drain on my energy. I'm losing all enthusiasm for my work.

"My" Christmas presents are almost complete. All I need now is something for Inge. I'd like to give her something really nice, but I don't have the cash. Could you possibly lend me 20? I'll naturally pay you back on January 1st. I earn enough, as you know.

I trust you aren't too overburdened with work during these pre-Christmas weeks. You'll need to rest for a long time yet.

Fond regards and much love for now,
Hans

The following letter was written on the second Sunday in Advent – and the day the Japanese attacked Pearl Harbor.

To Rose Nägele, Munich, December 7, 1941

Dear Rose,

I'm thinking of you on this second Sunday in Advent, which I'm experiencing as a wholehearted Christian[175] for the first time in my life. Perhaps this letter will follow promptly enough on the heels of my last, from which you could infer the existence of a lot of loose ends. Fundamentally, much has changed since then. That's to say, there's been a fundamental reinforcement of something that has become my mainstay in an age so eagerly searching for new values. I've discovered the only possible and lasting value – the place on one's pillow that never becomes hot or cold, as Cocteau puts it. There are things one can never fathom with rational thought, things that are outwardly incomprehensible but inwardly comprehended. I want to travel far, as far as possible, along the road of reason;

but I realize I'm a creature born of nature *and* grace, though a grace that presupposes nature.

I'll be able to describe this innermost development of mine better later on. I'm too much in the thick of it at present. At present I don't want to stray from the essential point at any price.

If I were near you, could you or couldn't you help being glad?

Hours of genuine contemplation and peace – that's what I wish you during these weeks before Christmas!

Yours,

Hans

To one of his sisters (either Inge or Sophie), December 15, 1941

A few lines[176] from a rattly express train. I'll put off writing yet again if I left it till later (would put it off, I mean). You sent Professor Muth 11 [marks] for me. I wish I knew what I'm supposed to do with them, but I don't, unless you expect me to conjure that banned and universally unobtainable book by Sigrid Undset [probably *Kristin Lavransdatter*][177] down from the sky or out of the ashes. But that's impossible. That Prussian-like, silly-sounding sentence conveys the sum total of my extensive and intensive research among my bookseller friends. Shall I send the money back [here there appears a slip of the pen] (this railroad car belonged to the Austrian State Railroad), or would you like me to buy something else?

I very much look forward to our skiing trip,[178] though I'm rather apprehensive of being outnumbered by the female element. (The train's stopping.) Signing off for now.

It's started again – we haven't reached Augsburg yet. Words of farewell. Words of pent-up nostalgia. When, oh, when? And finally,

All the best!

Hans

To Carl Muth, Munich, December 22, 1941

Dear Professor,

The few words of gratitude I want to send you are more easily written than spoken. It fills me with joy to be able, for the first time in my life, to celebrate Christmas properly and Christianly, with true conviction.

The vestiges of my childhood, when my carefree gaze dwelled on the lights and my mother's radiant face, were not obliterated, but shadows had fallen across them. I toiled in a barren age along profitless paths that invariably ended in the same sense of desolation and emptiness.

My loneliness was aggravated by two profound experiences of which I must sometime tell you, and last but not least by this terrible war, this Moloch that insinuated itself into the souls of all men from below and strove to kill them.

Then, one day, from somewhere or other, came the answer. I heard and perceived the name of the Lord. My first meeting with you coincided with that period. Thereafter it grew lighter every day, as if scales were falling from my eyes. I am praying. I feel I have a firm background and a clear goal. This year, Christ has been born for me anew.

Yours,
Hans Scholl

The skiing trip of Christmas 1941 made a profound impression on Hans, Sophie, Inge, and a few of their friends who accompanied them, and several of them wrote about it for Windlicht. *Sophie enlarged upon the idea of spiritual hunger that had been debated in the stone hut; Inge wrote directly of the experience: "Most of you will know how grand it is to sit around a stove by candlelight with a few friends, in the solitude that reigns at 2,000 meters, with wind-driven snow lashing the four walls outside and*

nothing visible to the eye but a grayish-yellow, swirling, drifting
mass. It's a good thing that the purity and peace prevailing
at such an altitude entails a certain amount of trouble and
exertion. . . ."[179]

To his sister Elisabeth, Ulm, January 6, 1942

Dear Elisabeth,

You mustn't think we forgot you at Christmas. On the
contrary, we'd hoped to be able to welcome you here on New
Year's Day and planned to keep our presents till then. Now that
this hope has also been dashed, you'll be getting a few little
things next Sunday. The only trouble is, I won't be seeing you
myself because I've got to leave for Munich tomorrow. That's
why I'm writing to you now.

Inge will tell you all about our skiing trip. I don't possess the
great writer's brilliant command of language needed to describe
that monumental experience. I can only mumble, "Good, very
good." If I abstain from all essential digressions into scenic
description, the following prosaic picture remains: a stone
hut perched on an unprotected hillside high above the tree
line, woefully exposed to every wind and storm but – being of
stone – firmly anchored there; facing it an open valley; looming
up in silhouette behind and on either side of it huge rock faces
productive of a triple echo; and trudging toward the said hut a
little band of people, half-despairing, weary, starting on their
second stormy ascent, panting, climbing, stumbling. . . .

In the next scene, sheer smoke prevents you from seeing a
thing until the outlines gradually take shape. Faces glow red in
the candlelight – serene, contented faces relieved of all fatigue
by their sense of snug security. Tea is drunk. Songs ring out. The
old forever becomes new.

There's only one basic difference between this gathering and earlier ones: a focusing of attention on our troubled times, the cross, and salvation.

Much love,

Hans

The first paragraph of the following letter exemplifies Hans's use of coded language to convey anti-Nazi sentiments, in this case by means of outwardly trivial allusions to the weather. ("Closer to spring" signified "nearer the end of the war.") Note the prefatory remark to the lines cited from Goethe, lines which are also to be found in the first White Rose handbill.[180]

To his parents, Munich, January 17, 1942

Dear Parents,

The severe cold, which has done you both no good, has been weighing relentlessly on our city, too, for the past week. It's a good thing, for all that. Even the cold is a factor that brings us closer to spring.

I'm worried about your state of health, though, and hope you're getting over your flu. It must have come at a very inopportune time for Father.

Many thanks for the parcel, Mother. I don't own a fur coat, unfortunately, and have no idea where I could get hold of one. . . .

I shall be paying another visit to Ulm with Hans R.[181] in a week's time.

Much love and best wishes for body and soul,

Hans

P.S. A poem by Goethe[182] from Parmenides, which the British might well bear in mind:

> Was aus dem Abgrund kühn entstiegen
> Kann durch ein ehernes Geschick

Den halben Erdball übersiegen –
Zum Abgrund muß es doch zurück.
Schon droht ein ungeheures Bangen,
Vergeblich wird er widerstehn.
Und alle, die an ihm gehangen,
Sie müssen mit zugrunde gehn.

[That which has boldly risen from the abyss can, by some harsh quirk of fate, conquer half the globe – but it must then return to the abyss. Mighty dread already looms. In vain will he resist, and all who have clung to him must perish too.]

To Rose Nägele, Munich, January 25, 1942

Dear Rose,

My promise was a rash one. Several weeks have gone by without my writing to you, but that's the way it is. I can never compel myself to write.

I'm now a *homo viator* in the best sense, a man in transit, and I hope I always will be. After a lapse of many largely wasted years, I've finally learned to pray again. What strength it has given me! At last I know the inexhaustible spring that can quench my terrible thirst.

That's the main thing I have to tell you.

All else is secondary!

I read your letter and rejoiced at your ideas. I too despise hard-hearted people, far more than grievous sinners. Spiritual harshness is the most abominable human trait. It stems from an extreme incapacity for life and robs people of their essential humanity. Courage is something altogether different. The meaning of courage is being utterly distorted at present.

Wasn't Christ the most courageous of all? Yet he asked for water when he was thirsty.

What a lot of harm Kant inflicted with his categorical imperative! Kant, harshness, Prussianism – the death of all spiritual life.[183]

I've no idea what will happen to us when the semester ends in a month's time, nor do I care in the least. I've dropped anchor, come what may, and nothing can really trouble me from now on.

I wish you all the best and God's blessing in the coming days. Expect another letter from me soon!

Yours,
Hans

P.S. I'm enclosing a picture for you.[184] Study it. I'll be writing to you about it before long.

Sophie Scholl
Winter–Spring 1942

After spending Christmas at home and seeing the New Year in at the skiing lodge, Sophie began the second half of her Blumberg assignment on January 6.

To Lisa Remppis, Blumberg, January 14, 1942

Dear Lisa,

. . . The very least I must do is thank you for your Christmas present, and now I'm finally getting down to it. . . . That's a handsome edition you sent me of the *Urworte*[185] (what does "orphisch" mean, actually?). The ornamentation is unusual and fraught with significance, though I find the style rather weird – strangely symbolic.

I'm back here with Christmas Eve and a few lovely days in the indescribably beautiful mountains[186] behind me – or rather, not just behind me but inside me as well, like all experiences.

I've become a pretty experienced nursery school teacher during my three months here (nearly four now). I doubt if many people get as much of an opportunity to learn as I do here, and I'm having a certain amount of success.

This evening I listened briefly to some music on the radio, by whom I don't know, but written in the time of Bach: a

marvelously lucid, majestic, joyous quartet, utterly unsenti-
mental and wonderfully "hard." (I'm reminded of the saying: *Il
faut avoir l'esprit dûr et le coeur tendre.*) That's good. If anything
can raise a storm in my stolid heart it's music. And that's essential – a prerequisite for everything else. And then (given my
surroundings at the time) I longed to breathe the same clear
air as those who had created the piece. And that desire proved
sufficient to distance me a little from the turmoil around me,
with its resemblance to glutinous, hostile mush. I'm going to try
to get permission to play the church organ again.

How did you get on? Will you write to me sometime?

Affectionate regards,

Sofie

Draft, possibly of a letter to Otl Aicher, possibly for a projected
Windlicht *article, Blumberg, undated [January 1942?]*

A conversation at the skiing lodge about spiritual hunger
steered my thoughts involuntarily to the subject you asked me
to explore in greater detail. I couldn't at that time have devoted
any thought to something that seemed so extraneous to my
current concerns. Your suggested theme was: Why do today's
concerts have a flavor of their own? —Since you recommend
that I write down what little I've been able to glean, I'm putting
it in a letter to you.

In the course of our conversation about spiritual hunger[187]
and the food that might assuage it, we got around to the subject
of music – not surprisingly, since one of our number was a
music student. Can music really satisfy spiritual hunger? Can
something that springs from the soul be its food as well? That
would be like a body having to construct itself out of itself
alone.

I've learned, however, that a hard mind without a soft heart
is necessarily as barren as a soft heart without a hard mind. *Il*

faut avoir l'esprit dûr et le coeur tendre – I think Maritain said that. A word unexperienced by the soul is a dead word, and an emotion that fails to engender a thought is a futile emotion. But music softens the heart; by resolving its confusions and relaxing its tensions, it enables the mind, which has previously knocked in vain on the locked portals of the soul, to operate within it. Yes, music quietly and gently unlocks the doors of the soul. Now they're open! Now it's receptive. This is the ultimate effect that music has on me, that makes it one of my life's necessities. I no more wash for the sake of the water I need to wash in than I listen to music for music's sake.

I should add that I'm not referring to each and every kind of musical composition, but I don't intend to write about that because I've still heard far too little and can't absorb it completely. Listening to music properly entails complete self-abandonment to it, a detachment from all that still holds me captive, even now, and a childish heart devoid of sophistication and the quest for ulterior motives. The reward is a liberated heart, an uninhibited heart, a heart that has become receptive to harmony and things harmonious, a heart that has opened its doors to the workings of the mind.

But why do the concerts of today have a special flavor? Even as I write that, I realize that I'm incapable of answering the question, clear though it is to me, because so many reasons can be cited. First I think of the people that go to listen. They don't want to listen at all, in fact, because their hearts are intent on so many little things they're reluctant to forgo. Miserly and pigheaded, they close their ears before the first note rings out. Why, in that case, do they go to concerts at all? Why indeed? We truly need to ask that question, because it's quite absurd to go to concerts without meaning to listen to them. But these people's sense of propriety demands the possession of some ludicrous crumb of knowledge about every subject.

They go to concerts as casually as they show off a new hat. They graciously commend what thousands have commended before them – whatever may be commended with impunity – and coldly condemn anything new to them until it has gained universal approbation. They go home as blinkered as they came. Most of them do, at least. Precisely the same applies when music has given them aesthetic pleasure, however great. It fruitlessly fades away unless the whole heart has absorbed and subjected it to its beneficent, liberating power.

The flavor of today's concerts is the flat, insipid flavor of the bourgeois mentality. And yet, couldn't it be that music sometimes stirs one among the many, and that the concert thus acquires meaning?

While pondering on the hunger that exists in mankind, for which music represents neither more nor less than the air that enables a flame to burn more brightly still – while pondering on this, I've become aware that we would starve to death if not sustained by God, and that not only one long thread attaches us to God through the creation, as I used to believe when I still didn't know what a life is, especially a human life.

Diary, Blumberg, February 12, 1942

I've decided to pray in church every day, so that God won't forsake me. Although I don't yet know God and feel sure that my conception of him is utterly false, he'll forgive me if I ask him. If I can love him with all my soul, I shall lose my distorted view of him.

When I look at the people around me, and also at myself, I feel awed by humanity because God came down to earth for its sake. On the other hand, this is what always strikes me as most incomprehensible. Yes, what I understand least about God is his love. But what if I didn't know about it!

O Lord, I need so badly to pray, to ask.

Yes, one should always bear in mind, when dealing with other people, that God became man on their account. To think that one feels too good to condescend to many of them! What arrogance! Where on earth did I get it from?

To Lisa Remppis, Blumberg, February 12, 1942

Dear Lisa,

Even if I can't answer your letters adequately, the least I want to do is thank you for them most sincerely. —I've abandoned my studies, at least while the war lasts. If one can't decide voluntarily to renounce the world's goods, including knowledge (of the sciences, anyway), and to love poverty, the war and the years ahead will inflict a lot more pain on us. It already does that, to me among others, but at least I try to regard such afflictions as secondary so as not to forget more important things.

Affectionate regards,
Sofie

To Lisa Remppis, Blumberg, undated [end of March 1942]

Dear Lisa,

I got your sweet letter today, and I'm writing by return just to tell you that, exactly like you, I believe that every little flower and stalk of grass has grown for my sake. I really don't think that's a delusion. Being as richly endowed as we are, shouldn't we rejoice wholeheartedly in spite of all the sorrow we're forever bringing into this beautiful world? I even believe that every star in the sky is there for my sake. Who can be sure that our world wouldn't perish if even one little heavenly body were missing from the great cosmic system? Indeed, we've so much additional evidence of all-embracing love that we could really be the happiest of mortals.

I go walking with my girls nearly every day. They've grown as fond of me as I am of them. Very few of them ever disrupt this harmony. It makes me happy to be able to leave on such a note. I'm taking them on a grand outing before I go. We're all looking forward to it. The spring, too, has made everything new again.

I'm going home in a week's time. I can't tell you how much I look forward to it. I haven't had a minute to myself lately. Every evening is crammed with RAD duties or other chores.

So I'll be at home from March 27th on. Write and tell me when you'll be free. I hope they'll let you do the Fröbel course. Lots of luck with your finals, and with everything you'll find them useful for.

Yours,

Sophie

Sophie was discharged from the war auxiliary service on April 1, 1942. She spent the month that remained before the start of the summer semester at home in Ulm.

To Lisa Remppis, Ulm, Easter Saturday (April 5), 1942

Dear Lisa,

The breakfast things are washed up and the beds made. So is the wine pudding, and since I'm all alone (Inge has gone for a walk with Traute[188]) I've time to write you a letter. I wonder if you'll be with Herr Schlehe when it turns up?

I've been back here a whole week. It's a tremendous change, and a tiring one, finding your way back into a circle of friends after a solitary and self-reliant way of life. I'm working in the house and the office. When the bulk of the work is done, I'd love to go on a trip with you, footloose and fancy-free, either by bike or on foot. Would you have the time and the inclination, say in a month or so?

Yesterday we got up early, at 3:45 a.m., so as to be in time for the Easter service at Söflingen church, but we got there a bit late all the same and didn't see them strike sparks from a stone to light the Easter candle. Much as I need that kind of service – because it's a real service, not a lecture like you get in a Protestant church – I'm sure it takes practice or habit to participate in it fully and not be distracted by the spectacle confronting you. If you have faith, that spectacle becomes a profound religious experience in itself. My trouble is this, however: I'd like to kneel down because it genuinely accords with my feelings, but I'm shy of people seeing, especially people I know. I'd like to bow down before an effigy of God because you shouldn't just experience such feelings but express them as well, but again I'm far too inhibited. The result is, I'm never whole-heartedly involved – or haven't been so far, at any rate.

Yesterday morning, when the baptismal water had been consecrated by dipping the Easter candle in it three times, a dear little newborn baby was brought forward. All one could see peeking out of the white wraps was a tiny red face and some even tinier fingers happily playing with each other.

Inge says to thank you for your nice Easter card. She'll be replying in due course.

Lisa, sometime you really must see Dieterle,[189] Klaus's baby brother – he's such a sweetheart. He toddles around all over the place and tries to get his hands on everything. Miraculous though I find it, he's even allowed into my stern father's office, where he loves to bang on the typewriter – in fact Father takes him on his knee and plays with him and talks to him. He's a regular little lady-killer. Yesterday, when I put him on the table to get him dressed, so that he was taller than me, he bent down and looked into my face with the sweetest laugh. He's like a little ray of sunshine stealing into your heart. Wouldn't you like to see him sometime?

Write and tell me how you are.

P.S. Again my love to your mother, and many thanks for my two days with you.

Hans Scholl

Winter–Spring 1942

The "most ridiculous 'offense'" to which Hans refers to in the letter below was described by Mario Krebs: "An incident occurred. A devoutly National Socialist professor of medicine was jeered while lecturing by members of the students' company. Because the 'ringleaders' could not be identified, the entire company was confined to barracks for four weeks – 'for the most ridiculous offense imaginable,' as Hans Scholl puts it . . . After the 'case' was forwarded to the judge advocate's department, the situation became more and more grave."[190]

To his sister Elisabeth, Munich, February 10, 1942

Dear Elisabeth,

Many thanks for your two nice parcels. Can you really spare that butter and sausage? At present I'm a prisoner of the state again, by which I mean that I am atoning for the most ridiculous "offense" imaginable with four weeks' confinement to barracks. What makes this unnecessary torment even more galling is that I had so many important plans mapped out in the next few weeks, and for those I definitely needed some quiet evenings in my room. *Ça passera.* Many more things lie in store, but they won't divert us by so much as a finger's breadth from what really matters.

It looks as if we may be able to continue our studies in the summer. That would be a great boon from my point of view.

Some friends and I are currently reading *Der seidene Schuh [Soulier de Satin]* by the French writer Claudel.[191] I regard this work as the greatest event in modern European literature. I wouldn't dream of comparing Claudel's language with Goethe's or Dante's. That would be as nonsensical as judging baroque art by Gothic standards, but Claudel's ideas are more profound and comprehensive than Faust's. You know the book, don't you?

I recently made the acquaintance of a very distinguished Russian philosopher, Fedor Stepun,[192] who last held a chair at Breslau University. A philosopher of history, he's one of those people who are so far above the age in which I myself moil and toil that he says the preservation of fundamentals is all that matters – and preserved they will be. He's right.

You'll be able to read something about our Christmas vacation at the Coburg skiing lodge in the next *Windlicht*. Inge wrote it,[193] and a good job she made of it.

I'm expecting Inge here next Saturday. What a great day that'll be!

I'll sign off for now.

Fondest love,

Hans

To his parents and his sister Inge, Munich, February 12, 1942

Dear Parents, dear Inge,

It was a big surprise today, on spending a few hours in my room for the first time in ages,[194] to find two parcels there full of delicious things. I gorged myself and then went to sleep. The last few weeks have been physically taxing, and for no good reason. The situation is becoming more and more tense. The judge advocate's office has reported our company to the OKW[195] for mutiny. Informers of the most loathsome kind are sprouting in our ranks. I find this incomprehensible, which may be why I'm feeling so depressed. I have no personal connection with the affair. Everyone was interrogated separately today. One of my best friends is among the accused.[196]

I hadn't expected the majority to react as they have to the least little threat, but I've learned a lot.

We're all delighted that Inge is coming on Sunday. Let's hope my time isn't preempted by the army, as it was last Sunday.

How are you, Mother?

All my love,

Hans

To his sister Elisabeth, Munich, February 28, 1942

Dear Elisabeth,

I'm always being confined to barracks. I reel willy-nilly from one punishment to the next. Before it's too late, I mean to make the most of this all-too-brief interlude of so-called freedom and quickly write you a letter. I've every reason to thank you for the dear parcels that reached me a considerable time ago. The charming donor of the bacon also merits my commendation. Please tell her so.

Now to your birthday. Since you weren't able to spend Christmas with your nearest and dearest (and mine), it may well come hard to you to have to celebrate your birthday, too, so absurdly near yet far. However, I still hope to be able to tell you more at Ulm tomorrow than one can say in a letter. (What I wish you most of all, and what is essential, is that you should soon be released from your all too narrow confines and no longer prevented from looking farther afield, both physically and mentally. The higher we climb, the deeper the abysses, and our aim should be to harness the peaks and troughs of the spirit. Those who fail to see the precipice fall into it; but those without a light search in vain, and their weary eyes are useless to them. Our present task is to find the light on our way. It always has been and thus will remain so for all time. What I wish you, I also wish myself and everyone else, but these days my thoughts are more than ever with you.)

You'll be interested to know that I'm doing a temporary internship at St. Ottilien am Ammersee[197] during the vacation. After that I hope to resume my studies.

We recently had a splendid evening at Professor Muth's. Professor Muth read passages from some of his own unpublished works to a small circle of students convened by me. What I liked best was an essay, "On Poverty,"[198] which you *Windlicht* readers will shortly be getting in the next issue, in connection with the subject I raised for discussion in the first *Windlicht*.[199]

I'm off to Ulm tomorrow with Traute Lafrenz.[200]

You often visit Leonberg, don't you? I'd be very interested to hear how Lisa's getting along.

That's all for now.

Fondest love,

Hans

After completing the winter semester 1941–1942 and working at St. Ottilien, Hans Scholl took on another internship, this time with the surgical unit of a base hospital at Schrobenhausen, a small town some forty miles northwest of Munich. The hospital was staffed by nuns belonging to the Orden der Englischen Fräulein.[201]

In the following letter Hans mentions the Gestapo: he took it for granted that the family's mail was being monitored because the Gestapo, acting on an informer's tip, had questioned Robert Scholl in February 1942 and threatened him with legal proceedings. The "west wind, with its renewed threat of cloud" is a coded

*reference to the expectation that Allied troops would soon be
landing on the Atlantic coast.*[202]

*To his parents and his sister Inge, Schrobenhausen, March 18,
1942*

Dear Parents, dear Inge,

I don't know if you received my last letter, because Mother's
made no mention of it. The mail I get here is very irregular.
I really sympathize with the Gestapo, having to decipher
all those different handwritings, some of which are highly
illegible, but that's what they're paid to do, and duty is duty,
gentlemen, isn't it!

I've nothing to complain of here. There's plenty of work for
me to do. Another batch [of casualties], including many cases
of frostbite, arrived here yesterday from Russia, and there's
only one doctor here apart from me. I get on tremendously well
with the nurses and the Englische Fräulein. Our joint efforts
on behalf of the wounded almost make us forget our own little
cares and concerns. The demands on us differ from those
involved in opening other people's letters and prying around in
them. I wonder if those gentlemen would be as courageous if
they had to slit open dressings sodden with pus and stinking to
high heaven? It might upset them, I fear.

How eagerly we longed for the warm March days, and now
they're here! We sun ourselves on the terrace at lunchtime. We
inhale the scent of spring in spite of everything. In spite of the
west wind, with its renewed threat of cloud. In spite of the smell
of hospital and army boots. In spite of my long hair, which for
some incomprehensible reason strikes certain of my fellow
men as *too* long, and on whose account I should really be at the
barber's instead of relaxing here.

I regret that nearly half my time here is up, and that I'll then have to move back to Munich. I'm looking forward to Munich too, though. If only I could come home sometime soon.

> Fondest love,
>
> Hans

To his parents, Schrobenhausen, March 29, 1942

Dear Parents,

Many thanks for the letters and the laundry. My quietest days here are over. Tomorrow another batch of badly wounded men arrives from Russia. I'll have plenty of work to do in my last two weeks.

Last Sunday, when I had to deputize for the senior medical officer, it became necessary for the first time (discounting the French campaign) for me to perform a vital operation during the night. It went well.

You wouldn't believe how kind these nuns are. They read your every thought. They're like that because they draw on another source of strength, one that never fails.

Not to mention the spring.

Best regards to everyone including the uninvited readers of this letter, especially Traute.[203]

> Yours ever,
>
> Hans

P.S. These are the kind of little treats[204] the "English" [nuns] slip me. (This sentence is quite innocent.) There are 7 (seven) in all. I mention this purely for the record.

To Rose Nägele, Munich, April 13, 1942

Dear Rose,

I've simply got to write to you at last. I've kept you waiting an awful long time. You've waited for many a melancholy hour, I know, but it couldn't be helped. I doubt if I'll ever be able to love anyone happily and contentedly. There's far too much afoot for me to keep a promise at this stage and say that my course is set for good and all.

I'd much rather have paid you a visit at Easter, instead of writing in this nebulous vein, but I couldn't get away. I didn't even get Easter off. I was satisfied with my internship, for all that. My four weeks in a medium-sized town in Upper Bavaria, rural and outwardly superficial, brought me much joy and a little, albeit genuine, sorrow. I breathed good air there and chatted with hospitable people. Now I'm back in Munich. The time of year is making me restless and rousing many a demon, contrary to my intentions. My most faithful friend is still Carl Muth. I'm to be found at his home every day. . . .

Best regards,

Hans

To his mother, Munich, May 4, 1942

Dear Mother,

The words of that fervent seeker after God, St. Augustine,[205] will convey more to you on your birthday [May 5] than mine ever could. That's why I'm putting them first of all, because I know that no one is closer to them than you. However great the turmoil prevailing today – so great that one often has no idea where to turn because of the multitude of things and happenings around me – elemental words of that kind loom up like beacons in a stormy sea. That's my conception of poverty, that one should fearlessly jettison old ballast at such moments and powerfully, freely, head for the One. But how rare such moments are, and how often and repeatedly man subsides into drab uncertainty, into the stream that flows in no direction, and demons are always busy grabbing him by the hair at every opportunity and dragging him down.

Hans Scholl | 219

Sophie has arrived here[206] safe and sound. She'll be staying at Professor Muth's for a few days[207] until the room's ready. She's well off there. Is Liesel coming next Sunday? Please write and tell me soon, so I can make arrangements.

Fondest love and best wishes on your birthday,

Hans and Sophie

Sophie Scholl

Summer 1942

On May 3 or 4, 1942, shortly before her twenty-first birthday,
Sophie was at last able to join her brother in Munich and begin
reading biology and philosophy at Munich University. Later
that month Hans, in collaboration with Alexander Schmorell,
wrote and distributed the first White Rose leaflet calling for
"every individual, conscious of his responsibility as a member
of Christian and Western civilization . . . [to] defend himself as
best he can at this late hour . . . [to] work against the scourges of
mankind, against fascism and any similar system of totalitari-
anism. Offer passive resistance – resistance. . . ."[208] That summer,
the students began to learn of German atrocities in Poland, and
subsequent leaflets published the information that since Poland's
conquest, 300,000 Jews had been murdered there.

After her arrival in Munich Sophie stayed briefly at Solln with
Carl Muth, then took lodgings with Frau Berrsche, the widow
of a Munich music critic, at No. 1 Mandlstrasse. It is likely that
Hans tried to protect her by keeping her ignorant of White Rose
activities, but evidence suggests that she became acquainted
with, and participated in, the distribution of leaflets early on.

To Lisa Remppis, Munich, May 30, 1942

Dear Lisa,

I got your card from Lake Constance yesterday. I now look forward to a more substantial letter. My new address is c/o Dr. Berrsche, 1 Mandlstr., M. 23.

I've a great favor to ask you. Could you spare me your tent? It would come in so useful here.

Hans and I, plus an occasional companion, often regret having to return to our far-flung lodgings on glorious nights to grab some much-needed sleep. It would be so practical if we could erect our own house on the spot!

There's something new for me to digest[209] here every day. Yesterday I had tea with Professor Muth and Sigismund von Radecki,[210] and in the evening Hans and I visited a friend whom we simply call "the Philosopher."[211] Three solid hours of tiring conversation ensued. —To be honest, I rather hanker to be on my own, because I've an urge to act on what has so far existed within me merely as an idea – as what I perceive to be right. —I'm glad of the opportunity to absorb things, though, even if I'm still uncertain of my ground.

Perhaps you could pay me a visit sometime? Hans is being a good brother to me. I'm growing fonder and fonder of him.

Don't leave me so long without news.

Affectionate regards,

Sophie

P.S. I'd so much like to spend a few days alone with you somewhere.

To her parents and her sisters Inge and Elisabeth, Munich,
June 6, 1942

Dear Parents, Inge, and Lisl,

The coats arrived yesterday, also the chop, which we devoured on the spot. Many thanks for them and the accompanying letter. —I've already been to Students' Administration about the munitions work,[212] but there isn't a hope of obtaining exemption. Not even girl students with the best of personal connections, daughters of current bigwigs, can get out of it on any grounds, however pressing. The most I can do is get deferred till September, which I naturally will.[213] I hope Mother's feeling a bit better. It was lovely at Passau last Sunday. We also made a brief excursion into the Bohemian Forest to see a friend of Professor Muth's, a highly original, most impressive parish priest in a little village[214] (where he's been sent for disciplinary reasons). We couldn't bring the Professor back as much stuff as we'd hoped, unfortunately. He isn't very well. Events are taking their toll, and the wartime food isn't improving his general condition. Could you possibly get him a pound or two of white flour – he can't eat black bread – and some trout[215] as soon as they're available again? Trivial though such things may seem, his state of health largely depends on them.

At Hans's request,[216] Sigismund von Radecki read some essays, poems, and translations to a group of around twenty of us the night before last. He reads aloud brilliantly, with sweeping gestures, and acts out everything he reads. How we laughed! He used to be an actor, and not a bad one by any means. Four of us joined him in my room afterward. He's going away for three months, unfortunately, but he'll be game for anything when he gets back.

Have you sent off my bike yet? I miss it terribly here, I waste so much time and money on streetcars. It's nice to be able to go off cycling on Sundays, too.

When is Inge coming? Is Werner still in Ulm? Fondest love to him and all of you from Sophie and Hans.

P.S. Have a nice Sunday!

Sheet from a letter, Munich, June 24, 1942

I very much hope that your next letter doesn't go to Ulm, so it won't reproachfully inform me at first glance that none of my letters has reached you yet. I suppose I can put half the blame on the army post office, which delivers springtime letters at the height of summer.

There's a bird squawking outside in a tree whose golden-green top is lighted by the mellow, slanting rays of the evening sun. I'm reminded of the passage in your nice letter from Russia in which you speak of Nature being "unredeemed." I've always felt, and I still do now, that I can hear the most consummate harmony resounding from field and forest. Last Sunday, as I made my way into a big, peaceful mountain valley bathed in warm evening air that was already obscuring little details and throwing big, clear-cut outlines into relief, all my usual worries seemed to fall away from me like useless leaves, and I began to judge my preoccupations by an entirely different criterion. It seemed to me that man alone had disrupted this wonderful harmony, which I can also detect in a Bach fugue. I felt as if man had set himself apart from this harmony, and that it was lingering on, but without him. That's why I found it inconceivable that Nature should be in need of redemption. —Yesterday evening, or rather, after midnight, while I was walking back with someone through the Englischer Garten (a small group of us had been reading Paul Claudel's *Le soulier*

Hans and Sophie Scholl with Christoph Probst (*right*), just before Hans and Christoph's student company left for Russia, July 23, 1942

Farewell scene later the same day at Munich's East Station; from left to right: Hubert Furtwängler, Hans, Raymund Samiller, Sophie, and Alexander Schmorell (*extreme right*)

de Satin), it suddenly occurred to me that Nature might have to be redeemed by death, however innocent the death that animals and plants must die. I can recall that, as a child, I felt that living without destroying others was an insoluble and terribly distressing problem. It still seems just as insoluble, but I'd forgotten about it, and how can a harmony still be complete if a note has forgotten its proper place? And the roaring of the offended earth – of things that have been displaced and become demonic, of machines that ought to serve mankind and are destroying it – soon seemed to swamp every vestige of peace. But that I can't believe, or I'd be done for.

To Lisa Remppis, Munich, June 26, 1942

Dear Lisa,

Yesterday I finally received another letter from you, for which many thanks. I think I'll be going to Ulm around the middle of July. Then we can either meet there or fix a rendezvous one Sunday. I look forward to meeting Gust. You presuppose a certain lack of enthusiasm on my part, but I don't think an initial failure to hit it off would be as tragic as all that. It would mean that both parties had been found wanting. I'm not sitting in judgment, after all, and I'd like to feel the same affection for Gust as I do for you. You'd never forgive me if I didn't. That's not the reason, though – you know what I mean.

I still have a vivid recollection of my time at the crèche.[217] I had ten babies to look after, too. It took me no time at all to form a personal relationship with them – a far closer one than I had with the other nurse. Each of the little things was a distinct individual, and I could have predicted what they would be like in twenty or thirty years' time. Not for sure, of course, but even with little creatures between two and ten months old, you feel you can tell how they'll turn out. My affection for them varied, too, even though their universal helplessness aroused the same degree of compassion. The one I like best tried to put all his various emotions into a single "da." A week ago I held another of the tiny creatures in my arms. It fills me with delight every time, quite a different feeling than the one I get with other children. The soft fragrance of their flowerlike flesh, their sweet, toothless mouths, their tiny, ever-fluttering hands, their almost vacant gaze – they really do resemble buds that have just opened: unique, sacred, and sublime, like miracles visited upon our everyday world.

I'm so pleased you're lending the tent. We'll make good use of it. But do me a favor and don't *give* it back. That would be awful for Hans, I'm sure, however little you mean to each other now. Think it over, and you'll refrain.

I'll write again when I get some more writing paper.

I'm going home today.

Affectionate regards,
Sophie

Robert Scholl, Hans and Sophie's father, a former mayor of the small town of Forchtenberg, had set up offices as a tax and financial consultant in Ulm, where his family regularly pitched in to help with the books. He was a pacifist who had refused to serve in the military during World War I, and his liberal ideas clearly influenced his children. One early morning in 1942 the Gestapo arrived at the Scholls' door in Ulm, searched the apartment, and arrested Robert Scholl. He had been denounced by an employee for remarks made during a conversation in his office when he called Hitler a "divine scourge" and added, "If he doesn't end the war soon, the Russians will be in Berlin two years from now" (a prophetic statement only about a year off the mark).

*As the summer progressed, the family anxiously awaited
Robert Scholl's trial, set for August 3; Sophie continued, with
dwindling hope, to try to get a deferral from war service work
at the munitions factory, and Hans's student company received
orders for the Eastern front, where Werner was already stationed.*

Diary, June 29, 1942

My God, I can only address you falteringly. I can only offer
you my heart, which is wrested away from you by a thousand
desires. Being so weak that I cannot remain facing you of my
own free will, I destroy what distracts me from you and force
myself to turn to you, for I know that I'm happy with you
alone. Oh, how far from you I am, and the best thing about me
is the pain I feel on that account. But I'm often so torpid and
apathetic. Help me to be singlehearted and remain with me. If I
could only once call you Father, but I can hardly address you as
"YOU." I do so [as one that speaks] to a great Unknown. I know
that you'll accept me if I'm sincere, and that you'll hear me if I
cling to you. Teach me to pray. Better to suffer intolerable pain
than to vegetate insensibly. Better to be parched with thirst,
better to pray for pain, pain, and more pain, than to feel empty,
and to feel so without truly feeling at all. That I mean to resist.

Diary, July 15, 1942

My soul is like an arid waste when I try to pray to you,
conscious of nothing but its own barrenness. My God, transform that ground into good soil so that your seed doesn't fall
on it in vain. At least let it bring forth a yearning for you, its
creator, whom it so often declines to see. I beseech you with all
my heart. I call aloud to you, I call "you," even though all I know
about you is that my salvation resides in you alone. Do not turn
away from me if I fail to hear you knock; open my deaf, deaf

heart. Make me restless so that I may find my way to the repose that dwells within you. I am so powerless. Receive me and do with me as you will, I beseech you, I beseech you.

Into your hand I give my thoughts of my friend, that little ray of solicitude and warmth, that modicum of strength. Do with me the best you can, for you wish us to call upon you and have also made us responsible in prayer for our fellow creatures. I think likewise of all others. Amen.

To Lisa Remppis, Ulm, July 27, 1942

Dear Lisa,

I got your letter just now, at coffee time on Sunday morning, and here I am already, sitting down to answer it and thank you. On August 18, when you aim to get back from your trip to the mountains, I shall be doing factory work at a small town near Ulm. I have to do two months of it. My break should more or less coincide with your fall vacation, I think (October). Still, how things will be with us by then I don't know, because my father's case comes up in a week's time, and there's little hope that he'll be allowed home again after that. If he isn't, I shall give up my university course for the time being.

Hans went off to Russia last week with all the other people I've made friends with over the past few weeks and months. I still preserve such a vivid recollection of every little farewell word and gesture. I'd never have believed I could become so attached to them all, especially Hans. Let's hope we'll all be reunited soon, safe and sound. Werner's first letter from Russia also turned up yesterday.

So, Lisa, I'd love it if you felt like coming via Ulm after all. . . .

Have a really nice vacation, and affectionate regards to you and Gust Schlehe!

Yours,
Sophie

On August 3, 1942, a special court sentenced Robert Scholl to four months' imprisonment for "treachery," and he was later debarred from practicing law.

Diary, August 6, 1942

I'm so weak-willed that I can't even fulfill and act on my own perceptions, nor can I ever renounce my personal volition, which I know to be imprudent and self-seeking, and surrender myself to His. Yet I'd like to, and I'm happy to reflect that he is the ruler of all things. Being unable to relinquish my foolish hold on it voluntarily, I pray every night that he may wrest my will away and subject me to his – if only I didn't stand in my own way. I pray for a compassionate heart, for how else could I love? I who am so shallow in everything must pray for everything. A child can be compassionate, but I too often forget the sufferings that ought to overwhelm me, the sufferings of mankind. I place my powerless love in your hands, that it may become powerful.

Diary, August 9, 1942

I've just torn a page out of my notebook because it was about Schurik [Alexander Schmorell], but why should I tear him out of my heart? I'll pray to God to assign him his rightful place in it. He shall go back into the notebook with the rest, and I'll include him in my prayers every night like Fritz and the others.

Many people believe that our age is the last. All the omens are terrible enough to make one think so, but isn't that belief of secondary importance? Mustn't we all, no matter what age we live in, be permanently prepared for God to call us to account from one moment to the next? How am I to know if I shall still be alive tomorrow? We could all be wiped out overnight by a bomb, and my guilt would be no less than if I perished in company with the earth and the stars. —I know all that, but don't I heedlessly fritter away my life all the same? O God, I beseech you to take away my frivolity and self-will, which clings to the sweet, ephemeral things of life. I can't do so myself, I'm far too weak.

I don't understand how "devout" people can fear for God's existence today because mankind is dogging his footsteps with the sword and vile atrocities. As if God didn't have the power (I sense that everything rests in his hand) – the power. All we should fear for is the existence of humanity, because it has turned away from him who is its very life.

I must write down a curious dream[218] I had – one of the few that haven't been dominated by a peculiarly oppressive sensation. I was out walking with Hans and Schurik, with them on either side of me and our arms linked. Half walking, half skipping along, I was lifted off the ground by the two of them and soared through the air for a little way. Then Hans began: "I know quite a simple proof of God's existence and intervention in the world of today. Human beings need a certain amount of air to breathe, so the whole sky would eventually become polluted by their stale breath. To prevent them from running out of this nourishment for the blood, God periodically injects our world with a mouthful of his own breath, which permeates the stale air and renews it. That's how he does it." And then Hans raised his face to the very, very gloomy sky. Drawing a deep breath, he expelled the whole of it from his lips. His breath streamed forth in a bright blue jet. It grew progressively bigger and rose high into the sky, driving away the murky clouds until the sky ahead and above us was as flawlessly blue as blue could be. It was beautiful.

With term over and Hans's student company serving in Russia,
Sophie had to qualify for permission to resume her studies during
the winter semester of 1942–1943 by devoting the months of
August and September to war work at an Ulm munitions factory.

To Fritz Hartnagel, Ulm, August 1942

My dear Fritz,

Did you receive my last letter enclosing the snaps of Professor Muth? I'm enclosing another to make sure you get one.

I still have several more weeks' work to do at the factory. It's an awfully soulless, loveless occupation, standing over a machine and going through the same motions all day long. All it requires is concentration, but a trained monkey could do it just as well – if it was stupid enough to be bullied into it. You go home in the evenings physically tired and mentally bored. The sight of so many people in front of so many machines is depressing and reminiscent of slavery, except that these slaves have appointed their own slave driver. Working alongside me is a Russian woman with a childishly naïve and touching faith in all and sundry, even the German overseers, whose fist-shaking and brutal yelling she merely greets with an uncomprehending, almost merry smile. She probably finds them comical and thinks they're threatening her for fun. I'm glad she works next door to me, and I do my best to try to correct her picture of the Germans a little. But a lot of the German women are also friendly and helpful to her, surprised to find that even Russians can be human beings, and unsophisticated ones at that, with no mistrust of others. But my judgment is only based on the Russian men and women working at my factory, numerous though they are. Yours would be more valid. Are you still down by the Black Sea, at the place [Stalingrad] whose name you weren't allowed to divulge? All my best wishes go with you.

Yours,
Sophie

To Otl Aicher, Ulm, August 14, 1942

Dear Otl,

It's ages since I sat in the garden at Solln,[219] pad on knee, meaning to write you a birthday letter,[220] but I gave it up as a bad job too soon, both then and later. It's my own fault, but as soon as I pick up a pen I feel more barren than a desert. It isn't inhibitions that make it hard for me to write, but a genuine emptiness [that afflicts me] the moment I feel like unbosoming myself.

Inge will have written about Muth in the meantime, better than I could have done. I'm glad I can at least send you a photo of him – and don't think I've forgotten who introduced us to Muth, and not to him alone.[221]

Maybe I'll manage a letter sometime, but I don't want to hold up the photo any longer. It comes with affectionate regards from

Yours,

Sophie

Hans Scholl

Russia: 1942

After the summer semester of 1942, Hans's students' company had to do a "combat internship" in Russia. He and his friends entrained at Munich on July 23 and reached Warsaw, their first stop, on July 26.

To his parents, Warsaw, July 27, 1942

Dear Parents,

We arrived here[222] after a long journey through Germany and Poland. The journey itself was pleasant enough. My friends and I had a section to ourselves, and whenever we weren't asleep, we passed the time conversing intelligently or playing games. We often gazed out of the window for hours on end at the passing countryside – the more so because the endless plains of the East cast their spell over us. There are two salient features here: trees and sky. The farmhouses are thatched with straw, and the farmsteads nestle picturesquely in little birch woods. The sunsets are indescribably beautiful, and when the moon comes up and bathes the trees and fields in its magical, silvery glow, one thinks of the Polish prisoners in Germany and understands their boundless love of country.

Warsaw would sicken me in the long run. Thank God we're moving on tomorrow. The ruins alone are food enough for thought, but an American palace towers incongruously into the sky from among shattered walls. Half-starved children sprawl in the street and whimper for bread while provocative jazz rings out across the way, and peasants kiss the flagstones in churches while the bars seethe with unbridled, insensate revelry. The mood is universally doom-laden, but I nonetheless believe in the inexhaustible strength of the Polish people. They're too proud for one to succeed in striking up conversation with them. And children are playing wherever you look.

Tomorrow morning we board an empty hospital train for Vyaz'ma. That's where we're supposed to split up.[223]

Have you heard from Werner yet? I'd be very interested to know what area he's in. I'll write you some more soon.

Fondest love,

Hans

Quite by chance, Hans and Werner were assigned to the same sector of the front. Werner was only a few miles away to the west, so Hans rode over to see him on several occasions.

To his parents, Russia, August 7, 1942

Dear Parents,

You'll have received our joint letter. Werner paid me a visit here yesterday. We went for a long walk together and wound up at a Russian farmhouse. There we drank several glasses of vodka and sang Russian songs as if we were in the depths of peacetime. Actually, there was still a bit of shooting in progress. The Russian fliers got especially busy, but why worry? It's amazing how quickly the Russians recover from extremes of terror. When evening comes and the sun goes down in all colors behind the fields, this country is overcome by a melancholia that weighs

Hans and Alexander Schmorell on the train bound for the Eastern front

even heavier than the war. That's when wounds are forgotten and voices are raised in song, as they have been in every age.

Werner has struck it lucky. He's back in the orderly room again. Although his clearing station is overflowing with casualties from Rzhev, he doesn't have much to do with it. The Russians have broken through at two points near Rzhev, but they never manage to exploit their advantage.

I myself am temporarily quite redundant. I either go walking or sit and sleep in my dugout. Who knows how much longer, though? It looks as if the Russians may be planning a major attack after all.

The partisans are incredibly active. They pose a genuine threat to our supply lines. I was talking with a dispatcher recently. In his area, which is roughly the size of Ulm–Geislingen, they blew up forty-eight trains in a single week. The locomotives were totally destroyed in every case. Throughout occupied territory, all young males are systematically recruited at night by the partisans. And paratroops land behind our lines, day after day and night after night.

For the moment I'm taking the best possible care of myself.
I've grown perceptibly fatter. I may have to live on it someday.
Fondest love,
Hans

*The following letter is addressed to Professor Kurt Huber,
lecturer in philosophy at Munich University, a noted authority
on folk songs and the aesthetics and philosophy of music. It was
signed by three other students who attended Huber's lectures
and who were already participating in the activities of the
White Rose: Alexander Schmorell, Willi Graf,*[224] *and Hubert
Furtwängler.*[225]

*Huber, who would come to write the last leaflet of the White
Rose, first met Hans and his friends at a private party in June
1942, and his relations with them grew steadily closer during the
month before the student company's departure for Russia. He
became one of the circle's older friends and mentors. Although
he stimulated their ideas, chiefly because of his emphatic and
uncompromising attitude when the glories and miseries of the
German nation were under debate, it is unlikely that they initi-
ated him at this stage into the White Rose handbill operations
already in progress.*[226] *The group had produced and distributed
a total of four leaflets before they were sent to the front in July.*

To Kurt Huber, Russia, August 17, 1942

Dear Professor,

Two weeks ago, after a long and eventful journey, we arrived
at this small, shell-torn town east of Vyaz'ma. Here we spend
our days in idleness. It's not that I yearn for "work." I busy
myself with medicine only to escape from exceptionally idle
hours. The incessant rain doesn't bother me in the least, either,
but I'm often immensely irked by our accursed inactivity in
more important respects, the hopelessness and isolation. I
meant to send you a postcard from Warsaw, while the whole of

the students' company was still together, but it all went far too quickly. The city, the ghetto, and the whole setup made a very profound impression on all of us. It's impossible to give even a vague picture of what has assailed me in Russia since the day we crossed the frontier. I don' t know where to begin. Russia is so vast, so boundless in every respect, and its inhabitants' love of their native land is boundless too. War sweeps across the countryside like a rainstorm, but after the rain the sun shines once more. Suffering takes total possession of people, purifies them – but then they laugh once more.

Three good friends of mine, whom you know, are in the same company. I find my Russian friend [Alexander Schmorell] particularly useful. I'm trying hard to learn the language. At nights we mix with Russians and drink schnapps with them and sing.

The Russians are attacking in strength, it seems, north and south of here, but it's still uncertain how things will turn out.

With best regards, yours sincerely,
Hans Scholl
and Alexander Schmorell
and Willi Graf
and Hubert Furtwängler

To his mother, Russia, August 24, 1942

Dear Mother,

Father's imprisonment starts today, and today I received your first letter and Sophie's. Your other letter arrived a week ago.

You can imagine that even though I wasn't surprised by the news, I didn't take it calmly. Indignation and turmoil filled my heart when I read your letter, and it took me a while to calm down again. I did so mainly thanks to your generosity of spirit and all-pervading love. However, I still can't bring myself to write an appeal for clemency. If I tried, I'd go off the rails. I told

Werner in a big-brotherly way what had happened. He took it calmly, on the surface, as he does everything else.

Father is in for a very hard time at first, as I know too well: starved of contact with the outside world, cooped up alone in a cramped gray cell. He'll survive, though. Being strong, he'll emerge from captivity even stronger. I believe in the immeasurable strength of suffering. True suffering is like a bath from which a person emerges born anew. All greatness must be purified before it can exchange the narrow confines of the human breast for a wider world outside.

We shall never escape suffering, not till the day we die. Isn't Christ being crucified a thousand times every hour, and aren't beggars and cripples still being turned away from every door, today as always? To think that human beings fail to see precisely what makes them human: helplessness, misery, poverty. . . .

Both of us[227] are still doing fine. Most days I stroll through the endless forests with my friend Alexander, and in the evenings we sit with Russian peasants, drinking tea or schnapps and singing.

We buried a Russian today. He must have been lying out there for several weeks, a hundred meters from our dugout. Werner still has a lot of dealings with the dead too.

I'll write again soon.

> Fondest love,
> Hans
> Best regards,
> Alex

*To his mother and his sisters Sophie and Inge, Russia,
September 2, 1942*

Dear Mother, Inge, and Sophie,

First let me thank you for your letters and parcels. Two letters from Mother, one from Sophie, and one parcel have reached me so far. I'm still waiting eagerly for a letter from Father.

Write to me often, because your letters are very reassuring. Since love grows with distance to the power of two, you can imagine how often I think of you, especially in the evening, when night descends suddenly on the Russian plains, and we have to sit there in the dark. The fall has already yellowed the first leaves in the treetops, and the birches, yes, the birches stand among the tall, solemn firs like young girls shivering with cold. It still isn't obvious to every eye, but there's a thin, delicate film over the trees and fields. It's Nature's mourning garb, which externalizes all sadness and converts it into beauty. I can't understand why so many people are such strangers to death. Isn't it death that makes life precious, or rather, has made it so? Death, like sin, is what makes us human. A flower is beautiful because it fades. The flower fades, but beauty endures. What is more, death transfigures beauty.

I have a great deal of time in which to do nothing, and consequently to think. We all need that. My last few weeks in Munich were grand and worthwhile but hurried, so they prevented many of my ideas from maturing.[228] If you could see me now, you'd be surprised how little I'm affected by all that happens here at the front. And my comrades like me for being down-to-earth. Tackling things with a totally different attitude of mind, that's what counts.

Alex has been very ill for several days. He developed diphtheria overnight, and now he's in bed with a high temperature. Hubert F. [Furtwängler] and Willi Graf had to deputize for a unit medical officer yesterday, up front with the infantry.[229]

That means I'm the sole remnant of our once proud "fifth column."[230] I'm never lonely, though. I've made friends with a grizzled old fisherman. We often sit on a riverbank from dawn to dusk, fishing like Peter in the days of Christ. I've also formed a choir here in camp from prisoners of war and a few Russian girls. Not long ago we danced half the night away, so energetically that our bones ached the next day.

I see Werner nearly every day. I shall certainly be staying here at Gzhatsk [Gagarin] another four weeks, and so will he. The Russian artillery shelled Gzhatsk every night to begin with, but that stopped about a week ago, so you've nothing at all to worry about. From the military aspect, we're in absolutely no danger at present. In fact, one of our senior medical officers has reinjected some iron into the peaceful atmosphere by lecturing us on infant nutrition. I couldn't help laughing heartily.[231] There are many amusing asides to this place, and it's fun to preserve such caricatures. I carry a little notebook in which I "record" trivialities of this kind. No room for more.

All my very fondest love,

Hans

To Rose Nägele, Russia, September 10, 1942

Dear Rose,

I've been in Russia over a month now, and almost all my ties with the old world have been temporarily severed. I've only one remaining desire, and that's to roam ever eastward, free from all constraints and far from the musty smell of European civilization. I'm exaggerating, but one has to exaggerate. . . . This country is so extreme that it casts its spell over you either completely or not at all. It obeys the all-or-nothing law, like one's heart. In reality, though, I'm every inch a European, an epigone, a guardian of a sacred heritage, and that's why I'll have to go back.

My mood changes like the autumn wind. Five minutes ago an officer bawled me out because of my long hair. Disagreeable incidents like these are capable of making my blood boil.[232] My mood is as fickle as a young girl's. "Russian fever" is definitely the wrong term for it. I can't express it properly, but it's something along these lines: You're dependent on your surroundings because your soul gets ruthlessly sponged down in Russia until it resembles a clean slate. This blank surface is subsequently assailed on all sides by various forces, good and evil, drastic and gentle.

Can you read my writing?

Regards to everyone, especially Eve!

Hans

To his parents, Russia, September 18, 1942

Dear Parents,

Yesterday, after an interval of several days, another of your letters reached me. I'll pass it on to Werner this afternoon. We still meet from time to time, though not as often as before. The fact is, I've developed a passion for riding, and it won't let go of me. There's nothing to beat galloping across the plain astride a fast horse, forging your way like an arrow through the head-high steppe grass, and riding back into the forest at sunset, weary to the point of exhaustion, with your head still glowing from the heat of the day and the blood throbbing in every fingertip. It's the finest delusion I've succumbed to, because in a certain sense you have to delude yourself. The men call it "Russian fever," but that's a clumsy, feeble expression. It's something like this: when you see the world in all its enchanting beauty, you're sometimes reluctant to concede that the other side of the coin exists. The antithesis exists here, as it does everywhere, if only you open your eyes to it. But here the antithesis is accentuated by war to such an extent that a weak person sometimes can't endure it.

So you intoxicate yourself. You see only the one side in all its splendor and glory. I know I haven't been here long, but I can see what an immense test of endurance a static war is.

Alex is fit again. I'm glad he's over it, but he'll have to take things easy for a while. I just missed getting it myself recently. I had a high temperature and severe pains in the throat, but it was all over in two days. We've both given too much blood, I suppose, so our bodies' natural resistance is low. And in Russia, especially in our area, which is teeming with infections like malaria, typhus, Volhynian fever, dysentery, etc., one needs resistance.

A strong wind has been lashing the forest since dawn and shaking the trees, but it's warm and snug in our dugout. A fire is burning and crackling in the stove, and the gloomy interior is thick with tobacco smoke.

I think of Father a great deal here. And, as one can only in Russia, I often run the entire gamut of my emotions within a few minutes, rising to a shrill pitch of fury and then, just as quickly, subsiding into an expectant, confident, equable frame of mind.

The fall bring so many things with it, among them a desire to burst one's bonds and fly south with migrant birds to a warmer home. Big flocks of jackdaws are gathering in readiness to fly to where the sun stands overhead at noon, and crows accompany them part of the way.

All my love,
Hans

P.S. I gummed up the envelope this way myself.

The following essays and meditations, beginning with the entry of July 30, are extracts from Hans Scholl's Russian diary, recorded in the "little notebook" mentioned in his letter of September 2.

Russian diary, July 30, 1942

The plain began in Russia. Before that we were traveling through a gentle morainic landscape. Songs with a youthfully zestful rhythm were awakened in my soul by rolling hills like a frozen sea and, floating above them in the blue sky, cloud-ships that gleamed white in the afternoon sunlight. I was thinking of airy baroque churches and Mozart when, beyond the frontier, there began the broad, boundless plain where every line melts away, where everything solid dissolves like a drop in the ocean, where there's no beginning or middle or end, where a man becomes homeless and his heart is filled with nothing but melancholy, and his thoughts resemble the ever-changing clouds that float past just as interminably, and his nostalgia resembles the wind that bears them along. All the handholds to which people cling so desperately, like home, native land, or profession, are wrenched off, as it were. The ground gives way beneath your feet, and you fall and go on falling, and just as you're wondering where to, and all your faithful companions are deserting their broken master because they've nothing left to hope for, you unexpectedly and gently land, as though wafted there by angels, on the soil of Russia: on the plain that belongs to God alone and his clouds and winds.

God is closest when home is farthest, hence the young person's desire to go forth, leaving everything behind, and wander aimlessly until he has snapped the last thread that held him captive – until he stands confronting God in the broad plain, naked and alone. He will then rediscover his native soil with eyes transfigured.

July 31, 1942

Gray clouds are hovering over the plain. The horizon looks like a silver ribbon dividing earth and sky. On earth, colors glow undiminished through the thin drizzle in every shade of brown, yellow, and green. When a shaft of light pierces the overcast in the far distance, an expanse of land gleams like a mirror, and the earth laughs like a child with a smile breaking through the tears in its eyes.

How splendidly the flowers are blooming on this railroad embankment! As if all had assembled so that no color should be missing, they bloom here with gentle insistence – everywhere: alongside ruined buildings, gutted freight cars, distraught human faces. Flowers are blooming and children innocently playing among the ruins. O God of love, help me to overcome my doubts. I see the Creation, your handiwork, which is good. But I also see man's handiwork, our handiwork, which is cruel, and called destruction and despair, and which always afflicts the innocent. Spare your children! How much longer must they suffer? Why is suffering so unfairly meted out? When will a tempest finally sweep away all these godless people who besmirch your likeness, who sacrifice the blood of countless innocents to a demon? The whole world is bright again, for as far as the eye can see, after this rain.

August 7, 1942

I'm tired of doing nothing, and the dugout is shuddering and groaning because the Russians are dumping one bomb after another onto the runway. I'm redundant here. I walk alone in the midst of meaningful absurdity. War holds me spellbound only between shot and impact. . . .

The Russians are a remarkable people. It's too noisy, though. I'll write about the Russians later on. About Marushka, Boris, and the farmer who sang songs that evening. And about all the others.

August 9, 1942

Today is Sunday. I'm sitting in the sun, smoking. Dimitri walks past and greets me with a laugh. He laughs every time he sees me.

A week ago today we were in Vyaz'ma. I managed a visit to the Russian church there. The service differed from those familiar to prosaic Central Europeans like us. I entered a spacious hall. The vaulted ceiling was black with soot, the floor made of wood. Warm semidarkness filled the interior, except where candles beneath the altar and the icons showered the sacred pictures with gold. People stood together in haphazard groups, bearded men with kindly faces, wearing the finest of sarafans [actually, caftans], women with their hair done up in colorful kerchiefs, forever bowing low and making the sign of the St. Andrew's cross with splendidly ceremonious gestures. Many bowed their heads to the ground and kissed it. The liquid gold of the candles tinged their faces with red, their eyes shone, and the murmur of voices gradually died away as the priest raised his own voice in song. A choir responded with some magnificent chords. Again the priest sang, and again the choir answered him, reinforced by many additional voices, bell-like tenors and wonderfully mellow basses. The hearts of all believers vibrated in unison. One could sense the stirring, the outpouring of souls unfolding after a long and terrible silence, souls that had at last found their way back to their true home. I could have wept for joy, because my heart, too, was loosing its bonds one by one. I wanted to love and laugh because I could see that hovering above these defeated people was an angel stronger than the powers of nothingness. Spiritual nihilism was a major threat to European civilization, but as soon as it underwent its ultimate development in the total war to which we have finally succumbed, and as soon as it veiled the mighty sky like a sea of gray cloud, it was vanquished. Nothing comes after nothing, yet something must come because all values can never be destroyed among all men. There still exist custodians who will kindle the flame and pass it from hand to hand until a new wave of rebirth inundates the land. The veil of cloud is rent asunder, as it were, by the sunlight of a new religious awakening.

I watched the Russian peasants' strong-featured faces spellbound. Then I caught sight of a shadowy corner where two women were seated on the floor, suckling their children. I was looking at a symbol of the inexhaustible power of love. I left the church and emerged into the harsh light of day. The sky was overcast, a light drizzle was coming down, and the roads had been transformed into bottomless slush. Shellfire rumbled in the distance.

August 12, 1942

Be honest, my friend! Skimming through what I've written, I realize what a pathetically poor description it gives of this country's real appearance. Where am I to get the colors required to paint just one of these flowers? And before me I see a field – no, more than a field: a sea of swaying, whispering grass that stretches away to the horizon and ends who knows where. How much grace there is in just one slender birch tree, and before my eyes there stands a whole clump of those lovely trees. A faint mist is rising from the grass, and a last vestige of daylight is dancing in the treetops.

Today I was lucky first and found a horseshoe after the event. Ludicrous ideas. Shall I make up a fairy tale or describe that encounter in plain language? Eyes forever changing, hard and uncommunicative one moment, exuberantly bright and laughing the next. Long lashes, full lips. A naturally graceful manner unclouded by a single shadow.

But even when looking into those eyes I encountered unfathomable depths, as I do with you. It's getting dark. I can scarcely see a thing, and my thoughts are winging their way over trees and clouds.

What scope there is here for a person's imagination! You need only sit down quietly on the edge of a wood, perhaps on the trunk of a fallen alder or beneath the broad, leafy canopy of a bush, and watch the living shadows on your hands while a magical fragrance comes wafting towards you from the south. There in the south, infinitely far away, white cliffs drop sheer to the sea below and foaming breakers roar while phantom birds plummet out of the clouds and hunt their prey with strident screams. The wings of your boyish imagination carry you farther still, to the most secret part of that azure sea, the birthplace of the wind to which you so often liken your thoughts. The air there is cool and chaste as the soul of a newborn child. Like a blank sheet of paper, the wind is ready to assimilate all it encounters, good and bad, fair and foul, noble and vile. But before it reaches you, it has sped across the steppes like galloping horses, drunk the noonday heat from sandy wastes, and, in the evening, cooled its wings above broad, silent seas. It scales lofty mountains and descends into the valley once more, and from everything it takes a little: a sound, a speck of dust, seeds from flowers, greetings from a passing traveler, a recollection of every fluttering hair. It plucks some doors open and slams others shut, ruffles water, cools farmers' brows. But of factories and coal dust and the stench of gasoline this wind can tell you nothing. It has forgotten all that on its long journey, just as you have forgotten it too. —

The army is the most unimaginative thing in the world, and what makes this war so foul, and distinguishes it from previous ones, is its very unimaginativeness. Never mind, though. Lie down in the grass and look up, and perhaps you'll doze off after all.

August 14, 1942

Now begins the season I love so much. The clouds are thin and transparent, and they scud along high above the trees. The wind never drops completely. It whips up the dust and carries ripe seeds in its arms, and sometimes it shakes the first weary leaves from the branches. Migrant birds are flying south because the nights are getting colder, and mist enshrouds the fields when evening comes.

August 16, 1942

Sunday again already. How time flies! Will I still be using such inane figures of speech eight weeks from now? Or will I employ a simile for the passage of time, or will I refrain from referring to the fourth dimension altogether? Time? History? Day and night, from far away, I can hear the barrage at Yukhnov fluctuating like thunder of varying intensity. It has been pouring incessantly since yesterday. Everything is dripping. The trees are glistening with moisture, and frogs squat sullenly on the edges of puddles, contemplating the water. That's how our modern philosophers, Klages[233] and the rest, view life. The dugout isn't waterproof, but the monotonous patter of raindrops enhances its coziness, like the smoke that blackens the roof. I'm holding a half-smoked cigar in my left hand while the candle's feeble light falls on my notebook from the right. Everything around me could serve as material for metaphors and imagery. But no sooner has an idea surfaced in my imagination, like a horse speeding out of the mist, than it disappears once more into the merciful, all-enveloping grayness which today signifies: do nothing, relax, immerse yourself completely in a pleasant, uniform haze; wait, wait without expectancy for the day when, lightninglike and vivid as sunlight, a new idea erupts (awakens) from the blurry, impenetrable haze, and new life sprouts from the tilth.

How Sundayish I felt this morning, when after tossing and turning awhile, I sloughed off all oppressive, earthbound emotions and looked up! I had the gall to liken myself to Dante, who was privileged to see Beatrice in a new light, exalted above all earthly things. It was over in a flash, but ever since then I've been filled with a kind of childish exaltation. I'm growing giddy and exuberant. What bliss!

I see Dostoyevsky differently than in Central Europe. Almost all men experience the same thing, daily and hourly. The chasm yawns unexpectedly in their heedless path. They trample purity with clumsy feet, and thousands unload their own guilt onto the shoulders of a frail, innocent child. Only one person opens his eyes and sees the world of men, sees that every creature seeks mercy and redemption, but he is Russia's greatest writer.

I'm ruining my eyesight in this gloom, but I understand Dostoyevsky here.

August 17, 1942

Sheer exuberance prompted me to get drunk on schnapps last night. I don't drink because I'm melancholy, or, as many would assert with a mournful air, to banish dismal thoughts – I hold melancholy far too sacred to avoid it. I drink with cheerful abandon, as an aid to singing and telling jokes. With rash presumption, I drew an analogy between wine and man. Man is composed of spirit and matter, and the former takes precedence. Isn't it the same with wine? What would its delicious material content be without spirit? There are unspiritual people and spiritless drunkards. Where there's wine, there's culture, and only the Americans have managed to breed a vine that doesn't require extremes of care and cultivation, of *cultura*. It thrives like a weed in any poor soil. I claimed that culture flourishes where there's wine, and in spite of anything more debatable I may have said, I'd like to maintain that proposition and hold it up for all to see.

If I were all alone, I could amuse myself for hours, collecting my curios in the gloom. The air may be damp and the bread's perpetually soft and gooey, but the soul remains dry.

On Melancholy

It's funny that I should write that first and follow it up with something else. What I mean is, I'm going to postpone "On Melancholy" for a while and begin by recounting a minor incident which, though trivial, is typical in its insignificance. We have a senior medical officer here. He's like a child. I took to him the very first day and so did the others. It wasn't until a few days later that I detected latent traits in his face that made me feel vaguely uneasy. I could be wrong – perhaps it's quite irrelevant. All that's relevant is that this pet of ours invited us – out here in the wilds of Russia, with the guns thundering nearby, at a stage when I was becoming increasingly acquainted with Dostoyevsky's infinite depth of perception, and when my initially merciless impressions had gradually sublimated themselves and put me in a strange but agreeably suspenseful frame of mind – that he issued an invitation, quite a casual and semi-informal invitation, less official than personal, men, if you know what I mean – that he invited us, rather like a priest inviting one for a chat about other topics (and that I could well have understood, here in this land of extremes, because I some-times feel badly in need of a priest, though I'm mistrustful of most theologians, who might disappoint me if I found I knew all they said before it left their lips; ah yes, if only Father

Schwarz[234] were here, or Muth, or Haecker, or preferably dear old Furtmayer,[235] or better still, I'd like a chat with an intelligent girl of fifteen and a half) – that he invited us, as I've already said, to a lecture – quite man-to-man, mark you – on infant nutrition. Well, I won't forget Pfaundler's Formula[236] in a hurry, nor the youngster who interrupted the lecture with a "Permission to address the Chief Medical Officer?" So I gleaned a few more professional tips, effortlessly and free of charge, as it were, but wouldn't it have been infinitely better if I spent a few hours watching the clouds go by?

On Melancholy

It isn't melancholy that drives a man to suicide. By the time he's ready to surrender by engaging in a last, monstrous act of self-destruction, melancholy has entirely deserted him, because melancholy was insufficient to restrain him. The melancholy man ceases to act altogether. He's chained to the immense and unfathomable depths of his own soul by a hundred anchors, so to speak, and every tempest rages over him unnoticed. Melancholy is both things at once, the spiritual abyss and the anchors that keep him there – indeed, it could be said that the man himself is both, one being inseparable from the other. The more unfathomable the abyss, the more his melancholy weighs. And here we meet a paradox that instills fear and brings the average person out in a sweat: The man whose soul grows steadily calmer as the storm rises, until it finally attains an outward state of deathly repose, is truly melancholy, truly great and profound. His average, superficial counterpart merely drifts, tosses hither and thither, and his soul bobs on the surface like a rowboat on the waves.

But not every great man is capable of waiting so steadfastly, trusting in the immense force that holds him in place. Unwilling to return to the shallows, he aspires to penetrate his own depths

and go farther. Violently, with an effort that passes all understanding, he smashes his soul and acts once more. When that
happens, destruction and deliverance are near neighbors.

Russia alters its appearance just when you least expect it. It's
as peevish as a child and as capricious as an old maid.

In quest of a comparison, you find, after three gray, rainy,
miserable days in the dim half-light of the dugout, that Russia
most resembles an old man forever gazing wearily at the same
corner of his death chamber with nothing in prospect but
death, waiting calmly and patiently for the end that must surely
come. And then, contrary to all expectations, the wall of cloud
overhead parts and the dawn light peeps forth, fresh as a baby,
and within a few hours the sky is blue all over. A gentle breeze
stirs the birch trees. Like pearls, a thousand droplets glisten on
the leaves once more and are promptly, heedlessly flung to the
ground.

August 18, 1942

Lunchtime. I'm smoking my usual cigar, but Willi [Graf] is the
only person who appreciates its aroma. The others prefer to
stick to cigarettes. Two or three puffs, and they're tossed away. I
take things more leisurely.

Mother wrote me yesterday that Father has been detained
on account of his well-known assertion that Hitler is a divine
scourge upon Europe. Now he's going to have to spend four
months in prison. Mother enclosed a draft petition for clemency. She wants Werner and me to send a petition too, in the
expectation that one written at the front will carry more weight
than hers. I won't do it under any circumstances. I won't plead
for mercy. I know the difference between false pride and true.

I plan to discuss it with Werner today.

My nights are filled with confused dreams. I wanted to get
away from the others for a better look at some mountains.

Hans Scholl | 253

Without saying good-bye, I left a sizable party of companions and made my way through narrow streets to the outskirts of town. There I lingered for a while, studying the view. Before me lay a deeply incised valley. I could make out the winding silver ribbon of a river. Everything else was green: grassy meadows and leafy woods. It was afternoon, and the treetops glittered in the sunlight. The shadows striking the ground were jet-black, but every color was absorbed, so to speak, by the dazzling light. The landscape was an incredible color, like velvet brushed the wrong way. I'd been dreamily surveying it for a long time when I noticed an exceptionally high iron bridge spanning the valley. I made for it without hesitation. Although my head swam a little when I stole an apprehensive glance at the chasm beneath, I briskly strode on. All at once it dawned on me: I had to cross this bridge or die in the attempt. Then the ironwork beneath my feet began to slope, more and more steeply, until it was vertically suspended over the chasm. Calmly, holding on tight, I descended step by step. I was an expert climber, so the procedure presented no difficulty whatsoever.

The only difficulty I could see was how to escape some men who were waiting to arrest me as soon as I reached the foot of this fantastic ladder. I debated what to do. There was nothing for it, I told myself, and when I reached the ground I voluntarily gave myself up. —And so on.

August 22, 1942, Sunday

That's all.

We Germans don't have Dostoyevsky or Gogol. Nor Pushkin nor Turgenev. What about Goethe and Schiller? someone retorts. Who does? A scholar. When did you last read any Goethe? I don't recall – in school or somewhere. I ask a Russian: What writers do you have? Oh, says the Russian, we have them all, all of them. There aren't any under the sun apart from them. What Russian is this? A peasant, a washerwoman, a mailman.

But I see you wrinkle your nose, my worthy academic: not a word against Goethe or Schiller. You aren't acquainted with Hölderlin or Stifter, I suppose? Well, why should you be? People can live without them. People can live without everything save vitamins and calories, entertainment and lechery. Have you any idea who founded your place of learning, you fat lump, you clothes horse and rice bag, as the Japanese would say? Oh, yes, you stand up for Western civilization, my dear fellow, even though you yourself equate civilization with your nail file and w.c. And, perhaps, with your marginal superiority over others and your stamp collection. What of Goethe and Schiller, those two fixed stars in the German firmament, whom you also defend against the storm from Asia? Having already made a whore out of Goethe (all can use him as they please), are you planning to do the same to Schiller? Never fear, you doughty Swabian, they can't harm a hair of your head, even if they utter your name in the same breath as the most vulgar and offensive word imaginable, which I can't use here. If we've read Dosto-yevsky, we're entitled to criticize Goethe, but first we must defend him. We must protect him by protecting ourselves. If there's a knife sticking in our body, let's not pull it out, or we'll bleed to death completely.

The bee would survive even if poets of every age hadn't sung its praises. If poets were no more, the world wouldn't perish, and the wind would continue to sing its song. But what is the bee, and what the wind, unless heard and listened to by man? Unless the eye of man looks up at the treetops, unless his spirit soars to the clouds, unless his love attains the sun. The spirit is endangered, not the poets' names. And if the spirit is endan-gered, so, to no avail, is human existence. It isn't enough for a person to ply his trade any old how. Merely doing one's duty is absurd and misleading. Man is born to think, says Pascal. To think, my worthy academic: I reproach you with that word. You're surprised, eh, you representative of the spirit? The spirit you serve at this desperate hour is an evil spirit, but you're blind to despair. You're rich, but you're blind to poverty. Your soul is withering because you refused to hear its call. You ponder on the ultimate refinement of a machine gun, but you suppressed the most elementary question in your youth. The question why and whither?

How small must a nation be that calls Frederick II "the Great"? That nation fought for its freedom against Napoleon, only to choose Prussian slavery. I know how limited human freedom is, but man is essentially free, and it is his freedom that renders him human. Freedom and poverty are human, enslavement and arrogance Prussian.

Did Goethe ever suffer extreme hardship? Did he sample destitution even once? That question, which intrudes discreetly at first, gains strength like a storm until it finally becomes all-embracing. When did he ever eat his bread with tears, and why? Wasn't he careful to avoid every sickness, everything ugly and evil under the sun, and didn't he himself fear death like the plague? Oh, yes, he sampled hardship, but only sampled it. Snugly ensconced in his silk and velvet coat, he strode through the depths of human misery like a horned Siegfried. Never once did he bow his proud head, never once did he lie naked and bleeding on the ground at night, and never once did hunger torment him to the point of despair. He knew neither the melancholy of a whore excluded from human society nor the sorrow of a homeless child. His mind was always focused on the stars. He was clear of voice and bright of eye. But who is more defenseless than man, a creature born to roam the world without respite, universally rejected by the strong as having been born in sin? Goethe brushed the fringes of hardship, nothing more.

Dostoyevsky didn't descend into hell – he was dragged down because he had eyes to see. His ear heard the lament that arose from his soul and joined in the terrible, discordant chorus of the defeated and forlorn. He didn't tear off the masks because he didn't notice them. He looked into the darkness and saw because his eyes weren't dazzled by a false sun. He found his way from sin to Christ because one repentant sinner is worth more to God than a hundred thousand of the righteous.

When I write a sentence down, I free myself from it. Even when I want to free myself from a sin I must write it down, as I do now. It's childish of me to do Goethe an injustice. It's simply a fear of great minds that impels me to attack them. I find Goethe alien because he confronts me with such unapproachable grandeur, almost like a false god. I'd like to pierce his side with my spear, wound him, and see him bleed – then I could take compassion on him and love him. I wouldn't for one moment dare to question the beauty of his characters and imagery. No one could write more beautifully than Goethe. He was, perhaps, the only man to have embraced the whole of creation in his unclouded gaze. Stirred to the very depths of his soul, he hymned the beauty of the cosmos.

But he never sang of chaos. He never divested himself of his sumptuous attire, never mingled with the poor and sick. He couldn't, because he would have had to descend from his throne, and his lucid mind told him that merely descending isn't enough. One has to be drawn down as though by a magnet, so that one casts off every tie at a stroke and becomes poor oneself and forgets all that went before. In that context I see Francis of Assisi and Beethoven and Rembrandt: beggars and sinners whom Christ redeemed.

My father's in prison. I'm sure he's thinking of me at this
moment. I'm sitting on a wooden crate. A candle is burning
fitfully. Strange shapes are flowing down it, waxen forma-
tions that are either haphazard or, for all I know, fashioned by
fate. The candle will get smaller and smaller and eventually
go out. What is death? Why are people so afraid of it? Why do
your fingers tremble when you touch the dead? Ah, and your
thoughts turn with a faint trace of pleasure to your mother's
tears, or a beloved's anguished heart that yearns to stop beating,
and a thought sneaks into your mind, just a thought with which
you casually toy – strictly in secret, of course – to the effect that
you're still alive, that your heart is still beating, and that death
really matters as little to you as your neighbor's corns. My father
in prison. Detonations outside. Bombs. How long is it since I
left prison! I was still quite young in those days.[237] Wrote a girl's
name in breadcrumbs on the table in my cramped, vaulted cell.
The red notice hanging on the door said "Juvenile."

She got engaged to someone else because I treacherously
abandoned her. She wanted to die at first, but she did the right
thing. A person has to go on living, come what may. Yes, and
shun death at all costs, even when the fall arrives and the whole
of Nature, in an extremity of grief, externalizes melancholy and
transforms it into beauty – yes, beauty. You, too, were once as
beautiful.

If there's one thing I'd still like to do, should I ever be able
to breathe freely again, it would simply be to head for Asia
as a beggar and roam from village to village across desolate
plains and through mysterious forests. To sleep beneath over-
hanging fir trees or in ditches and roam farther, ever farther
afield. May God never grant me an earthly destination, so that
I never come to rest till the end of my days. Will I have to leave
you too, beloved, because you don't understand; because I don't

Hans as a medical corps sergeant, Russia, 1942

even dare to sow such seeds in your heart; because you're still a delightful child, a cornflower, a wisp of a girl and a kiss? I mean to forsake all the gardens of delusion and coat my feet with dust, renounce the writers and talkers and seek wisdom among the stars. Perhaps I'll go to prison a second time, perhaps a third and a fourth. There are things far worse than prison. It may even be among the best.

Father may undergo a religious awakening there. I found the love that death inevitably follows because love flows gratis and cannot be repaid.

Ten die here daily. That's not many, and nobody makes a fuss about it. How many flowers are heedlessly trampled? Isn't Christ crucified a hundred times every hour? Even so, don't children continue to spring up irresistibly, like young birch trees, tender and bright-eyed?

Recently Alex and I buried a Russian. He must have been lying there a long time. The head had come away from the trunk and the soft parts were already decomposed. Worms were

Hans and an unknown comrade beside the grave of an unknown soldier

crawling out of the rotting clothes. We'd almost finished filling in the grave when we found another arm. We ended by nailing a Russian cross together and sticking it in the ground at the head. Now his soul is at rest.

Art's function is to make the world a more cheerful place, Hubert said today. But, oh, I'm tired. At present I've lost sight of that kind of art.

Where is it now? Not in Dostoyevsky. Not here. Not in the dugout and not outside in the moonlight. I don't have any music with me. All I hear day and night are the groans of men in pain and, when dreaming, the sighs of the forlorn, and when I think, my thoughts perish in agony.

If Christ hadn't lived and died, there really would be no escape. To weep at all would be utterly futile. I should have to run full tilt at the nearest wall and smash my skull in. But not as things are.

September 5, 1942

A bizarre idea has kept me brooding incessantly for several days now. I'd like to create a utopia, but not like those we so often give vent to when we let our hair down: what the postwar world would be like if, etc. No, that would be too easy. One would only have to exaggerate all our present circumstances to a grotesque extent, but the idea [of nonfulfillment] would be lurking there all the time, and everyone would sense that things could never turn out that way because the whole utopia was linked to a single condition that could never be fulfilled. No, what haunts me is the strange notion that a time may come when the war is entirely forgotten, because a kindly providence has effaced its memory from every book. A truly golden age will dawn such as no one could now conceive of in his wildest dreams: peace on earth and universal contentment in every country under the sun. And then, while playing one day, a child unearths a frag-ment of some object from the sand and shows it to his bosom pal, and the two of them go on looking until they've assem-bled all the pieces. They eventually discover that it's a weapon, scuffle over it, one of them kills the other with the newfound weapon, etc., etc.

War has finally returned. The whole world goes up in flames. This war is a feeble version of the present one – everything is carried to extremes, notably human stupidity and cowardice on the one hand, *hubris* and *superbia* on the other.

I was hard hit by the news of Ernst's death.[238] Not that death as such would have surprised me – it will never surprise me again – but I sense the wound in my sister's side [Inge's] and cannot heal it. I see the void and cannot fill it, nor do I wish to. I know that it shouldn't be filled. It must remain empty until, through grief, he is with her again in spirit, transfigured.

September 11, 1942

I wrote Lisa a letter in a dreamlike state. Today I'm writing another. Why? I don't know myself. I see her every night, but enough of that. —The Germans are incorrigible. Their duplicity is so deep-seated by now that it couldn't be excised without killing the entire body. A doomed nation.

My pessimism gets worse every day. Skepticism is poisoning my soul. I want to save it by running away, but where to? In desperation, I erect a wall around me. It consists of sarcasm and satire.

To his parents, Russia, October 3, 1942

Dear Parents,

Your kind birthday present reached me the very day before I was transferred. Needless to say, it took eight candy-starved men only a few minutes to devour the contents. I'd made some good friends in the dugout, but farewells are so commonplace here, even farewells to life, that I packed my belongings without saying much and set off. First a car took me part of the way. Next I had to plod along an interminable corduroy road until a cyclist took pity on me and put my things on his carrier. Last of all I was overtaken by a rider with a spare horse, and that encounter was like a gift from the gods. I swung myself into the saddle and trotted to my destination past a burning village. Here as elsewhere the dugouts are concealed among the trees, and few of their occupants have any conception of the beauty of the country they're living in. But luck hasn't entirely deserted me, even here. Today I was detailed to tour the positions on horseback and inoculate the men against cholera. I have only to mount a horse and all my constraints disappear. The landscape stretches away before me, open and unconfined, and off I gallop.

My regimental MO and the officers here are ultramilitary, because they're serving in a regular regiment, and they're all terribly dull. They're friendly, though, not that I take much advantage of it.

I managed to say a quick good-bye to Werner, but I hope to see him again soon. At all events, I shall be returning to Gzhatsk before my final departure.

I marvel anew every day at the beauty of Russia. I think I'll often be overcome with great nostalgia for this place when I'm back in Germany. The birch trees are gilded all over now, with a blue sky above. The jackdaws flew south in such numbers that they blotted out the sun.

You've no cause to worry about me.

All my fondest love,
Hans

To Otl Aicher, Russia, October 9, 1942

Dear Otl,

Since I'm now enjoying some quieter days than in weeks gone by, and since I've long been meaning to thank you for your two letters, one nice and the other no less so, and since my mind is pervaded this particular evening by a genuinely late-summer mood, I've picked up my pen and am writing you a letter in the hope that it will reach you quickly. I don't need to tell you what

I always wish you. Those two letters of yours brought you very close. I could clearly discern both sides of your youthful soul. I saw yet again how alike we can be in our effusions.

On the other hand, I saw how different in direction our ideas are. My present state of mind is such that I'm increasingly abandoning the abstract for the sensuous, the pictorial and corporeal. Perhaps I'm doing so because of some internal crisis, and perhaps I'll change direction again someday. There are many times when I feel quite clearly that I've left my salad days behind, and that, being a man, I quite often rediscover the boy in me. Discounting all political ideas (to which I'm not averse on principle, but more attached than ever – more of that later), I'm grateful to God that I had to go to Russia. I've experienced a change of scene that has cut me off from all the flower gardens of the past and set me down in the great plain, where I've found a solitude for which I've been thirsting for years. You won't misunderstand me, I know. There's surely nothing greater than this solitude. It doesn't in any way conflict with the commandment to love one's neighbor. It's only here that I've finally learned to stop taking myself so infinitely seriously, to turn my aimless contemplation inside out and direct my mind outward, at material things. The old affliction often sneaks back into my soul, of course, and I long to return to my lost dream-love, which once meant everything to me. Believe me, though, my best plan would be to cut loose right now and tramp east, alone and devoid of material possessions, on and on across the Urals and Siberia to China – if only, yes, if only I wasn't a European and unable to desert Europe at this eleventh hour. That's my sole reason for wanting to return to Germany: that the West and I shouldn't lose touch.

I hope you'll gather what I meant to say but couldn't.

Best regards,
Hans

P.S. I'll be back in Munich four weeks from now, so please write to Ulm.

Hans wrote the following letter after receiving the news that his father, in prison since August, had been granted two months' remission and was to be released from prison October 25.[239]

To his family, Russia, October 13, 1942

Dear Ones,

Today I finally got your news.

My thoughts are with you every hour. But what shall I write? I'll be setting out for home in two weeks' time. Nothing could be more important than to rejoin you right away, I realize that. The Russians are 80 meters from our trench, but life here is more peaceful than ever. As long as one doesn't mind the din.

I paid Werner a visit the day before yesterday, and we spent a few enjoyable hours together. One of the reasons why I'm writing so little is that I don't have any paper or envelopes or anything. My departure from Munich was far too hurried, but we'll be seeing each other in a few days' time, and then everything will be fine. I'm able to report that Werner is currently in good hands. The Russians have stopped shelling Gzhatsk. Alex is fit again. I myself am reading Stifter's *Nachsommer*[240] and a history of the church in my spare time. I find the chapter on the persecution of the Christians especially interesting. The fall will soon be subsiding into winter. I look for the first snow daily. More tomorrow.

Much love,

Hans

Ernst Reden, whose death Hans mentions in his diary entry of September 5, was a close friend of Inge's.

To his sister Inge, Russia, October 15, 1942

My dear Inge,

I've meant to write to you every day since I left you all, but I've never been more conscious of my inadequacy and poverty of expression than during these twilight weeks. I can tell you this much: every letter I've had to write was pain and agony. The result is, I've neglected the people whom I know to be aware how erratic I am in these matters – not that I haven't waited impatiently for letters from these very people. However, I now feel an inner compulsion to say what really goes without saying but must be said for all that.

I'm with you in spirit every hour of the day. When I wake in the mornings, and also in the evenings, when I review my innermost thoughts, my love speeds on its way to you. I know how little I am compared to what you've lost, but the little I am wants to be as much use to you as it can. "The fall is here, and I'm sad and weary. I'm not eager for the spring because I must die first, and because falling leaves mean more to me than vigorously bursting buds. . . ." So says Nature through the medium of every flower, of every blade of grass turning yellow at the tip, and of the evening mists that gather above the fields and enshroud us.

Why should we resist the fall? Fall days are days of great sorrow from which love doesn't disappear, even though joy fades. "For it's love that makes me sad," says the forest whose trees are almost bare.

I'll take you to Russia with me after the war. You're bound to love the country as much as I do.

By the time this letter reaches you, it won't be long before I'm with you again. All my love, and see you soon!

Yours,

Hans

As October drew to a close, so did Hans's time in Russia.

To his parents, Russia, October 18, 1942

Dear Parents,

Don't write to me here after you get this letter. I gather we'll be leaving before the week is out. I don't yet know what they'll do with us in the interval before lectures start – nothing, I hope. Then I would be able to spend four weeks at home or go off to the mountains with Inge. It's very lovely there, too, in the late fall.

I received a parcel from Inge and another from Lisl. Both were much appreciated.

I'm not certain if I'll be able to see Werner again before I go, but I very much hope so.

There's virtually nothing for me to do here, but spare time isn't much use up front because we can't go for walks – and what else would one do? You gradually turn into a mole, stuck in a dugout day after day and night after night. It's too crowded to do much reading.

Only a few more days till we see each other again!

> All my love,
> Hans

P.S. I've saved all my APO parcel stamps so I can send Werner something at Christmas.

On October 30, 1942, the Munich medical students met up at the forward assembly center in Vyaz'ma. Willi Graf noted in his diary: "Now we're back together again: Hans, Alex, Hubert, and Hans G. We strolled through the town, swapped accounts of the last few weeks, and sat down in the sun somewhere. . . . Alex is thoroughly exhausted by our departure. October 31: Our last night in Vyaz'ma, and thus the end of our months here. I'm leaving Russia with a heavy heart."

Sophie Scholl
Autumn 1942

To Lisa Remppis, Ulm, September 2, 1942

Dear Lisa,

I've just finished my contribution to Father's letter. We're allowed to write him every two weeks. He has already written us a lovely long letter (he can only write once a month). I'm not really worried about him, even though it often grieves me to know he's there, but that it's for his own good. "For his own good" – how happy that knowledge makes you when you really think about the phrase. It's the best thing that could have happened to him. —That's why I haven't forgotten a word they said, the people who brought him to his present pass. This, like so much else, must be remembered, not from motives of hatred or revenge, but for their own sake.

I'm finding my factory work awful. It affects one not only physically but above all mentally, this deadly, soulless work, this purely mechanical activity, this minute contribution to a task whose entirety is beyond our ken and whose purpose appalls me. The state of one's nerves isn't improved by the incessant din of machinery, the dreadful wail of the knocking-off siren, and the degrading spectacle of people tending machines as if they're completely in their power. Farmers, craftsmen, even road sweepers – how much finer their work is in comparison! The most stimulating part is cleaning the machines on Saturdays. Then you have a definite object and a complete job to do, which is to polish your machine till it's nice and shiny. You get the same sort of pleasure from that as a housewife does from her spotless kitchen.

Working alongside me is a delightful Russian woman. I'm trying to make use of the little I've learned, and I've even picked up a few additional words, e.g., *cepzibs,* meaning earrings. The Russian women take a childish delight in jewelry, and nearly all of them wear cheap earrings in their earlobes. They're far more childlike in general than the German women workers, among other things in their attitude to Germans, which is utterly guileless and devoid of mistrust. It's a charming, touching trait. If somebody swears at them, no matter how fiercely, they don't understand a word and burst out laughing. What a pity it would be if they, too, became infected with the suspicion and commercialism of "superior" Europeans like us. Schurik had the same typical characteristics, the same faith in others coupled with an infinite readiness to help them.

I'm already looking forward to my time with you. I'll at last be able to sketch and paint in perfect peace, with you as my loveliest of models. Before that, though, I'm planning a trip to the Bohemian Forest with Lisl.

Best regards to everyone including Gust (I'm so glad he liked your picture), and extra special love to you,

Sophie

P.S. (If I were at Leonberg now, we'd go stealing plums.) I've acquired a huge great roll of drawing paper – from an unknown soldier!

To Otl Aicher, Ulm, September 5, 1942

Dear Otl,

Thank you for the two letters I've received from you here. The other little Reclam books[241] I found for you in Munich may have reached you by now. I'm afraid they won't yield much more than the Goethe-Zelter correspondence. The best sources of material are some of the poems and *Faust*.

Much as I'd like to say something that would demonstrate the falsity of your existing conception of Goethe (and I know you're only looking for some way of refuting it yourself), I can't. The same goes for his conversations with Eckermann. I couldn't resist the feeling that overcame you on reading the said correspondence: that one's confronted by a pair of jumping jacks. They're sometimes reminiscent of passengers on a sinking ship who do their hair, powder their noses, and dress with the utmost care instead of making a dash for the lifeboats. I occasionally feel when reading a poem: now he's bound to open his eyes to his own circumstances, because he's very receptive to impressions of all kinds, especially those derived from Nature – in fact I think he possesses a very special capacity for sorrow and joy and a very special need to love and be loved. —Isn't it their conceit that makes the two of them so ridiculous in their letters: their self-esteem, which suggests that they themselves aren't products of creation like everyone else? I read a passage from St. Augustine yesterday: "The poor are the humble of heart. The more they lack the things of this world, the more they indulge themselves, but the less this satisfaction with the world, the greater their hunger [for the next]." —Even if Goethe hankered after such food, he would have to refuse it, because he's full up! The only thing is, how does this fit in with the end of *Faust*?

As for the letter on music[242] which I meant to produce for *Windlicht*, I haven't managed it yet, because fresh perspectives keep opening up. I heard Bach's Brandenburg Concertos this summer, and they just don't tally with what I wrote you in my letter: that music enriches the soul. —The music I heard then isn't enriching like that of Beethoven, for instance, who stirs and plows you up and leaves you feeling like a furrowed field. No, that music doesn't resemble a plow – it's more like seed corn, because you sense that it contains an element of crystal-line clarity, of indestructible order. Even playing a piece of Bach on the piano strikes me as more demanding than playing one by Beethoven: that you can play when you're in a gloomy, less cheerful mood, but if you try to play Bach in that state, it doesn't come off, because every passage is absolutely transparent and lucid and can't be glossed over, and you have to take hold of yourself like mad if it's going to come off after all. But the compensation afterward is that you get up feeling exhilarated. —I don't want to say too much at this stage, though. I'm still not through with the subject, and I might regret having broad-cast my present view too widely because it's still open to dispute from many angles.

I took little Dieter over to your parents' yesterday lunchtime and helped to strip the pear tree, but my head for heights isn't as good as it was that time at Suppingen,[243] when you unsuccess-fully bombarded me with stones from below.

To her father, Ulm, September 7, 1942

Dear Father,

We were all delighted to get your letter, though I was never afraid your spirit would be broken by your so-called punish-ment. I'm convinced that you need this interlude – even, in some way we still don't grasp, that it's the best possible thing for you, though I haven't forgotten a word that was uttered by those who engineered it. Not from any motives of revenge, but from quite another aspect of which you're doubtless aware. —Well, now you're no longer here to keep us up to date, I conscientiously listen to the news and often study the map of Europe. You've received the *Frankfurter Zeitung,* so you know the main points. —I've survived almost half of my "factory service." The work doesn't appeal to me in the least, and I'm appalled that so many people should have their entire lives taken up by this dull, soulless activity for ten hours a day, and that they not unnaturally lack the energy to apply themselves to other things at nights. Most of them feel unhappy, too, but it's a wartime business, and things will change afterward. Let's hope so, anyway. I've been far more deeply affected by the fate of all these people than if I'd only formed an opinion from outside.

The news from the front is invariably good. Many of the friends I wrote to about you send their regards. They're all at work on the wall of thoughts[244] surrounding you. You can sense you're not alone, I'm sure, because our thoughts can breach any gate or wall: thoughts – !

Yours,

Sophie

To her father, Ulm, September 22, 1942

Dear Father,

I completed my factory work last Saturday, which means that another month is up for you too – half your involuntary vacation, let's hope. As soon as Lisl comes home, we plan to go to Munich together to reorganize my room and, if need be, give Professor Muth a bit of a helping hand. After that we'll spend a few days in the mountains[245] at a lonely farmhouse, where we'll be out of sight of man and his works for a while and find compensation in the natural order for all the terrible things that are happening. The sight of the mountains' quiet majesty and beauty makes the reasons people advance for their disastrous doings seem ludicrous and insane, and one gets the impression that they've lost control over themselves and their actions and are impelled by some evil power. I got the same impression when I surveyed the big factory floor and saw a hundred-odd people standing over their machines as if they were unwittingly yet sadly obeying a power which they themselves had created, only to promote it into their own tyrannical master. Machines are acquiring a demonic quality here, and all that's needed to restore them to their proper place is a change of mental attitude on the part of mankind. —But the sight of an evening sky above the mountains and the gentle sound of bells inspire another vision of humanity in me. I look forward to breathing that air again, and I'd like it even more, and would gladly sacrifice my vacation, if you could do the same. But you still have that ahead of you in spite of everything.

All my fondest love,
Sophie

To Otl Aicher, Munich-Solln, October 9, 1942

Dear Otl,

I'm just reading *Schöpfer und Schöpfung.*[246] Do you know it? "A theodicy which fails to perceive that all tragedy is resolved not only in heaven and eternal salvation, but in hell and eternal damnation, has justified nothingness, not God." Those words revived a long unanswered question in me.

I fully agree with the proposition. The only thing is, why should all tragedy be resolved in hell? How can I be happy, knowing that fellow creatures of mine are unhappy?

I always found it equally incomprehensible (though I sought the error in my own inadequacy, nowhere else) that Lazarus in Abraham's bosom[247] should have refused the rich man thirsting in hell even one little drop of water.

I find that incomprehensible, and perhaps you can render it comprehensible to me.

Perhaps Lazarus failed to hear the rich man's plea?

I recall a passage in *Diary of a Country Priest:*[248] "Eternal damnation is the inability to love anymore."

Perhaps it's also the fact of not being loved anymore?

I find this question terrible and insoluble. Perhaps the answer to it can only be taken on trust, for hell is as much a mystery as heaven.

I see this letter is one big "perhaps." Can you help me to eliminate it?

Even if it has to persist, however, it doesn't imply any doubt in my mind or on my part. Why should I doubt a truth simply because it's still hidden from me?

Affectionate regards,
Sophie

Diary, October 10, 1942

Whenever I pray, the words drain out of me. The only ones I can remember are "Help me!" I can't offer up any other prayer for the simple reason that I'm still far too abject to be able to pray. So I pray to learn how to pray.

This morning I was at the Schmorells', looking for some books in Schurik's room. How often one wishes oneself into a state of self-deception! Months ago I still believed my affection for Schurik was greater than for many others, but how false this illusion was from the start. It was simply my vanity that wanted to possess a person who was worth something in the estimation of others. Oh, how I disgust myself! How ludicrously I distort my own image, and – no, I long for the chance to prove myself in a different way.

How beautiful the sky was today, how wonderful and beautiful the innocent trees and plants, yet the sight of them didn't make me happy; it filled me with gentle melancholy. [They were] an innocent reminder of guilt – my own guilt.

Dear Lisa,

This time last year we used to sit around the sandpit in the last of the warm, late fall sunshine. (By "we" I mean myself and the children I was then looking after.) It's pleasant to recall those days,[249] which were almost like vacation days. I would play with my handful of children without any preconceived plan. Far from feeling like an "auntie," I felt like one of their number who, by virtue of her seniority in age, was responsible for warning them of the unexpected approach of cars on our lovely walks to the herd of sheep or through the colorful, autumnal woods – not that that often happened on those tiny side roads. And then . . . My mouth waters when I recall the meals I was served at the Gasthaus zum Grünen Kranz, on a white tablecloth shared with the man who was guarding the Yugoslavs there. The landlord and his wife were so friendly to me, and almost friendlier to Fritz, who paid me a visit there once, and whom they warmly commended to me afterward. It was almost as if I'd been privileged to play a carefree role in a pleasant, heartwarming, sunny little episode. Or so it seems now, at least. The reality was somewhat different, no doubt, but I felt at home there.

Now I'm delighting once more in the last rays of the sun and marveling at the incredible beauty of all that wasn't created by man: the red dahlias beside the white garden gate, the tall, solemn fir trees, the tremulous, gold-draped birches whose gleaming trunks stand out against all the green and russet foliage, and the golden sunshine that intensifies the colors of each individual object, unlike the blazing summer sun, which overpowers anything else that tries to stir. It's all so wonderfully beautiful here that I've no idea what kind of emotion my speechless heart should develop for it, because it's too immature to take pure pleasure in it. It merely marvels and contents itself with wonder and enchantment. —Isn't it mysterious – and frightening, too, when one doesn't know the reason – that every-thing should be so beautiful in spite of the terrible things that are happening? My sheer delight in all things beautiful has been invaded by a great unknown, an inkling of the creator whom his creatures glorify with their beauty. —That's why man alone can be ugly, because he has the free will to disassociate himself from this song of praise. Nowadays one is often tempted to believe that he'll drown the song with gunfire and curses and blasphemy. But it dawned on me last spring that he can't, and I'll try to take the winning side.

I'll be busy at Muth's for another few days.[250] My fondest love to you, and let me hear from you again.

> Yours,
> Sophie

To Fritz Hartnagel, Ulm, October 28, 1942

My dear Fritz,

I received a letter from you today, and I thank you for it with all my heart. I wish I could back you up with what I know and am in the arguments you're so often compelled to have with your brother officers. The fact that their whole inner being doesn't rebel at that law of nature, the conquest of the weak by the strong, strikes me as dreadful and degenerate, or utterly and completely insensitive. Even a child is filled with horror when forced to witness the defeat and destruction of a weak animal by a strong one. I was always deeply moved and saddened by that inescapable fact, not only as a child but later on as well, and I racked my brains for some way of remaining aloof from this universal state of affairs. The sight of an innocent little mouse in a trap always brought tears to my eyes, and I can only attribute my regained and continuing happiness to forgetful-ness, which is no solution. Nor *can* there be any solution here on earth. It says in Romans:[251] "For the earnest expectation of the creature waiteth for the manifestation of the sons of God. For the creature was made subject to vanity, *not* willingly, but by reason of him who hath subjected the same in hope." Fritz, you simply must read that chapter yourself, either when you've finished this letter or right away. And read the wonderful words at the beginning:[252] "For the law of the Spirit of life in Christ Jesus hath made me free from the law of sin and death." Aren't they terribly, terribly poor, the people who neither know nor believe that? Their poverty ought to make us eternally patient with them (that, and the knowledge of our own weakness, for what would we amount to by ourselves?), even if their stupid arrogance tends to infuriate us. If they believe that might must prevail, ask them if they think that man and beast should be placed entirely on a par, or that man additionally shares in a world of the spirit. Ask them – they're bound, in their arrogance, to endorse the latter. And then ask them if it isn't ignominious for the flesh and brute force to triumph in the world of the spirit, if other laws don't prevail in that world than in the world of the flesh, if an ailing inventor or – to get away from the dubious realm of technology – an ailing poet or philosopher doesn't count for more and command more strength in the world of the spirit than a brainless athlete – a Hölderlin more than a Schmeling[253] (may Hölderlin pardon the juxtaposition, which pains me too). Yes, we do believe in the victory of the stronger, but the stronger in spirit. And the fact that this victory may perhaps come to pass in a world other than our own limited one (beautiful though it is, it's nonetheless small) – no, it already does so here, but only as a radiant prospect visible to all – makes it no less worthy of attainment.

When they say that Nature is good because it was created by God, they forget that man, and the whole of Nature with him, fell after the creation, which God had described as "very good."

How meekly they submit to God's judgement all of a sudden! I've never, ever believed that anyone thinks it is good for a weak country to be attacked by a powerful army. Even the worst of men, however pleased he may be in other respects, won't regard that as a good thing. The supremacy of brute force always implies that the spirit has been destroyed or at least banished from view. Is that what they want, the people who argue with you? Oh, those lazy thinkers with their sloppy notions of life and death! Only life engenders life, or have they seen a dead woman give birth to a child? Or what about a stone, which can't be denied a semblance of life, since it exists and has a fate of its own – have they ever seen one reproduce itself? They've never reflected on the absurdity of the proposition that only death engenders life, and their urge for self-preservation will lead to their self-destruction. They know nothing of a world of the spirit in which the law of sin and death has been overcome.

It's too annoying that you aren't exempted from nights in the officers' mess, even out there – laughable, too. How relieved you'll be when it's all behind you. How relieved we'll be when that time comes. It won't be too long now. Will you be getting some leave at Christmas? Hans will be home before long, and Werner has similar hopes. You haven't used up your annual quota of leave, have you? Not entirely, anyway. I'd be so pleased.

One more thing: I'm still waiting vainly for a parcel stamp [issued by the army post office]. I'm almost tempted to be angry with you! The others send them, so why not you? I'll have to borrow one of Werner's stamps, just so you get something for Christmas. Will you make a careful note? You shouldn't find it too hard to get hold of one.

And now I'll close on a conciliatory note: fondest love from
Sophie

To Fritz Hartnagel, Ulm, November 4, 1942

My dear Fritz,

Since my letter of yesterday will probably turn up late, I'm sending you another today. The thing is, yesterday's letter was enclosed in your Advent parcel, which you owe to one of Werner's APO stamps. I made your Advent wreath weeks ago. Waldemar helped me to pick the sprigs of fir in the Kloster-wald on a lovely sunny afternoon that seemed an age away from Christmas. That evening we made a lot of wreaths in the hallway and, although it was only October, sang a lot of Christmas carols. They weren't a great success, not because it was too early but because Inge laughed too much, and because W. just sat there like a spectator. . . . I didn't say much – I left him to Inge most of the time, but I feel I made something of an impression on him. —Establishing contact with someone new is a momentous occurrence, a simultaneous declaration of war and love.

It's ages since I heard from you. Day after day I return from the mailbox empty-handed, disappointed but not disheartened. Are you so very busy?

I've been giving a lot of thought lately to the kind of job you might take up after the war. If money still possesses any value, your poultry farm idea might come to something, though an ordinary farm would be more to my taste than a poultry farm. For that you'd need roughly three years' training. I'm still thinking. I've no doubt you'll make a success of something once you start on it (in fact I feel quite certain of it).

For the moment, though, we've both got other things on our mind.

And we're both happy, come what may, and the common ground we stand on is the strongest bond between us.

Fondest love and best wishes,
Sophie

To Fritz Hartnagel, Ulm, November 6, 1942

I'm still waiting in vain for a letter from you. The longer the interval, the more often I'm impelled to write to you. Tonight is no exception. After playing a piano awhile, bathed in candle-light and the delicious scent of burned fir twigs, I'm determined to drop you a line, however brief. And I'll think of you as I make my way to the station mailbox through streets whose gloom the stars do little to dispel, even though they're once more looking down on us through the clouds. And on you as well! But for that, one would sometimes be tempted to lose heart, there's so much preying on our minds.

Such of the family as are here have asked me to send their fond regards.

> All my love and best wishes,
> Sophie

After a long train journey interrupted at numerous points – for example, Brest-Litovsk, where Willi Graf noted: "We nearly got into trouble for giving cigarettes to some Russian pris-oners" – Hans's student company reached Munich on the evening of November 6, and traveled home the following day. When Sophie remarks, in the letter below, that she can't feel "whole-heartedly happy," it is one of the few indications of how heavily her knowledge of the handbill campaign in the summer of 1942 was preying on her mind. She felt that her brother's return would spell the end of her short span of relatively "normal" existence, free from a constant sense of menace and dread. The words acquire redoubled force and convey an even more vivid impres-sion of the shadow under which Sophie lived in Munich when one compares them with the following passage from a letter to Fritz Hartnagel written nearly three years earlier, on February 1, 1940:

"I pity people who can't laugh at every little trifle, i.e., who can't find something to laugh at in everything, the salt and pepper of daily life. That doesn't necessarily have anything to do with superficiality – in fact I think I could still find something to laugh at, if I had to, even at the saddest of moments."

To Fritz Hartnagel, Ulm, November 7, 1942
[inadvertently dated October 7]

My dear Fritz,

Hans gets back from Russia tonight.[254] I suppose I should be glad he's back with us, and I am. I can already picture the times we'll spend together in our modest Munich lodgings.[255] They may well turn out to be productive times.

But I can't feel wholeheartedly happy. I'm never free for a moment, day or night, from the depressing and unremitting state of uncertainty in which we live these days, which precludes any carefree plans for the morrow and casts a shadow over all the days to come. When will we finally be relieved of the compulsion to focus all our energy and attention on things that aren't worth lifting one's little finger for? Every word has to be examined from every angle before it's uttered, to see if it carries a hint of ambiguity. Faith in other people has been forcibly ousted by mistrust and caution. It's exhausting – disheartening too, sometimes. But, no, I won't let anything dishearten me. Trivialities like these can never master me while I'm in possession of other, unassailable joys. Strength flows into me when I think of them, and I'd like to address a word of encouragement to all who are similarly afflicted.

It's been so long since I heard from you that I'm prey to all kinds of misgivings. . . .

I'd like to go walking with you through the woods again, or anywhere at all, but that's still a remote prospect, if not an unattainable one.

A sheet of writing paper will have to suffice for now. It brings you many loving thoughts from
Sophie

P.S. From December 1 my address will be c/o Fr. Dr. Schmidt, rear entrance, 13B Josefstr., Munich 13.

To Fritz Hartnagel, Ulm, November 18, 1942

I really meant to write to you last night, but circumstances prevented me. You'll never believe how much and how long I'd been looking forward to a letter from you, and how many fears and conjectures were bred in me during my long wait – fears I couldn't explain away by ascribing them to your laziness at letter writing. Now, however, [I know that] all is as well with you as it ever was, meaning not so much well as unchanged. I'm glad you're determined to overcome the boredom that was bound to infect you in your work and isolation (you've been living in that wasteland for five years or more). If I could, I'd redouble my efforts to arm you against potential apathy, and I wish your thoughts of me were a permanent incentive to resist it.

If only you could go to church sometime and take Communion. What a source of consolation and strength you might find it.

The only remedy for a barren heart is prayer, however poor and inadequate.

As I did that night at Blumberg, I'll keep on repeating it for us both: we must pray, and pray for each other, and if you were here, I'd fold hands with you, because we're poor, weak, sinful children. Oh, Fritz, if I can't write anything else just now, it's only because there's a terrible absurdity about a drowning man who, instead of calling for help, launches into a scientific, philosophical, or theological dissertation while the sinister tentacles of the creatures on the sea bed are encircling his arms and legs and the waves are breaking over him; it's only because I'm filled with fear, that and nothing else, and feel an undivided yearning for him who can relieve me of it.

I'm still so remote from God that I don't even sense his presence when I pray. Sometimes when I utter God's name, in fact, I feel like sinking into a void. It isn't a frightening or dizzy-making sensation, it's nothing at all – and that's far more terrible. But prayer is the only remedy for it, and however many little devils scurry around inside me, I shall cling to the rope God has thrown me in Jesus Christ, even if my numb hands can no longer feel it.

Please remember me in your prayers. I won't forget you either.

Yours,
Sophie

To Fritz Hartnagel, Ulm, November 19, 1942

My dear Fritz,

Today my father was notified that he can no longer prac-tice his profession because he's politically unreliable. Although the news came as no surprise, we still had some hopes of a petition signed by thirty of our biggest clients (including the [Nazi] district commissioner for Ulm). This ban is uncon-nected with my father's court sentence. It was imposed by the NS-Rechtswahrerbund [a Nazi legal watchdogs' association] at the Party's prompting.

This is another blow, naturally. If one couldn't count on the war being over in the foreseeable future, it would be a very painful one, because a bookkeeper's salary (my father could still be employed in that capacity) isn't sufficient to feed a large family, support children at university, and maintain an expensive apartment. However, my father doesn't want to give up the apart-ment for the sake of a year, or however long the war goes on.

You already offered us your help from the financial aspect, so now it will come in useful. . . .

Hans and Schurik have been here for some days. We start again at Munich next week. We'll have to economize from now on, but I'll be glad to.

Affectionate regards from all, and especially from
Sophie

P.S. Could you get me a pack of envelopes sometime?

Hans Scholl

December 1942

After three weeks' vacation Hans Scholl's student company resumed the life they had led until July 1942: studying, attending Huber's lectures, going to concerts, singing in the Bach Choir, reading and debating with their mentors at Manfred Eickemeyer's studio. But as Sophie anticipated in her letter of November 7, other things were afoot.

In the following letter to Otl Aicher, Hans refers to "urgent business in the offing." He had made a similar allusion two weeks earlier, on November 22, 1942, in a letter from Ulm to his girlfriend Rose Nägele:

"In recent weeks I've taken on a major task, one that is seldom far from my thoughts. I'd have liked to tell you about it if we'd been alone together."

Apart from half a sentence in a letter to Otl Aicher dated January 19, 1943, these two passages are Hans Scholl's sole references to preparations in progress for a new handbill campaign. This was prefaced in November and December 1942 by an attempt to expand the circle of potential helpers and establish contact with resistance groups in other towns and cities. Hans's friend Traute Lafrenz paid a visit to the Hamburg resistance group centered on Heinz Kucharski and Felix Jud; Willi

Graf sounded out his old friends at Saarbrücken and Freiburg; and the Munich-based painter Lilo Ramdohr, a friend of Alexander Scholl's, formed a link with another friend of hers, Dr. Falk Harnack of Weimar, to whom Hans and Alexander paid a joint visit at Chemnitz late in November. Falk Harnack, brother of Arvid Harnack, imprisoned leader of the "Red Orchestra" spy ring (the Harnack/Schulze-Boysen group), undertook to establish contact with the Bonhoeffer/Dohnanyi group. A personal meeting with Bonhoeffer, scheduled for February 25, 1943, did not take place because of Hans Scholl's arrest.

To Otl Aicher, Munich, December 6, 1942

Dear Otl,

The longer I leave it, the more my brain amasses things I should write in answer to you if the inadequacy of modern correspondence didn't muzzle me after every other sentence. . . . Much of the blame lies with me, at least to the extent that I shrink from the effort of lending an idea the requisite outward form in a sentence. I've temporarily lost my zest for writing, which used to give me such a pleasurable sensation when I covered a blank sheet with words. Nowadays I prefer to leave a sheet blank, not for aesthetic reasons, but because it's still devoid of lies and threadbare assertions, because potential strength resides in a blank sheet, and because I can restrain myself and wait for the day when writing becomes a pleasure to me again.

How often over the years have I written "my love" and "my beloved" with an aching heart, and later it proved to be a delusion. Not a disillusionment (I cite this only as an example), but a delusion and therefore a lie. —I'm writing you something quite other than I meant to. Forgive me, but that often happens to me. I merely wanted to let you know that my silence doesn't stem from laziness at letter writing. Your last letter made a grand tour through Russia, Poland, and Central Europe before it caught up with me. When it came into my hands, I resolved in spite of everything to make a bit of an effort and write you from time to time after all, so we don't go groping in the dark and neither of us knows where the other happens to be. This will probably be the only correspondence I keep up.

Don't misunderstand me: I'm a sociable person in spite of my solitariness. (The reverse order would be more apt.) I'm surrounded here by a circle of people whose company you'd enjoy, and it would be a pleasant and tempting occupation to expand and cultivate such a circle if I didn't at present have more urgent business in the offing.

The best thing from every angle would be if you could spend a few days of your convalescent leave here with us in Munich.

I'll write again soon, dear Otl. Meantime, accept these few lines as a thank-you for your splendid letters. And get well soon! (Have you got infectious hepatitis?)

Best regards,
Hans

P.S. This morning we heard Handel's *Messiah*.

To Rose Nägele, Munich, December 14, 1942

Dear Rose,

How am I to answer your letter? I lovingly laid it aside after reading it, thought over what you'd said, and came to no conclusion. Valid and true though it is, your advice can't help me now. It can't, during these present months, steer me back to meditative introspection. Once wild beasts have burst their bars and are roaming the streets, every able-bodied person must take up arms, irrespective of class and inner vocation. To employ an old metaphor, man doesn't travel one road, but many roads at once, high and low, so it's immensely difficult to form a true appreciation of the doings and intentions of another. If you knew Alex and me better, you wouldn't advise me to emulate my friend's down-to-earth attitude. Perhaps the reverse applies, and I ought to cultivate an even more active relationship with the purely spiritual. . . . What ultimately matters is to find the proper relationship between character and intellect. I've never taken the view that those two antagonists can be divorced. A person's nature is as much a creation of God as his spirit, but in the divine order of things, the spirit takes precedence.

You can see for yourself that letters aren't a sufficient aid to mutual understanding. Only conversational give-and-take can resolve the hundred questions we append to every written word – for instance, what do you mean by "nature"? But where among our unphilosophical fellow creatures is one to find the right conversational partner? At present, for understandable reasons, I prefer to cultivate the company of older people, but those whose hinges haven't yet been rusted by bourgeois thinking, and who can still provide access to the troughs and peaks of human thought. As you'll well appreciate, I don't attach much importance to the views of people who are fundamentally alien to me.

Instead of the above, I'd sooner have told you about yesterday's walk beside the Ammersee, and the shells cast up on the shore, and the colorful pebbles, and the mist on the heath, and the glimmer of the pale evening star, and how later we cowered in the lee of the warm smokestack, shivering, and sang songs while the ship inscribed a broad dividing line on the water as it slowly headed for the opposite shore. . . .

But first my heart had to write the rest down. Many a fine speech remains sealed within our lips because disaster looms over us. Leafing through a review when I got home, I came across this poem by Verlaine:

Le ciel est, par-dessus le toit, si bleu, si calme!
Un arbre, par-dessus le toit, berce sa palme.
La cloche dans le ciel qu'on voit doucement tinte.
Un oiseau sur l'arbre, qu'on voit chante sa plainte.
Mon Dieu, mon Dieu, la vie est là, simple et tranquille.
Cette paisible rumeur-là vient de la ville.
—Qu'as-tu fait, ô toi que voilà pleurant sans cesse,
Dis, qu'as-tu fait, toi que voilà, de ta jeunesse?

There's music for you! Finer than Rilke.

Yours,

Hans

To Rose Nägele, Munich, December 18, 1942

. . . You mustn't forget that, fundamentally, man was *created*
intellectual! So he can't blithely and unwittingly vegetate in a
state of nature, like plants or animals, because his mind won't
leave him in peace, because he's conscious of the ambiguities
of this world and aware of the death that threatens him. Only
when the mind has overcome Nature does death, too, cease to
exist. Nature is as much of divine origin as the mind, but it has
been thrown off its peaceful course by the intervention of man.
It has been largely perverted (man's nature) and needs redemption. But it wasn't this that prompted me to give you an objective
answer – it was your advocacy of contemplation. I know you
think as I do, but this is precisely the answer that unites us:

We shouldn't contemplate ourselves so much as things, the
world, and the way ideas can exist without us and independent
of us. From there it can't be far to genuinely universal love.

It would be better, undoubtedly, if we could see one another
from time to time, so that we could discuss problems like
these. I rate good conversation higher than any letter because
the spoken word carries conviction, whereas the written word

seems dubious at a distance. I'm sure I've already pointed out elsewhere that I suffer so badly from verbal diarrhea that my own letters strike me as downright inadequate. All the same, I do my best.

Perhaps you might like to visit Ulm during the vacation, or come here later on. I'd be so pleased.

A very happy Christmas.

Hans

Sophie Scholl
Winter 1942–1943

To Lisa Remppis, Munich, December 17, 1942

Dear Lisa,

I've been vainly expecting a line from you for ages. I hope it's only school and Gust that have kept you from writing.

I'm probably coming to Stuttgart Monday afternoon (they don't know that at home!).* Let's hope we can meet. I'll call you at the college.

All the best till then.

> Yours,
> Sophie

Presumably an indication that her visit to Stuttgart was connected with the activities of the White Rose.[256]

To Fritz Hartnagel, Ulm, December 30, 1942

. . . Another quiet evening at home. I coaxed some lovely old music[257] out of the radio, the kind that soothes your senses and tidies up the turmoil in your heart. Beauty of that kind can never be bad, redolent as it is of the existence of a pure mind – a lucid, sometimes mathematically lucid mind. Modern music in general has ceased to be entirely pure – mental images are required to absorb it. It has already deserted the realm of music proper. I'm far from failing to appreciate it, though – why shouldn't one? I'm very fond of the sound pictures of Saint-Saëns, for instance, but in my view they never come up to Mozart, let alone Bach.

The photo was taken around a year ago. I tore it out of an album of Hans's because the pose was ridiculous, and I've only left you the head. I don't look the same these days. My hair will soon be down to my shoulders unless Lisl takes pity on it again.

Let's hope we'll soon be able to stroll through town again, as we did last year. It doesn't have to be Freiburg, after all. I couldn't help remembering that this evening because my composition soles kept slipping so terribly on the fresh snow, as they did then.

All my love,
Sophie

The young Scholls spent a few days at home in Ulm until lectures restarted after the January 6 holiday.

To Fritz Hartnagel, Ulm, January 1, 1943

My dear Fritz,

Today we went for a splendid walk to Geislingen, along the foot of the hills and through the open beech woods and the glorious, freshly fallen snow. Snow in broad daylight can inspire you with such wild exuberance that you romp and frolic around like overgrown children. But when twilight descends on the snowy woods or the tall, narrow, snow-mantled houses, this mood becomes transformed into its opposite: a solemn and expectant hush like the eve of Christmas.

I'm sharing the little upstairs room with Hans. The silence before we go to sleep is punctuated by isolated remarks uttered at long intervals, retrospective comments on the day or questions raised by what we've discussed or read. Last night, for instance, Hans said that Leibniz (I'm just reading his theodicy) had been the first to restrict God's omnipotence on the ground that he can only accomplish good, not evil. I claimed it was a question of volition, not ability, but I soon had to abandon that argument and enlist the aid of a simile: God's inability to be evil is exactly like the inability of the wise to be foolish. Although Hans rejected that comparison, I myself find it more and more cogent. If God weren't good, he wouldn't be wise, and vice versa. His failing is an inability to have any failings.

But how will what I've just written strike you in your noisy, warlike surroundings? As far as I can be, I'm with you.

Yours,
Sophie

To Fritz Hartnagel, Ulm, January 3, 1943

My dear Fritz,

Maybe an airmail letter will have a better chance of reaching you, so I'll use up the blank side after all. I'm following the news with far more interest now that I know where you are. I hope you're all right, and that not even hardship and the din of battle can throw you off course. Hardship tends to blunt the senses, I'm sure, but remember: *Un esprit dûr, du coeur* TENDRE! It often makes me unhappy that I'm not a vehicle for universal suffering. That way I could at least remove part of my guilt from those who are undeservedly having to suffer so much more than I. I'm so much with you in spirit these days that I often feel we're bound to bump into one another, but I keep on worrying and wondering how things are with you. You know the value of a human life, and we have to know what we're risking it for. What a responsibility you bear! However, you do know a source of strength.

And now, God bless you.

Yours,
Sophie

*Upon Hans and Sophie's return to Munich in January, as
German armies were falling prey to stiffening Russian resistance
and bitter cold on the Eastern front, the Munich circle drew up
its next leaflet, no longer referred to as a leaflet of the White Rose
but titled* Leaflet of the Resistance.

*Hans and his circle had been befriended by the Munich archi-
tect Manfred Eickemeyer, who had given them the information
about the German atrocities in Poland presented in one of the
handbills distributed the previous summer. The White Rose
circle held readings and discussions at Eickemeyer's secluded
studio in a garden on Leopoldstrasse, and it was in the studio
basement that the students produced the handbills on a hand-
cranked duplicating machine, using quantities of paper and
supplies the very purchase of which tended to arouse suspicion.*

This straightforward leaflet, headed A Call to all Germans!*,
was briefer than earlier leaflets and included no literary quota-
tions. It said that Hitler could not win the war, that he was
"leading the German people into the abyss. . . . The guilt of Hitler
and his minions exceeds all bounds. Retribution comes closer
and closer. But what are the German people doing? They will not
see, and will not listen. Blindly they follow their seducers into
ruin. . . ."*[258]

To her sister Inge, Munich, January 12, 1943

. . . I always find the change of climate between home and here
a bit of a strain. It always takes me several days to learn to
dispense with all the little kindnesses I receive from Mother
and you, and your daily concern for me (if only as regards my
digestion, which is absolutely fine now), and to reaccustom
myself to my independence and, in a certain sense, to being on
my own.

Herr Geyer[259] has already moved into Eickemeyer's studio.
We'll probably see a lot of him in the evenings. His presence is
very reassuring. He genuinely radiates an aura of confidence. . . .

Diary, January 12, 1943

Predestination and free will, those apparently irreconcilable opposites, have ceased to trouble me much anymore, even though I find them as inexplicable as ever. I believe in God's omniscience, and the logical inference is that he knows what happens in the afterlife of every individual and of each and every one of us. His status as an eternal God entails this.

I can sense my free will, but who can prove its existence to me? What I don't understand is hell and the refusal of Lazarus in Abraham's bosom[260] to give the rich man in hell a drop of cool water from his endless abundance of it.

I think there's a difference between predestination and foreknowledge. Predestination I find far harder, if not wholly impossible, to reconcile with free will. Foreknowledge I find much easier, even though it remains an unfathomable mystery. Besides, "foreknowledge" is a human term. God isn't tied to our own time, so we ought to delete the syllable "fore" and simply say "knowledge."

Diary, January 13, 1943

As soon as I'm alone, melancholy suppresses any desire in me to do anything at all. When I pick up a book, I do so without interest, as if someone else were doing it. There's only one remedy for this awful state of mind.

Extreme pain, even if only physical, would be infinitely preferable to this vacuous inactivity.

To Otl Aicher, Munich, January 19, 1943

Dear Otl,

Forgive me for not having written, even though this won't be a real letter. I'm just not myself at the moment, and it's an entirely novel sensation. My thoughts flit to and fro without my being able to control them properly. I'm suffering from some pretty bad headaches, which may be to blame, partly at least. If I'm to get over this malaise soon, I'll have to be patient with myself.

When I realize something, it's as if it has had to grow inside me beforehand and is suddenly unfolding, leaf by leaf. I used to balk at the idea of an eternal order of things in which some are superior to others, but now I suddenly find it far less absurd, if not absolutely as it should be. I discovered this within myself, in a characteristic I used to think I lacked, namely, ambition. I utterly reject and condemn ambition because it seeks to overthrow every established order by promoting those obsessed with it into positions they don't deserve. To my consternation, it suddenly dawned on me that all the apparent good I'd done had been done, not for its own sake, but to make me look good in other people's eyes, or to catch up with a good person for my own sake, like one runner overhauling another, instead of acknowledging that person to be the better runner and modestly accepting my second or twentieth place as wholly fair.

Or do you think these scribblings of mine are wrong? I'm very preoccupied with the subject just now, because I keep on having little tiffs with myself. It's beyond me that some people have moments of temptation only. I have moments of greater lucidity, and I'm very grateful for them, but the rest of the time I'm paddling around in the dark.

I feel I've rattled on too long already. That's why I'm so averse to writing these days, because I produce too little that's rounded off and fit for others to read.

I hope you aren't having a bad time. I look forward to your getting some leave, so we can spend at least some time together.

Affectionate regards for now,
Sophie

Hans Scholl

Winter 1942–1943

Notes scribbled on an envelope, undated [probably winter 1942–1943]

I'm not speaking of the masses, but a national elite responsible for the spiritual substance and orientation of the entire nation: [an elite] which has failed so badly in this century, and doubtless in previous ones, that the spiritual plane has been deprived of its supports and plunged into chaos. Today, having a presentiment of impending doom, this elite is capable of making an even bigger mistake: of shutting itself and its blunders away from the real world and leading an existence of its own – of pursuing *l'art pour art* in the wildest sense. But nothing could be more dangerous to it than fleeing into the realm of aesthetics. [remainder indecipherable]

To Rose Nägele, Munich, January 5, 1943

Dear Rose,

I was secretly expecting you the whole time over Christmas. I've been back in Munich since yesterday, on my own, because Sophie won't be following for a day or two. I can imagine how pleased you were that the whole family congregated on Christmas Eve. Eve wrote me an amusing little letter about it.

(Actually, it was slightly out of keeping with her rather quiet and dreamy nature.)

I was delighted with your present. Bergengruen, whom I know personally,[261] I value above all other living German authors including Carossa.

The Munich air has stimulated me like mad again, so much so that I lay awake all last night. But I love these transitional periods. They may be hard to endure, but they whet the intellect. It's the same impulse that makes waiting at big railroad junctions appeal to me so much. I know someone of whom it could be said that, wherever he goes, he never takes his coat off and always remains a passing stranger, though he doesn't keep mum or play the mystery man. When you speak with him, you feel he may conclude every sentence by abruptly pulling out his watch and saying, "Time to go." I like him a lot.

I'm still waiting for a reply to my last letter. —

I've never really known why I study medicine. What primarily decided me to apply myself to that field was a love of the sciences, a penchant for the most general education going, and, last but not least, a measure of uncertainty: what else to do?

There's no philosophy at present. Nor any political science. Freedom was my overriding principle, both in choice of profession and field of study. So I chose, not knowing why. A reaction was bound to set in. After my preliminary examination I developed an aversion to anything connected with medicine. I thought my salvation lay in philosophy alone. Then came a period of intense concentration on problems relating to political theory and politics. It's only now that I've really succumbed to a love of medicine.[262] This, I realize, is where I can achieve most. I realize that a doctor *must* be a philosopher and a politician as well, so the intervening years have been a gain rather than a loss. I'll soon have made up any ground I've lost in the way of purely technical know-how. On the other hand, I'm now able to locate man, who has always been the focus of medical thought, in his proper place in the world and the political system. I don't like specialization. A great dilettante knows more about the meaning of things than a great specialist.

Fond regards for now,

Hans

While paying Otl Aicher a visit in the hospital near Bad Hall, near Linz, Sophie had told him about Hans's and their friends' activities and made him promise to come to Munich as soon as he was discharged – a promise he duly kept in February.[263]

To Otl Aicher, Munich, January 12, 1943

Dear Otl,

Your last letter arrived at the ideal moment, like a messenger from a better land. What I wrote you in my last is now superseded, and the present surmounts the shadows of the past in a different light. One should repay candor with respect. You did that, and I'm duly grateful.

We're all waiting eagerly and impatiently for the day when you pay us a visit here. I'm looking forward to it, if only because I can get far closer to you in conversation than on paper. I'm still rather chary of all this letter writing. In conversation, by contrast, one word coaxes another one out, and the other person's inner mental framework soon becomes visible.

You'll already have heard about the circle of people I've brought together here. Their faces would delight you if you could see them. All the energy one expends flows back, undiminished, into one's heart. Only weaklings stint their strength. Fools remain silent because they can't speak, and the unimaginative act tough and inflexible. Making a virtue out of a shortcoming, that's what I call that brand of Prussianism.[264] It's a virtue we disown.

Best regards,

Hans

Hans Scholl | 299

To Otl Aicher, Munich, January 19, 1943

Dear Otl,

Replying in great haste. We're just back from the mountains, tanned and refreshed.

I can't get away from Munich on Sunday for reasons I'd rather tell you about than write. But you'll be here soon!

Best regards,

Hans

P.S. It's Professor Muth's birthday on January 20. Did you remember?

Sophie Scholl
Winter 1943

Although the Munich circle viewed the German reversals in Russia as another step toward the downfall of Hitler's regime, they were appalled at the casualties, and Sophie grew increasingly fearful for Fritz Hartnagel's safety.

To Lisa Remppis, Munich, February 2, 1943

Dear Lisa,

   Rain is dripping onto the windowsill outside. There's a clock ticking inside the wall, a kind of phantom clock, because you can very seldom hear it, mostly around midnight. Sometimes it goes slowly, sometimes faster and faster, sometimes it sounds as if it's about to stop, and sometimes it sounds like a lot of clocks ticking all at once. Other times it ticks nice and steadily for hours on end, as a good, respectable clock should. Actually, I suspect it isn't a clock at all, tempted though I am to think so, but the central heating. The floor lamp sheds a small circle of light that doesn't even include the whole of this sheet of paper. Good conditions in which to write, but only outwardly, and in other respects I'm in a bad way. I can't remember when I've felt so unable to concentrate (except once, when I was in love, and that doesn't apply at present). I'm often tempted to blame it on headaches. That's never the reason, of course, but I've learned to be patient with myself.

Once upon a time – I'm reminded of this by your reference to the innocent suffering of trees – I occasionally used to wish I was just a tree, or better still, just a fragment of bark from a tree. I entertained such whims very early on, but nowadays I take care to stifle them and resist the kind of fatigue that seeks fulfillment in nonexistence. It isn't because I've conquered the feeling, far from it, but I'm often, almost constantly, overwhelmed by a feeling of melancholy of which I'm becoming almost fond. Do you know what I mean? It's dangerous and even sinful to cherish one's own agony of mind. It was a female mystic, I think, who said: "When I praise God, I feel no joy whatever. I praise him because I *want* to praise him." How well I understand those words.

I ought to feel half ashamed of this letter, but why shouldn't you know how things are with me? I'm so much at sea, I can barely manage to write about anything else. Besides, I'm writing this to *you*, and you alone, and I'd prefer you not to keep this letter.

I had a letter from Fritz dated January 17. His battalion, too, has been wiped out, and all he now expects is to be captured or killed. He got frostbite in both hands after spending weeks in the open, day and night, in thirty degrees of frost. It may be the last wartime letter I'll get from him (he thinks so). The end is drawing perceptibly nearer.

Affectionate regards to you and Gust,
Sophie

P.S. I'd already put this in the envelope when a call came through from home: Fritz is in the hospital at Stalino. He's lost some fingers and may lose his heels as well, but he's safe. Thank God!

Sophie, 1940 or 1941

*On February 3, the day after Sophie wrote to Lisa Remppis, an
OKW communiqué announced that the Germans encircled at
Stalingrad, after enormous casualties, had surrendered. Out of
420,000 German troops, 90,000 remained. Fritz Hartnagel had
been evacuated on January 22, 1943, by one of the last German
aircraft to leave the Stalingrad pocket.*

From Stalino, in the Donets Basin, Fritz was moved again, farther west, traveling for six days with a batch of casualties before reaching the hospital at L'vov. There, on February 4 – his birthday – two of his frostbitten fingers were amputated.

In the early morning hours of the same day, Hans Scholl and Alexander Schmorell painted their first slogans – "Freedom" and "Down with Hitler" – on the walls of Munich's university quarter.

Sophie left for Ulm shortly afterward and spent February 5 through February 15 in Ulm, helping her sick mother. Although she didn't know his exact schedule or whereabouts, she knew Fritz was scheduled for further evacuation, and so she was able to write to him in the knowledge that he was safe at last.

To Fritz Hartnagel, Ulm, February 7, 1943

My dear Fritz,

Haecker[265] was with us[266] on your birthday. It was a memorable occasion. He lets his words fall slowly, like drops you see gathering beforehand, and expectancy lends their descent a special kind of momentum. He has a very serene face and an introspective look. I've never seen a face that carries more conviction.

Otl's on leave at present. I've spent many hours with him in the last few days because he's been modeling me. Now my hands are itching to emulate him. I look forward to it. Pen and pencil are far too impatient to capture a face, and I don't feel the same assurance when using them as I do at the almost seductive touch of clay.

I'm eager for your next letter. I hope you've been moved on [from Stalino] by now, and that you'll contrive to end up somewhere near me, at least. In other words, provided I'm still free[267] (my freedom is very limited) I'll naturally come to see you. I'm overjoyed already at the thought of being with you. New plans sprout inside me every other minute, like weeds on a dungheap, but they're bright, many-splendored weeds.

Don't worry though, I'll restrain myself.

All my fondest love,
Sophie

To Fritz Hartnagel, Ulm, February 10, 1943

My dear Fritz,

I hope the address[268] your mother gave us over the phone is sufficient. If so, you'll at last be getting more news of us again. First, welcome back with all my heart, after being so far away from us for so long. Our forthcoming reunion now seems so different to me from all the rest, as if you're back to stay for good. Although I've been too tired till now to make plans, since the war would bring them all to nothing, they're now springing up like jungle flowers after a long, warm downpour, gaudy and outrageous. Except that they don't seem the least bit outrageous to me, but all very feasible.

Forgive me for letting my pen run away with me and losing my sense of proportion. I'd sooner not write again before you get back, because I'm so impatient I'd like to see you here tomorrow. You say there's little hope of that, but I believe it just the same.

My hands are all clumsy, hot, and trembly from wringing out masses of washing. I'm helping out at home this week because Mother and Inge aren't too well (diarrhea and vomiting), and there's a christening next Sunday. You probably aren't aware of it, but we've had a Frau . . . living with us for the past five months, and she's had a baby. Now it's to be christened, but that's just by the way.

As soon as you can, write and tell me your exact address, when you'll be allowed to travel, whether I'm to pay you a visit, and anything else it's important for me to know.

Forgive me once more for my peals of joy – I hope they haven't been too much for you – and get well soon.

All my love,

Sophie

To Fritz Hartnagel, Ulm, February 13, 1943

My dear Fritz,

I run to the mailbox every day, on the theory that there's more likely to be something there for me if I go and look in person. So far my hopes have been dashed, but I don't suppose you can write yet, with your frostbitten fingers.

It's regular April weather here. Snow alternates with sunshine, and I must confess to being in an equally childish frame of mind, for no special reason. Probably in reaction to all that has gone before, I keep on having colorful, innocuous dreams about the future. I realize how innocuous and trivial they are, thank goodness, or I might easily become immersed in them, like so many people, and rejoice on their sole account that the war will soon be over. But they aren't my grounds for rejoicing – far from it.

I shall probably be redrafted for war work next semester. I'm not too unhappy about it, because I'd prefer to go on suffering for the duration (that's an overstatement, but I do want at least to be directly affected). Fellow feeling can often be hard to muster, and it tends to become a mere figure of speech unless your own body hurts.

I so much look forward to being able to speak with you once more, because anything I write is just a drop from a big reservoir that has built up by slow degrees.

Shall I pay you a visit? You need only write and say.

All my love,

Sophie

*Sophie returned to Munich on February 15. According to
the testimony of Joseph Söhngen,*[269] *the Munich bookseller,
the last handbill,* Kommilitonen! Kommiltoninnen! *[Fellow
Students – Men and Women!] was printed on February 16. It
began: "Shaken and broken, our people behold the loss of the
men of Stalingrad. Three hundred and thirty thousand German
men have been senselessly and irresponsibly driven to death and
destruction by the inspired strategy of our World War I Private
First Class. Führer, we thank you!"*[270]

*According to Söhningen, "On Thursday, February 16, 1943,
Hans came to see me, in some agitation, and gave me the already
printed handbill to read. I felt obliged to raise a few objections
to the wording, but he told me he wouldn't and couldn't make
any more alterations at that stage. He proposed to distribute
these handbills at the university in the next few days but wasn't
entirely sure how to do it. I begged him under no circumstances
to employ the method he had in mind, which was to leave
substantial numbers of them outside the doors of the various
institutes, or on the stairs, or in the cloakroom, because the risk
of his being spotted was far too great."*[271]

To Fritz Hartnagel, Munich, February 16, 1943

My dear Fritz,

   Just a brief line before I dash off to my lectures. I think I
already told you I spent ten days helping out at home. Being
there always does me good, though I don't get much time for
personal activities, if only because my father's so pleased when
I turn up and so taken aback when I leave, and because Mother
shows her concern for me in a thousand little ways. There's
something wonderful to me about such an altruistic love. I
regard it as one of my life's greatest blessings.

The 150 kilometers between Ulm and Munich produce such a rapid change in me, I find it surprising myself. They turn me from an innocent, exuberant child into an independent, self-contained person. But being on my own does me good, even though I sometimes feel ill at ease because people spoil me so much. However, I only feel really secure when I recognize the presence of selfless love, and that's comparatively rare.

How are you? It's been two weeks since your last letter from Stalino, and I feel a bit unsure when I write to you, not knowing how things stand with you and what emotions I'm allowed to show. Rest assured, though, they're never anything but love and gratitude.

Yours,
Sophie

Hans Scholl
February 16

To Rose Nägele, Munich, February 16, 1943

Dear Rose,

    Your last letter saddened me. I saw your tears shine through the words as I read it, and I can't dry them. Why write that way? Although I live in a permanent transition from yesterday to today to tomorrow, the beauty of the past remains intact and no less beautiful. That bygone summer still reflects its light into the present. Must its radiance be extinguished by shades of melancholy?

    Nowadays I have to be the way I am. I'm remote from you, both outwardly and inwardly, but never estranged. Never has my respect for your purity of heart been greater than it is now, when life has become an ever-present danger. But because the danger is of my own choosing, I must head for my chosen destination freely and without any ties. I've gone astray many times, I know. Chasms yawn and darkest night envelops my questing heart, but I press on regardless. As Claudel so splendidly puts it: *La vie, c'est une grande aventure vers la lumière.* [Life is a great adventure toward the light.]

It might be better in the future if the sentiments conveyed in our letters owed less to emotion and more to reason. I'd welcome another letter from you soon.

Affectionate regards,
Hans

Sophie Scholl

February 17

To Lisa Remppis, Munich, February 17, 1943

Dear Lisa,

I've just been playing the Trout Quintet on the phonograph. Listening to the andantino makes me want to be a trout myself. You can't help rejoicing and laughing, however moved or sad at heart you feel, when you see the springtime clouds in the sky and the budding branches sway, stirred by the wind, in the bright young sunlight. I'm so much looking forward to the spring again. In that piece of Schubert's you can positively feel and smell the breezes and scents and hear the birds and the whole of creation cry out for joy. And when the piano repeats the theme like cool, clear, sparkling water – oh, it's sheer enchantment.

Let me hear from you soon.

Lots of love,
Sophie

February 18

On February 18, 1943, Hans and Sophie Scholl were arrested at Munich University. They had left the bulk of the handbills

*printed on February 16 outside the university lecture halls, and
when they sent the last few copies fluttering down over the balus-
trade of the atrium into the courtyard below, they were spotted
by a university janitor.*

*On February 22 the so-called People's Court presided over
by Roland Freisler sentenced them to death. Late that same
afternoon, Hans and Sophie Scholl and their friend Christoph
Probst,*[272] *who had helped draft the last handbill, were sent to
the guillotine at Stadelheim Prison, Munich.*

*Before leaving his cell in the Palais Wittelsbach, Hans
penciled on the wall the quotation "Allen Gewalten zum Trutz
sich erhalten."*[273] *His last words were: "Es lebe die Freiheit."
[Long live freedom.]*

*At the end of February Fritz Hartnagel, still in the hospital at
L'vov, received a letter from his mother informing him that Hans
and Sophie Scholl had been sentenced to death. He discharged
himself from the hospital and went at once to Berlin to petition
the People's Court for clemency. Reaching Berlin on the evening
of February 28, he telephoned Werner Scholl in Ulm, only to be
told that the sentence had already been carried out.*

*Alexander Schmorell, Kurt Huber, and Willi Graf were
arrested soon after Hans and Sophie and were sentenced to
death on April 19. Schmorell and Huber were beheaded on
July 13. Graf was held until October as Gestapo interrogators
attempted to induce him to reveal the names of friends and
accomplices. Staunchly silent to the last, he was guillotined
at Stadelheim Prison on October 12. Eleven others implicated
in the activities of the White Rose, including eight from the
Hamburg group, were killed, forced to commit suicide, or died in
prisons or concentration camps, and many others were arrested
and served prison terms.*

The rest of the Scholl family, excluding Werner who, being a serviceman, was not under civil jurisdiction, were taken into "kinship detention" and served prison terms of varying lengths before being released. Werner Scholl was killed in Russia.

Acknowledgments

The foregoing material has been selected from some seven hundred documents compiled over the years by Inge Aicher-Scholl. It should, of course, be borne in mind that the documents preserved on file at Rotis/Allgäu, of which approximately half are published here, represent only a part, albeit a substantial part, of the young Scholls' total correspondence. Many potentially incriminating letters were destroyed by their recipients when the White Rose was smashed; others – whole bundles of them, for all we know – have never been returned to the family.

Some of the cuts made in individual letters, which are indicated by marks of ellipsis (. . .), relate to passages whose publication would infringe the privacy of the writers, their correspondents, or the third parties they mention. Elsewhere, I have eliminated trivial repetitions, e.g., frequent requests for money and clean laundry or expressions of gratitude for parcels of food and the like. Any reader who still feels that too many mundane details have been retained should take into account that the editor has been at pains to leave the letters' general tenor intact, rather than to retouch them by concentrating on significant points. I have merely corrected the writers' more obvious solecisms and expanded abbreviations such as "H." for "Hans" and "S." for "Sophie" without mentioning this in every case. Excessive philological accuracy would, I feel, impair the freshness of the letters which, far from being proclamatory in style, were written spontaneously and for the nonce, with open, unguarded candor.

My thanks must go first to Inge Aicher-Scholl, who has spent years assembling the documents that form the makings of this volume, and whose expert assistance proved indispensable to the elucidation and annotation of the letters. I am also indebted to Otl Aicher, who provided me with a comprehensive account of the "climate" of events and its sociocultural context as seen by someone intimately involved. Above all, he explained the philosophical and theological basis of Hans's and Sophie's rebellion, an analysis and summary embodied in the Notes. I should further like to thank all those whose detailed replies to my numerous questions helped to reconstruct the sequence of events. Finally, my thanks are due to J. Hellmut Freund for his help in suggesting many improvements and additions.

I should like, in conclusion, to make two personal comments. In the first place, I have developed my interpretation of the spiritual and intellectual bases of the White Rose (notions of friendship, influence of the youth movement, concept of an elite, experiences in Russia, Christian orientation, etc.) in an essay entitled "Über die 'Weiße Rose'" in *Neue Rundschau*, Vol. 95 (1984), no. 1–2, pp. 193–213. Secondly, my editing and annotation owe a special debt to the following publications about the White Rose: Inge Aicher-Scholl, *Die Weiße Rose*, 1st–4th eds. (S. Fischer Verlag, Frankfurt) new enlarged ed. 1983; Klaus Drobisch, *Wir schweigen nicht*, 1st and 4th eds., Union Verlag, Berlin, 1968 and 1983; Richard Hanser, *Deutschland zuliebe*, Kindler-Verlag, Munich, 1980; Ursel Hochmuth and Gertrud Meyer, *Streiflichter aus dem Hamburger Widerstand 1933–1945*, Röderberg-Verlag, Frankfurt, 1980, reprint of the 1969 ed. in *Bibliothek des Widerstandes*, chapter entitled, "Weiße Rose Hamburg;" Clara Huber (ed.), *Kurt Huber zum Gedächtnis*, Regensburg, 1947; Karl-Heinz Jahnke, *Weiße Rose contra Hakenkreuz*, Röderberg-Verlag, Frankfurt, 1969, *Bibliothek des Widerstandes*; Günther Kirchberger, *Die "Weisse Rose,"* Ludwig-Maximilians-Universität, Munich, 1980; Christian Petry, *Studenten aufs Schafott*, Verlag R. Piper und Co., Munich, 1968; Michael Verhoeven and Mario Krebs, *Die Weiße Rose*, Fischer Taschenbuchverlag, Frankfurt, October 1982; Klaus Vielhaber, Hubert Hanisch, and Anneliese Knoop-Graf, *Gewalt und Gewissen*, Herder-Verlag, Freiburg, 1964; Hermann Vinke, *Das kurze Leben der Sophie Scholl*, Otto Meier-Verlag, Ravensburg, 1980.

Notes

Hans Scholl, 1937–1939

1. Abbreviation of *Deutsche Jungenschaft, November 1* (the date in 1929 on which this branch of the youth movement was originally founded).

2. Hans Scholl's nineteenth birthday present from his sister Inge was a copy of Stefan George's *Stern des Bundes*. Above the dedication, "Hans zum 22. 9. 37," she had encoded the motto *"Die Gedanken sind frei"* [Thoughts are free] – from a popular song – by giving the musical notation for the melody.

3. A dramatic novel published in 1934 by the best-selling Swiss author John Knittel (1891–1970).

4. The conductor Wilhelm Furtwängler (1886–1954).

5. Unidentifiable.

6. A reference to the arrest of Werner and Inge, his brother and sister. For details of proceedings taken against the Ulm branch of the illegal dj-1/11, see Hermann Vinke, *Das kurze Leben der Sophie Scholl*, (Ravensburg, 1980), p. 50ff.; Richard Hanser, *Deutschland zuliebe* (Munich, 1980), p. 74ff.; Inge Aicher-Scholl, *Die Weiße Rose*, new enlarged ed. (Frankfurt, 1983), p. 22ff.; and Mario Krebs in Michael Verhoeven and Mario Krebs, *Die Weiße Rose* (Frankfurt, 1982), p. 52ff.

7. The campaign launched by Party, Hitler Youth, and Gestapo authorities against the allegedly subversive activities of the Bündische Jugend.

8. A Nazi propaganda film by Karl Ritter (1937).

9. *Stuttgart, December 20, 1937*

    Dear Herr Scholl,
        I called on Judge E. on Friday afternoon and spoke with the judge advocate on Saturday. The main problem is that, as a youth leader, your son may be held to have abused his senior status. But for this, the whole business would probably be dropped. I informed Judge E. what a lenient view the judge advocate takes of the case. I also submitted a written recommendation that your son be released from custody, adding that he would continue to perform his normal duties with us and not be detained. The awkward feature of the whole affair is that the preliminary proceedings are being conducted at

Düsseldorf, which is holding everything up. I hope, however, that your son's case will subsequently be transferred to Stuttgart. The first step, I imagine, is for you or your son to put in an application for his release, which will be forwarded to Düsseldorf and relayed from there. We must then wait and see when and where the hearing will be held and how the public prosecutor handles the case.

> Yours sincerely,
> (Scupin), Captain and Squadron Commander.

Bad Cannstatt, December 30, 1937

Dear Herr Scholl,

Like you, I much regret the delay in securing your son's release. I went to the criminal court in person on the morning of December 27 to urge that it be expedited, but, as Dr. E. has already informed you, his papers hadn't turned up yet. I did, however, receive a renewed assurance from Judge K. and Judge E. that the local authorities will release your son the moment they receive his file. I found your son quite calm and composed when I paid him another visit in the remand prison on December 24. He had undergone further questioning about his membership in the Bündische Jugend, but feels confident that no charges can be brought against him on that score. I was displeased to find that your son had been housed with two other prisoners. I raised this with Judge K., who assured me that he would remedy the situation if at all possible. Since I shall be going on two days' leave tomorrow, I have instructed my sergeant-major to furlough your son if he is released before the New Year.

> With kind regards and best wishes for the coming year,
> Scupin.

10. Lisl (also Liesel or Lisel): Hans's middle sister Elisabeth, b. 1920, m. Fritz Hartnagel. Inge: his eldest sister, b. 1917, m. Otl Aicher. Sophie (also Sofie): his youngest sister, b. 1921. Werner: his younger brother, b. 1922, reported missing in Russia during the summer of 1944.

11. Hans's squadron was due to be transferred there.

12. First performed at Berlin's Lessingtheater on December 21, 1900.

13. Probably at the suggestion of his father, who had occasionally consulted the same Stuttgart palm reader.

14. A favorite sport in the dj-1/11.

15. Renée Sintenis (1888–1965), graphic artist and sculptress, principally noted for her portrait busts and small figures of young animals. Although she was expelled from the Akademie der Künste in

1933 and some of her works were denounced as degenerate art, photographs of her sculptures and copies of her numerous book illustrations continued to enjoy widespread popularity, especially during the Nazi era. The young Scholls were admirers of her work. The book referred to by Hans Scholl was probably Hanna Kiel's biography (Rembrandt-Verlag, Berlin, 1935), which Sophie extolled to her sister Inge in a letter dated June 16, 1938: "Yesterday I read a biography of Renee Sintenis. It's fantastic the way she struggled to practice her profession in spite of all the obstacles in her way, lack of money and so on. I'm very fond of her animal sculptures. She hasn't done many sculptures of people. They're all so tremendously animated. You're planning to buy the Polo Player and the Daphne, aren't you?"

16. Mathilde Pflanz, whom Hans's parents had employed as a maid-servant when he was a small boy.

17. It is clear from Hans Scholl's letters in the ensuing months that he was not assigned to Ludwigsburg after all, but to the base hospital at Tübingen.

18. Hans Scholl debated the merits of several universities, including Freiburg and Tübingen as well as Munich. On his release from the army in the spring of 1939, he enrolled as a full-time student of medicine at Munich's Ludwig-Maximilian-Universität.

19. *Eine Mauer um uns baue . . .* in an edition produced by the Mainzer Werkstatt für Buchdruck. Hans Scholl inscribed it for his sister with a quotation from Rilke: "He that holds his peace is wise, but he that speaks, speaks not for his own time." The friend of Wiechert's in Stuttgart was probably Gerhard Huber, owner of Stahl's bookstore at 15 Poststrasse, who had invited Ernst Wiechert to a public reading at the Haus des Auslandsdeutschtums, Charlottenplatz, on November 13, 1937.

Ernst Wiechert had been released on August 30, 1938, from Buchenwald concentration camp, to which he had been sent at the beginning of July 1938, after being arrested on May 6 and remanded in custody for several weeks.

The immediate reason for the Gestapo's intervention had been Wiechert's public protest against Martin Niemöller's arrest and his refusal to participate in the so-called plebiscite of April 4, 1938, which was designed to endorse Hitler's annexation of Austria after the event. Wiechert had first aroused the authorities' displeasure in April 1935, when he gave a lecture in the main auditorium at Munich University. Delivered under the auspices of the National Socialist Cultural Association, it was entitled "The Writer and His Time." He was regarded as an undesirable element from then on.

Notes | 319

It is uncertain which book Hans Scholl meant when he stated that Wiechert's "latest book is banned from publication." No publication ban was ever imposed on Ernst Wiechert under the Third Reich. Stories of his were published in 1938 by Piper (Munich) and Grote (Berlin); on November 4, 1938, just three months after his release from Buchenwald, Heinz Hilpert premièred his play, *Der verlorene Sohn*, at the Deutsches Theater in Berlin; *Das einfache Leben*, a novel completed on January 23, 1939, was published the same year by Langen-Müller of Munich and had sold over a quarter of a million copies by 1942. (For further information about Wiechert see Guido Reiner, *Ernst Wiechert im dritten Reich: Eine Dokumentation*, published by the author, 1974.)

20. A slip of the pen. Hans Scholl was referring to Hans Carossa's lecture to the Goethe-Gesellschaft at Weimar on June 8, 1938, "Wirkungen Goethes in der Gegenwart," which Insel-Verlag had published the same year in booklet form.

21. Ernst Karl von Baumbach, a friend of Hans Scholl's from Ulm.

22. The dead man's sister, a friend of the Scholl girls'.

23. Hanns Rückert of Tübingen (1901–1974), the ecclesiastical historian.

24. Hans Scholl had to prepare for his proficiency examination in that language.

25. The father of one of the young Scholls' girlfriends, who owned a well-known photographic shop in Ulm. Some of the townsfolk decried and ostracized him as a "Jewish lackey" for defying Nazi propaganda and continuing to serve his Jewish customers.

26. Sophie Scholl's projected trip to Yugoslavia with Fritz Hartnagel (see her letter to him of July 28, 1939, page 37).

Sophie Scholl, 1937–1939

27. A village near Oberstaufen im Allgäu, where the young Scholls proposed to spend several days at a skiing lodge after Christmas.

28. Charlotte Thurau, a Junior Girls' Hitler Youth leader from Ulm, whom the Scholl sisters much admired.

29. Inge began work as a governess for the Eggers family at Lesum, near Bremen, in 1938.

30. Erika Reiff, a friend of the young Scholls' from Ulm.

31. Dr. Else Fries, Sophie's biology teacher, with whom she remained on friendly terms after leaving school.

32. Daughters of the family for whom Inge was working. Sophie had already mentioned this plan for a communal excursion to her friend Lisa Remppis in a letter dated May 19, 1938: "Inge suggests we go to Lesum this summer. Then she'll be able to come touring for a week with the two daughters, Susi (eighteen), who's going to be an actress, and Annelieschen (sixteen), a budding violin teacher. It's bound to be tremendous fun. It was a wonderful idea and a brainwave on the Eggers' part!"

33. An art teacher at Sophie's school.

34. Manfred Kyber (1880–1933), *Gesammelte Tiergeschichten*, Leipzig, 1922.

35. Martha Vogeler (1879–1961), wife of Heinrich Vogeler, a painter and graphic artist who had emigrated to Russia in 1923 and died there at seventy in 1942, had her own weaving mill at Worpswede.

36. The painter Paula Modersohn-Becker (1876–1907).

37. The painter Lovis Corinth (1858–1925). Sophie's visit to the Kunsthalle at Hamburg was her first introduction to his work.

38. Unidentifiable.

39. Housemother of the Worpswede youth hostel.

40. Hanspeter Nägele had retranslated *Peter Pan* by J. M. Barrie (1860–1937) and asked Sophie to supply the illustrations for a projected new edition. Individual drawings from the series, which survived the war, are reproduced in Vinke, op. cit.

41. Hermann Vinke, op. cit., p. 67.

42. Hans Scholl was into his second semester (reduced to a trimester) as a medical student at Munich University. (See his letter dated December 1, 1939, page 43.)

43. In addition to producing drawings for Hanspeter Nägele's translation of *Peter Pan*, Sophie was engaged in illustrating *Ein Nachmittag*, a story by Georg Heym (1887–1912), at the request of Ernst Reden, her sister Inge's friend, who was planning to publish it.

44. Insel-Verlag, Leipzig, 1933.

45. The Bund Deutscher Mädchen, the branch of the Hitler Youth for girls age fourteen and over. Girls age ten to fourteen were enrolled in the JM, or Jungmädel.

46. Unidentifiable.

47. See note 43.

Hans Scholl, 1939–1940

48. While reminiscing over his diary, Hans Scholl may here have been
identifying with various modes of existence sampled during his
vacations. A letter from Inge Aicher-Scholl alludes to the restlessness
these images convey, which was one of her brother's principal traits:
"The rover and adventurer are restless souls, unpredictable both
to others and to themselves, impelled by an unfathomable urge for
independence whose negative side can be rootlessness, homelessness,
and loneliness. Associated with the rover and adventurer is the
lumberjack, likewise the fisherman, who often recurs in Hans's life:
the poor, undemanding individual who lives from hand to mouth,
without ballast, similarly independent in his strength or quiet composure. One is here reminded of the parable of the prodigal son."

49. The parents of Hans Scholl's friend and fellow student Hellmut
Hartert owned a vacation house at Bad Tölz, where Hans spent many
weekends during the winter of 1939–1940. After the war, Hellmut
Hartert recalled his friendship with Hans and their joint visits to
Tölz in a letter to Inge Aicher-Scholl dated February 26, 1946:

> I got to know Hans at Munich in 1939. We enrolled the same
> semester. My only friend in Munich at that stage was Peter Kiehl
> from Berlin. Hans and I took to one another greatly, and I soon
> formed a closer friendship with him than I had ever known
> before. To begin with, our main interest in common was modern
> literature, notably modern French writers like Bernanos, Jammes,
> Claudel, etc. We were together all day long, and eventually moved
> into a small attic room at 4 Athenerplatz, Harlaching. We already
> entertained some very definite political views but didn't seriously
> consider engaging in any form of agitation, unless you count our
> more or less jocular discussions with Jürgen Wittgenstein, whom
> I also got to know at this time, about the best way to kill Hitler.
>
> Hans and I often visited my parents' vacation house at Bad
> Tölz and went on cycle tours from there. It was there, too, that I
> introduced Hans to Professor Borchers, a friend of my father's.
> He fell passionately in love with the daughter, Ute, when we
> spent several weeks at Tölz during the winter. We were often cut
> off from the outside world for days on end by storms and snow.
> Among our other literary efforts at this period were preliminary
> drafts for appeals to the young people of Germany, prompted by
> the growth of conscription for military service and an extremely
> unpleasant speech addressed to young people by a Hitler Youth
> leader. In March 1940 we were both drafted. We shared the same
> barrack room and were initially sent on assignments together. We

weren't strictly confined to barracks at this early stage in our war service, and had only to turn out for musters at longish intervals. Meantime, Hans and I went off on long cycle tours, most of them starting at Tölz. On the trip I recall most vividly we spent several days as guests of the St. Ottilien Monastery on the Ammersee, where Hans knew the father librarian. We also made the acquaintance of a very modern-minded cardinal, who showed us some magnificent Leica photographs when we told him we planned to bring out a small book containing Leica photographs of the woodcarvings in Bavarian baroque churches.

50. Probably at the home of Hartert's friends, the Borchers family mentioned above. An extant letter from Hans to his parents, dated June 9, 1941, describes a similar excursion:

> Over the weekend I went on a wonderful cycle tour of the upper Isar valley. It rained so hard on the way back that I got soaked to the skin and had to stop. It wasn't far to Tölz, luckily, so I took refuge with the Borchers, where I received a rousing welcome, changed my clothes, and hung the old ones up to dry beside the fireplace, in which a huge fire had been lighted. We all sat around the open fire and told tall stories. It was very pleasant. After a positively peacetime lunch, we played all kinds of party games in the garden till coffee time. Then I rode on.

51. *Ortsunterkunft,* or simply "billet," the conventional military address in wartime. Hans Scholl's letter to his parents dated May 2 indicates that it here stood for Bad Sooden.

52. For further information about Ernst Reden, see Hanser, op. cit., pp. 66–67, and Krebs, op. cit., pp. 55ff.

53. This numbering resulted from the introduction of three-term academic years.

54. Ernst Jünger (b. 1895).

55. Fragment 53: "War is the father of all things, of all things king. Some it shows to be gods, others men; some it makes slaves, others free."

56. On May 27, Sophie Scholl relayed Hans's news to her boyfriend Fritz Hartnagel: "Hans has already written twice in cheerful vein. He's a dispatch rider. They must be in France by now. His last letter was from Neufchâteau. He appears to be getting along fine with the local inhabitants (this means a lot to Hans) and is acting as interpreter for the entire unit!"

57. Georges Bernanos, 1936. (English translation, *Diary of a Country Priest,* 1937.)

58. Georges Bernanos, *Sous le soleil de Satan,* 1926. (English translation, *The Star of Satan,* 1940.)

59. A cheap 6 × 6 box camera, superficially but not technically similar to a reflex camera.

60. Lion, Hans Scholl's puppy.

61. Hugo (1802–1885), compelled to emigrate to the Channel Islands after Napoleon III's coup d'état, was unable to return home until 1870, when the Second Empire fell.

62. Gide (1869–1951) withdrew to the unoccupied zone after the fall of France in 1940 and became an associate of Les Éditions de Minuit, the Resistance press.

63. The French novelist Georges Bernanos (1888–1948), one of the chief pioneers of the Renouveau Catholique. His "Lettre aux Anglais," written at the outbreak of World War II, fiercely attacked Hitler's expansionist policies.

64. Like Paul Claudel, Léon Bloy, Julien Green, and François Mauriac, the French novelist and poet Francis Jammes (1868–1938) was an adherent of the Renouveau Catholique, a philosophical, sociocritical, and literary movement founded at the end of the nineteenth century. Its aim was to revive the French ethos in the light of Roman Catholic tradition.

Sophie Scholl, 1939–1940

65. Christian Mergenthaler, provincial premier and education minister of Württemberg since 1933.

66. A classmate of Sophie Scholl's whom Fritz Hartnagel had met at dance classes.

67. Fritz Hartnagel's unit had been transferred around Christmas 1939, first from Calw in the Black Forest to Düsseldorf and later to Gelsenkirchen.

68. Hans Scholl and Hanspeter Nägele.

69. The Scholls had an apartment on Münsterplatz, Ulm. Klaus Rennicke, then three years old, was the son of some neighbors who lived in the same building. Many Klaus anecdotes occur in Sophie's letters at this period. Peter was Klaus's brother.

70. Sister of Sophie's friend Lu Hörsch.

71. A toy construction kit.

72. According to Inge Aicher-Scholl, this quotation from Goethe was a kind of family motto. Abbreviated to the single word *"Allen!"* it was often used by one member of the family to encourage another. Hans Scholl scribbled the poem on the wall of his cell before being conducted to the courtroom for trial. The full text is as follows:

> *Feiger Gedanken* *Allen Gewalten*
> *Bängliches Schwanken* *Zum Trutz sich erhalten,*
> *Weibisches Zagen* *Nimmer sich beugen*
> *Ängstliches Klagen* *Kräftig sich zeigen*
> *Wendet kein Elend* *Rufet die Arme*
> *Macht dich nicht frei.* *der Götter herbei.*

[Craven thoughts and of timid vacillation, unmanly dread and fearful lamentation can avert no affliction nor render you free. Stand firm against all the powers that be, never yield, be strong, summon the arms of the gods to your aid.]

73. Cf. Vinke, op. cit., pp. 71–74.

74. Exodus 17:11–12: "And it came to pass, when Moses held up his hand, that Israel prevailed: and when he let down his hand, Amalek prevailed. But Moses' hands were heavy; and they took a stone, and put it under him, and he sat thereon; and Aaron and Hûr stayed up his hands, the one on the one side, and the other on the other side; and his hands were steady until the going down of the sun."

75. Cf. Hans Scholl's letter dated July 12, 1940.

76. Probably an allusion to Italy's entry into the war. Mussolini had declared war on June 10, 1940, when France was already defeated. On June 24, two days after the Franco-German armistice was signed at Compiègne, war between Italy and France ended too.

77. A wry allusion to general expectations that after the defeat of France, Britain would be invaded.

78. An elliptical reference to a saying coined by Hans, which had become part of the young Scholls' stock vocabulary: "Be glad it's raining. If you aren't glad, it'll rain anyway." The family often employed it as an antidote to minor irritations.

79. Sophie's subsequent letters indicate that she went to Bad Dürrheim, near Donaueschingen, not to the northern part of the Black Forest.

80. Unidentifiable.

81. Gottfried Dinkelacker, a small boy whom Elisabeth Scholl was temporarily looking after. His father was a parson at Suppingen.

82. To start training as a children's nurse.

83. Rainer Maria Rilke, *Das Stundenbuch, enthaltend die drei Bücher: Vom mönkischen Leben, Von der Pilgerschaft, Von der Armut und dem Tode*, Insel-Verlag, Leipzig, 1905, and many subsequent editions.

84. "Can love be a sin?" The opening words of a song sung by Zarah Leander in the movie *Es war eine rauschende Ballnacht* (1939). It proved an immediate hit.

85. A mountain near Steeg in the Tyrol.

86. Sophie Scholl's talent for the graphic arts was above average. The numerous examples of her work that survived the war include portraits of children as well as her oft-cited illustrations for Hanspeter Nägele's *Peter Pan* and Georg Heym's *Nachmittag*. Some of these are reproduced in Hermann Vinke, op. cit., together with an account by Inge Aicher-Scholl of the influence exerted on Sophie's work by Bertl Kley, Wilhelm Geyer, and Otl Aicher. Sophie's own letters frequently refer to her experiments with various techniques.

87. While based in France, Fritz Hartnagel had made several trips to Amsterdam on duty. After one of these, in March 1941, he must have told Sophie about the Germans' anti-Jewish measures in that occupied city. Sophie's reply reflected the same uncompromising mental attitude as that which Fritz Hartnagel cited to Hermann Vinke (op. cit., p. 74ff.) as having stimulated his own development of political maturity: "I can only welcome the fact that they're being as ruthless everywhere [as in Amsterdam]. It confuses one's perception of the whole issue less than if one came across a mixture of good and bad and didn't know which was the real thing." (Sophie to Fritz Hartnagel on March 7, 1941.)

Hans Scholl, 1940–1941

88. Hans Scholl had a prepared skull at home in Ulm.

89. See Hans's letter of March 19, 1940, page 48, and note 49.

90. Landlords of Hans Scholl's Athenerplatz lodgings.

91. Hans Scholl's landlady in Amalienstrasse, where he rented a room when he first entered the university.

92. Hans Scholl was reading James Joyce's novel in the two-volume German translation by Georg Goyert, published in 1930 by Rhein-Verlag, Zurich/Munich.

93. Ute Borchers. See Hellmut Hartert's letter cited in note 49.

94. Olga Habler, a singer at Ulm's municipal theater and a staunch opponent of the National Socialist regime. She was a friend of the young Scholls' and occasionally gave informal house concerts at their Münsterplatz apartment.

95. Fair copies of Robert Scholl's annual accounts.

96. Swiss journalist (1901–1974), far east correspondent of the *Frankfurter Zeitung* from 1936 to 1943, subsequently on the editorial staff of the *Frankfurter Allgemeine Zeitung.*

97. At the home of Major Wagner, 9 St. Paulsstrasse.

98. Rainer Maria Rilke (1875–1926), *Die frühen Gedichte,* Insel-Verlag, Leipzig, 1909 [*Mir zur Feier,* poems, Berlin, 1899].

99. Herman Grimm (1828–1901), *Michelangelo,* 2 vols., 1860–1863, and many subsequent editions.

100. Romano Guardini (1885–1968), *Weltbild und Frömmigkeit,* 1939.

101. Ignaz Günther (1725–c. 1775), German rococo sculptor and wood-carver whose chief works, apart from Weyarn, include the decoration of the former Benedictine abbey at Rott am Inn and the parish church at Starnberg.

102. Wilhelm Geyer, the Ulm painter, was a family friend of the Scholls'. See Geyer's account in Aicher-Scholl, op. cit., p. 207ff.; Hanser, op. cit., pp. 241 and 259; and Christian Petry, *Studenten aufs Schafott* (Verlag R. Piper und Co., Munich, 1968), pp. 115–18.

103. Pus discharged from a draining wound was once regarded as a sign that the injury was healing.

104. A cordial handshake.

105. Inge Aicher-Scholl confirms this figure of speech, which appears in a letter dated April 14, 1941, from Robert Scholl to his daughter Sophie:

> Lately I'm of the opinion that the war will last somewhat longer. From a superficial aspect the barometer has risen a little and may rise a little more in the immediate future, but a change is absolutely inevitable. The development of any given process is as completely unaffected by intermediate episodes as a river in flood is unaffected by the backup of water upstream and in its tributaries.

106. Blaise Pascal (1623–1662), *Pensées: Fragmente zu einer Apologie des Christentums,* 1904, the still-definitive German edition, edited by Brunschwicg.

107. Alois Dempf (1891–1982), *Christliche Philosophie*, 1938.

108. Rainer Maria Rilke (1875–1926), *Briefe aus Muzot* 1921–1926, Insel-Verlag, Leipzig, 1936.

Sophie Scholl, 1940–1941

109. A novel published in 1933 by Karl Benno von Mechow (1897–1960). Mechow, who coedited the (temporarily banned) review *Das innere Reich* with Paul Alvardes between 1934 and 1944, was an author much admired by the young Scholls. (See Hans Scholl to Sophie on March 9, 1941: "The *Frankfurter* is currently serializing Mechow's very fine *Novelle auf Sizilien*. It makes edifying reading. It's so good to be able to approve of an author with genuine, wholehearted enthusiasm.")

110. Psalms 13:3. Inge Aicher-Scholl recalls that this psalm was one of the Ulm circle's favorite texts.

111. The winter vacations were regularly prolonged in wartime to save fuel.

112. Emma Kretschmer, sister of the Tübingen psychiatrist Ernst Kretschmer, ran the Fröbel courses at Ulm.

113. *Augustinus: Die Gestalt als Gefüge*, Jakob Hegner, Leipzig, 1934, a selection annotated by Erich Przywara, S.J.

114. The two-volume edition of 1924.

115. "One must have a hard mind and a soft heart." Otl Aicher had introduced the Ulm circle to this quotation from Jacques Maritain, and it became a kind of motto. Explaining its significance, Inge Aicher-Scholl called it "a little fixed star in our religious history" and cited a passage from Maritain's last book, *Le paysan de la Garonne:* "I once told Jean Cocteau: 'One must have a hard head and a soft heart.' Sadly, I added that the world was full of hard hearts and soft 'beans.' You have to be particularly wary of this in ecumenical discussions."

116. Hans Scholl was a friend of Lisa's.

117. An evacuee from the Rhineland who had been billeted with the Scholl family.

118. Francis Jammes, *Ma fille Bernadette*, 1910; first German translation 1927.

119. One of Otl Aicher's contributions to *Windlicht* was an essay entitled "Die Philosophen." It dealt with the spiritual and intellectual status in Athens of Socrates, Plato, and Aristotle.

120. Sir James Jeans (1877–1946), *The Universe Around Us* (1929), German edition 1931. Otl Aicher stated in 1983 that, where the sciences were concerned, the Ulm circle preferred to read and discuss books whose interest lay in their formulation of philosophical problems. In this context he cited works by the biologist Hans Driesch, the physicists Arthur Eddington, Niels Bohr, Louis de Broglie, and Werner Heisenberg, and the astronomer James Jeans. He also drew attention to Sophie Scholl's choice of subjects at Munich University: biology and philosophy.

121. Unidentifiable.

122. German: *Internat*, here used for its "internment" connotation.

123. George Bernard Shaw's *Saint Joan*, translated into German by Siegfried Trebitsch, S. Fischer, 1924.

124. Gisela Schertling (b. 1922). Later, while studying at Munich, she became a friend of Hans Scholl's and was sentenced to twelve months' imprisonment for "failure to denounce" at the second White Rose hearing of the People's Court.

125. Sophie gave a detailed description of these surreptitious visits to the church in a letter to her sister Elisabeth dated August 29, 1941:

> Saturday afternoon all I did was wait for you. In the evening I went for a bit of a stroll in the village with a friend, and we suddenly hit on the idea of playing the organ. Once we'd obtained the priest's permission and the key, we played and sang till it was time for bed. The next morning we went off to early Mass at 6:30, just the two of us. Any later and we'd have been spotted, and church attendance is forbidden. (We sleep in on Sunday mornings.) Afterward we went back to bed, and that afternoon we played the organ again. Later we cycled to Sigmaringendorf for outside work, by way of our lovely old route. We had to be back by eight. Really nice, eh?

126. She had already expressed similar sentiments when writing to her sister Inge on June 23, 1941: "Yesterday evening Gisela and Trude and I sat behind a haystack, smoking in a mood of childish defiance. Ridiculous it may be, but this act (and it is an act) gives you a Götz von Berlichingen feeling. If you can't do something straight out, do it in a roundabout way." ["Götz von Berlichingen" is a polite reference to Goethe's drama of that name, in particular to a specific line from the play that translates, "Kiss my ass."]

127. Eckart Peterich (1900–1968), *Sonette einer Griechin*, Freiburg, 1940.

Hans Scholl: Summer–Fall 1941

128. Alexander Schmorell collaborated with Hans Scholl in drafting the first White Rose handbills during the summer of 1942. In the ensuing period he played a leading and decisive part in all of the circle's ventures, nocturnal slogan-painting expeditions included. On February 18, 1943, after Hans and Sophie Scholl had been arrested, he sought refuge with a friend of his, the painter Lilo Ramdohr, who forged him some papers with the aid of a woman bookbinder resident in the same building. Alexander planned to pass for a Russian-born Yugoslav and go underground in a Russian PW camp near Innsbruck. This scheme was thwarted by an unlucky combination of circumstances. By now a wanted man, he returned to Munich, where – according to Frau Ramdohr – he was recognized and detained by two antiaircraft gunners in an air raid shelter near the central railroad station. Other sources state that he was inadvertently betrayed by a female fellow student in whose cellar on Habsburger Platz he had sheltered during an air raid.

   Alexander Schmorell was arrested on February 24, 1943. Together with Willi Graf and Kurt Huber, he was condemned to death barely two months later by the People's Court under Roland Freisler.

129. At 4 Athenerplatz, Harlaching. (See notes 49, 50, and 89.)

130. The pianist Elly Ney (1882–1963).

131. Piano composition by Franz Schubert (op. 15).

132. The extension of Sophie Scholl's stint in the Arbeitsdienst ended her hopes of joining Hans at Munich University for the winter semester 1941–1942. (See also Sophie's letters of August 2, 4, and 16, 1941, page 156, page 157, and page 159.)

133. Virgil, *Georgics*, I, 145: *labor [omnia vincit] improbus* [unremitting toil conquers all things].

134. Genesis 3:19: "In the sweat of thy face shalt thou eat bread. . . ."

135. *Das Jahr der schönen Täuschungen*, Insel-Verlag, Leipzig, 1941.

136. Unidentifiable.

137. Sophie would ordinarily have completed her Arbeitsdienst service on October 1, 1941, and the Scholl family still hoped they could obtain her recall to Ulm to help at home.

138. Miniature camera manufactured by the German Kodak factory at Stuttgart.

139. French philosopher (1884–1978), whose principal field of research was medieval philosophy. A German translation of the book mentioned here, *Introduction à l'étude de Saint Augustin* (1929), had appeared in 1930.

140. Dante's *Divina Commedia* in the German translation by Stefan George, Berlin, 1925.

141. Nickname of Wilhelm Habermann, a friend from Ulm and contributor of poems to *Windlicht*.

142. One of Hans Scholl's classmates at Ulm.

143. The Benedictine abbey of Melk on the Danube.

144. Youth movement pseudonyms for Sepp and Karl Saur, twin brothers from Ulm. Having belonged to the dj-1/11 in 1935, they were arrested, questioned, and detained with the Scholls in 1937.

145. Léon Bloy (1846–1917), French novelist and leading light of the Renouveau Catholique. *Das Blut des Armen,* the first German edition of Bloy's *Le Sang du Pauvre,* completed in 1909, was published in 1937 by Pustet of Salzburg, translated by Clemens ten Wolder with a foreword by Karl Pfleger entitled "Das Mysterium der Armut bei Léon Bloy."

    Among the *Windlicht* relics Inge Aicher-Scholl found a copy of Bloy's diary entries on the subject of poverty taken from Pfleger's introduction. They included the following passage:

    > I am the anvil in the deepest abyss, the anvil of God, who causes me to suffer so because he loves me, that I know full well.
    > The anvil of God in the nethermost abyss! So be it. That is the [proper place from which to groan up at Him. All that happens is worthy of adoration, entirely worthy of adoration, and I am scalded by tears].

146. *Pèlerin de l'Absolu,* title of the sixth volume of Léon Bloy's diaries, published in 1914. *Bloy, Pilger des Absoluten* is also the title of one of a collection of essays by Karl Pfleger, *Geister, die um Christus ringen,* published in 1934 and containing pieces on Péguy, Gide, Chesterton, Dostoyevsky, Soloviev, and Berdyaev. This did much to further Bloy's adoption by German Catholic intellectuals opposed to the regime. It is fair to assume that Hans Scholl had been introduced to this book by Carl Muth, and that he was citing Pfleger's title. This supposition is reinforced by his subsequent allusion to Berdyaev.

147. Nikolai Aleksandrovich Berdyaev (1874–1948), Russian philosopher. Under the influence of Jakob Böhme and Dostoyevsky, he abandoned an initially Marxist position and turned to mystical Christianity.

Berdyaev, who had studied at Heidelberg under Windelband, lost his Moscow chair of philosophy in 1922. He then spent two years in Berlin, where he founded a religiophilosophical academy, but moved to Paris in 1924 and lived there until his death. His *Das neue Mittelalter: Betrachtungen über das Schicksal Rußlands und Europas* was published by Otto-Reiche-Verlag in Darmstadt, 1927; *Die menschliche Persönlichkeit und die überpersönlichen Werte,* by Bermann-Fischer-Verlag in Vienna, 1937. Hans Scholl inscribed his copy of the latter work with Christ's words from Matthew (26:52): "'All they that take the sword shall perish with the sword.' In the wartime year of 1941."

148. Alsace and former province bordering Germany.

149. Looking back on the origins and objectives of this amateur periodical, which resembled a literary review, Inge Aicher-Scholl writes:

> As far as I can recall, we launched this circular letter, which we christened *Windlicht,* sometime in the summer of 1941 . . . Our circle, which ranged in age from eighteen to twenty-three, consisted mainly of friends from Ulm who were striving, like my brothers and sisters, to base their attitude on a firm spiritual foundation and shield their questions and problems from the tempest of spiritual terrorism raging in the soul-destroying environment of the political system.
>
> The members of our circle, around ten young people in all, had been scattered throughout Europe by the war: on the Russian front – Pripet Marshes, Caucasus – or the Western front – Brittany, Guernsey – or in Munich, where they divided their time on call between the university, the barracks, and the hospital; in the Upper Danube Valley as labor corps conscripts, or at my father's office in Ulm, where I myself was working. We felt badly in need of the contact supplied by *Windlicht* if we were to endure those dark days. All recipients of the circular letter had undertaken to collaborate on it, if only by commenting on other people's articles, or contributing book reviews, etc., or copying out some poem to which the others no longer had access. Hans obtained contributions for us – mostly unpublished – from Professor Muth, Theodor Haecker, Sigismund von Radecki, and others, together with translations by Muth of excerpts from manuscripts by contemporary French authors. To us, in our hermetically sealed environment, this modest peephole into a wider world was a boon. Hans was inspired to write one article using information from Carl Muth about the Turin Shroud and a photograph of the same. Sophie agonized over an essay on the significance of music to mankind.

Grogo contributed poems of his own, and Otl churned out pieces on philosophical and theological subjects. . . .

I don't think more than two or three issues of this circular letter had been produced when I returned to our apartment after visiting Hans in Munich, one Monday morning in February 1942, and ran straight into the Gestapo with the latest issue of *Windlicht* in my little traveling bag. The Gestapo officer, Herr R., ordered me to accompany him, bag and all, to the Gestapo's Neuer Bau headquarters, where I was promptly interrogated. To my surprise, his secretary turned out to be a former classmate of mine. When Herr R. left the room for a moment, I impulsively decided to ask her if I might remove a personally compromising sheet from the folder. Though unable to give me explicit permission, she jumped up and went to the telephone in the adjoining office. I was instantly seized with uncharacteristic coolness and sangfroid. Grabbing hold of the piece on Napoleon, which was strongly reminiscent of Hitler, I crumpled the wretched piece of paper into an unrecognizable ball and slipped it into my purse.

We later learned from a friend of my father's, who had once been at university with the then Gestapo chief of Württemberg, that anyone who persisted in [free] youth movement activities – and *Windlicht* could have been construed as such – was liable to sixteen years' imprisonment. That was the end of this innocent creative endeavor to keep our communal lamp alight and shield it from the hurricane. We had to renounce it just when Hans was seeking to involve his Munich friends in the venture. How greatly it would have been enriched by talented writers like Christl Probst or Willi Graf, Traute Lafrenz, and others! The first of the White Rose handbills appeared four months later, but that was designed for public effect, not private, and fraught with harsher consequences than a "lenient" sentence of sixteen years' imprisonment.

150. This plan was formally adopted two months later, on January 20, 1942, at the so-called Wannsee Conference chaired by SS Gruppenführer Reinhard Heydrich [second in command to Himmler] and expressly confirmed by Hitler in his speeches of January 30 and February 24.

Theodor Haecker, Carl Muth's friend and comrade in arms, had already recorded an apocalyptic interpretation of these measures in his diary on September 13, 1941:

It was announced today that from September 19 every Jew must wear on the left-hand side of his outer clothing a yellow star, the star of David, the great king of whose line the Son of Man, Jesus

Christ, the second person of the Trinity, was born. The time may come when Germans abroad have to wear a swastika, in other words, the emblem of the Antichrist, on the left-hand side of their outer clothing. Through their persecution of the Jews, the Germans are inwardly drawing ever closer to the Jews and their destiny. After all, they're crucifying Christ a second time today, as a *people!* Isn't it probable that they will also have to live through similar consequences?

A year later, the White Rose handbills enlisted similar interpretations in proclaiming it "the moral duty" of all Germans to dissociate themselves from the guilty parties.

151. Presumably the piece entitled "On Poverty."

152. It has proved impossible to find or reconstruct this.

153. Carl Muth (1867–1944), Catholic journalist, founder and for almost forty years (1903–1941) editor of *Hochland,* a periodical devoted to the dialogue between devout Roman Catholics and prominent artists and scholars. *Hochland* very soon became the principal forum at which progressive Catholics debated topical issues of a literary, social, philosophical, political, and theological complexion. To cite Walter Dirks' "Nachruf auf Karl Muth" in *Frankfurter Hefte,* vol. I (1946), p. 9ff.: "In this monthly, German Catholicism overcame its inferiority. For forty-odd years it inspired and fortified two whole generations of educated Catholics."

   Founded with the intention of extricating [German] Catholicism from the cultural ghetto in which it had resided since 1866, politically in consequence of growing Protestant and Prussian dominance, and theologically because of the Vatican's rigidly antimodernist stance, *Hochland* continued, even after 1933, to preserve its characteristic independence and critical detachment. In July 1941 the National Socialist authorities banned this periodical, whose status was such, in the words of Walter Dirks, "that it contrived to imbue hearts and minds with productive disquiet while simultaneously rendering their faith more assured and confident."

   By the fall of 1941, when Hans Scholl first met Carl Muth through the good offices of his friend Otl Aicher, *Hochland* had ceased to exist. Werner Bergengruen's "Erinnerungen an Carl Muth," *Hochland,* vol. 46 (1953–1954), p. 57, stresses Muth's "bent and talent for teaching" and his "passion for molding the people around him . . . in his own image." Just when the banning of his periodical had deprived him of an outlet for that urge, he encountered, in Hans Scholl, a young man who must have impressed him as a kindred spirit in many respects. Both loved literature, especially French literature, just as both had a liberal cast of mind and a capacity for spontaneous enthusiasm. Was it any wonder that Muth, already in his seventies, should have cultivated the young Scholls and their friends when he realized that he could trust them politically as well? That he should have encouraged them in every possible way, discoursed with them, given them books to read, tutored them in theology, and introduced them to people from whom they could learn? "I presume that Hans will have told you about his afternoon with Professor Alfred von Martin and his family, when the Stepuns were there," Muth wrote to Otl Aicher on February 28, 1942. "If he remains here this summer, his circle of acquaintances will become much wider still. Then he'll get to know Catholics of a caliber he's seldom come into personal contact with before."

Further insights into Muth's character can be gleaned, not only from the works listed in the acknowledgments to the present book and the previously cited articles by Dirks and Bergengruen, but also from Franz Joseph Schöningh's obituary, "Carl Muth: Ein europäisches Vermächtnis," *Hochland*, vol. 39 (1946–1947), p. 1ff. and pp. 17–18, and relevant passages in Hanser, Aicher-Scholl, Petry, and Krebs, op. cit. Schöningh, who worked closely with Muth on *Hochland*, confirmed what Bergengruen felt about him, namely, that:

> . . . he was able, throughout his life, not only to understand the concerns of the younger generation, but to share them in a loving manner. This was especially evident in the septuagenarian's frequent endeavors to make the acquaintance of young men, explore their ideas and aspirations, and enlighten and encourage them by dint of serious conversation and correspondence. Even after *Hochland* had been suppressed, Muth still had his young "associates" just as he used, when still editing it, to lavish solicitude and encouragement on all the gifted young people who came his way, even more for their own sake than for that of *Hochland*.

Among those young people was Hans Scholl, that martyred testimony to the existence of a secret Germany. During the summer of 1942, when he was cataloging Muth's library, Scholl and the elderly scholar held long and almost daily conversations that confirmed the younger man in his Christian-German opposition to an inhuman regime. Scholl and many of his contemporaries prevented Muth from losing hope that the German people, purified by the dire suffering in store for it, would rediscover its own character and regain its "European and Christian" conscience – a hope he had vainly cherished during World War I. After Hans Scholl's arrest, Muth . . . was distressed less by the house searches he had to endure and the fears he had to entertain for his own safety than by the news of the young man's death. . . . [He] spoke of him and his sister – he spoke of all the young, openly or mutely protesting people who were falling prey to the greatest strategist [Hitler's description of himself] and executioner of all time – with the sorrow of a bereaved father . . .

154. Carl Muth had persuaded Hans Scholl to reorganize and catalog his vast private library, as witness his letter to Otl Aicher dated October 24, 1941:

> I shall also be writing to your friend the medical student, because Inge has informed me that her brother is free and will gladly help to catalog my library. You see how much help you mobilized for me when you yourself had to go away? I shall thank you *ante faciem Dei* [before the face of God]!

In the ensuing period, Hans Scholl spent many hours at Muth's house, which he frequented almost daily. (Carl Muth to Otl Aicher, December 19, 1941: "Hans is a frequent visitor and a dear and much appreciated friend of the house. He often stays for meals, too, and comes into contact with a variety of people who interest him." April 3, 1942: "Last week Hans rearranged the entire series of *Hochland* issues and bound volumes.")

155. See note 179.

156. N. A. Berdyaev, *Die Philosophie des freien Geistes*, first published 1927, German translation 1930.

157. A relic preserved at Turin and revered as the shroud of Christ. A photograph taken in 1898 caused a furor when the negative revealed the impression of a human body whose owner had died in agony. The question of the relic's authenticity was debated with particular vehemence during the 1930s, when Giuseppe Enrie took another series of photographs employing more sophisticated techniques. These photographs, which received worldwide publicity, prompted physicians, chemists, and ethnologists to join in the debate. A German edition of Enrie's volume of plates had appeared in 1939, and Hans Scholl must have seen it at Carl Muth's house. At all events, a letter from Muth to Otl Aicher implies that Otl had requested a photograph of the relic at Hans's suggestion, possibly for inclusion in *Windlicht*. Muth wrote on January 2, 1942: "Herewith the face of Christ from the Turin Shroud. I never saw anyone as engrossed as Sophie Scholl was today in the big picture in the main volume I have here. It made an impression on me. She seems to be a very thoughtful and serious girl."

We cannot ascertain whether Hans Scholl had come across the book by chance while reorganizing his mentor's library, or whether

Muth had drawn his attention to the debate rekindled by Dr. Ralph Waldo Hynek's article in the *Eichstätter Klerusblatt* of September 10, 1941 (vol. 22, no. 37), which defended the shroud's authenticity against the results of recent research. What is certain is that Hans himself had absolutely no doubt that the relic was genuine. He devoted letters and notes to the history and, more particularly, to the effect of what he regarded as a unique historical document. Found among his papers was a letter ("B. 16. August 1935") dealing with the significance of the shroud to contemporary Christianity: the translation of a letter from Paul Claudel to M. Girard-Cordonnier, Brangues par Morestes (Isère), dated August 16, 1935, and included in a Paul Claudel booklet, *Toi, qui est-tu?* (Collection Catholique, Gallimard, Paris, 1936), under the title "La Photographie du Christ" (from *Position et Proposition*, vol. 2). The *Windlicht* article, which Hans deliberately prefaced with a Claudel dictum, "Night had to be, that this lamp might appear," is further evidence of how deeply moved he was by what he firmly believed to be the only palpable evidence of Christ's Passion.

Sophie Scholl, Fall 1941

158. Nationalsozialistische Volksversorgung.

159. Either *Über das Verhältnis der Poesie zur Religion* by Martin Deutinger, Augsburg, 1861, which Carl Muth had republished in 1915, or Deutinger's *Im Geist und in der Wahrheit,* which is still in the Scholl library. Inge Aicher-Scholl states that the latter had a considerable influence on her circle at the time. See also Sophie's draft letter (undated, November/December 1941) on page 192.

160. This visit is mentioned in an extant letter from Carl Muth to Otl Aicher: "The Pascal head is still lying in my studio where I put it when your friends, the medical student and his sister, brought it to me on your behalf" (September 12, 1941).

161. Hildegard Schüle from Blumberg, with whom Sophie had become friendly during her spell as a war auxiliary.

162. Sophie's fears proved groundless. She was able to stay on at the Blumberg day nursery.

163. Sophie's attempts to draw little Dieter Rennicke's head have survived. See also Vinke, op. cit., p. 33.

164. A piece by Wilhelm Habermann, a biology student, in which he pondered the question "What is life?" and debated whether it was a chain of biological reactions or a "mind-governed enlistment" of parts in the creation of a new whole.

165. Not extant.

166. Sophie used to rendezvous there with Fritz Hartnagel whenever he could get away from Weimar. Fritz Hartnagel, reminiscing in the spring of 1983: "On Saturdays I would catch the eleven o'clock train from Weimar and get to Freiburg, where Sophie would be waiting for me at the barrier, around six in the evening. I made the return trip over Sunday night so as to be back on duty at Weimar in the morning."

167. Youth movement pseudonym of Eugen Schneider, an acquaintance of Otl Aicher's and, through him, of the Scholls'. He belonged to the banned Catholic youth movement, Neu-Deutschland.

168. This piece has not survived.

169. Nikolaus von Kues, *Der verborgene Gott*, Erich-Wewel-Verlag, Krailing vor München, 1941.

170. Bishop and Cardinal Nikolaus von Kues (1401–1464, Latinized name "Nicholas of Cusa") was a medieval authority on canon law, mathematician, and philosopher from Kues on the Mosel.

171. Psalms 13:3. See Sophie's letter dated November 7, 1940, page 131.

172. Not extant.

173. *Kristin Lavransdatter,* a trilogy for which the Norwegian novelist Sigrid Undset (1882–1949) was awarded the Nobel prize in 1928. She fled from Norway to the United States in 1940, when the Germans marched in, and returned to Oslo in 1945. (See Hans Scholl's letter dated December 15, 1941, page 200.)

Hans Scholl, Winter 1941–1942

174. One of Hans Scholl's young friends from Ulm. No particulars known.

175. This novel experience, for which Carl Muth and Theodor Haecker were primarily responsible, is even more clearly conveyed by a letter to Rose Nägele dated December 20, 1941: "For me the birth of Our Lord represents the supreme religious experience, because he has been reborn for me. Either Europe will have to change course accordingly, or it will perish!"

176. They were written on the back of a *Süddeutsche* Konzertdirektion program sheet, announcing a concert to be given by the cellist Rudolf Hindemith on Saturday, December 13, 1941. The program included works by Dvořák, Chopin, and Schubert.

177. See note 173 and Sophie's letter to Lisa Remppis dated December 12, 1941, page 195).

178. See Hans's letter dated January 6, 1942, page 202.

179. A copy of Inge's *Windlicht* contribution, "Our Days at the Skiing Lodge," has survived. The following (partly abridged) text seems worthy of reproduction here because it so vividly conveys the atmosphere prevailing in the young Scholls' circle of intimates and the topics they discussed:

> Our Days at the Skiing Lodge. . . . The next morning we were able to set out for the Coburg hut, where we were to stay all by ourselves. After a short climb we reached a level track leading through a truly fairy-tale forest. . . . We progressed in single file, following the trail left in the snow by Hans's skis. At one stage the ballad of the worthy Emperor Barbarossa made its way along our little snow-caravan, probably started by one of the three young Swabians present. The next person continued quoting, and the next, one after another of us merrily capping each line in turn as though playfully batting a ball to and fro. . . . We ascended the side of a valley in zigzags, Hans and I a little ahead of the rest, to locate the position of the hut. Once the broad slope was behind us, crags began to loom on either side, and we made our way up a kind of steep gorge whose sides progressively closed in the higher we climbed. . . . When we reached the notch, it was as if the wind were whistling up from the valley and squeezing through the narrow pass with all its might. The snow was pretty windblown there, and it didn't matter where I placed my skis. Either they promptly slithered sideways, or the snow slid away from under them and rolled downhill in miniature avalanches, like mocking laughter. I toiled across this hopelessly impassable stretch while Hans, who had traversed it with ease, was already out of sight. . . . Suddenly Hans reappeared above. He had white hair, white eyebrows, and a patch of white fuzz over his mouth. It was genuinely heartening to see him standing there, calling to us that the hut was only a few steps farther on. He told us to remove our skis, hand them to him, scramble up after them, and put them on again. Sofie's confident face appeared below me. They all passed their skis to me in turn, and I handed them up to Hans. A few minutes later we were inside the hut. The blizzard that had sprung up outside made the first night's snowstorm seem like a gentle breeze.
>
> . . . Most of you will know how grand it is to sit around a stove by candlelight with a few friends, in the solitude that reigns at 2,000 meters, with wind-driven snow lashing the four walls outside and nothing visible to the eye but a grayish-yellow,

swirling, drifting mass. It's a good thing that the purity and peace prevailing at such an altitude entails a certain amount of trouble and exertion, not only because those incapable of appreciating and making the most of it would fill the silence with noise, but on our own account, too, because the communal exertion and discomfort of such a climb, and its occasional difficulty, create a special bond between us. The "us" that can be engendered by an outward experience of this kind forms a perfect basis for another, inwardly and invisibly constituted "us" to which we aspire and on whose account the *Windlicht* [Hurricane Lamp] has been lighted. It isn't that we want to sacrifice our "I" to this "us," but rather that we seek the "us" for the sake of the "I," so that it may derive sustenance for its continued development and contemplate its reflection in this "us" as though in a mirror. . . .

When all was in readiness [after a day's skiing] and our things were hanging up to dry on the rail above the stove, and Wulfried had made sure that his beloved dynamo lamp – an unfailing source of amusement – was in its rightful place, and the candle was to hand (because the hut was always in semidarkness), and all of us had crowded as close as possible around the stove, in which logs were crackling and flickering, it was time for the book entitled *The Double*, by Dostoyevsky. . . .

Books lent our days in the hut a very special flavor because they focused everyone's thoughts on the same subjects. But the comical aspect of Goldyakin's recurrent turns of phrase gradually rubbed off on us to such an extent that we often spoke of "a person known to us all" whom we addressed: "Reprehensible creature . . . all I mean is . . . you aren't a drunkard at all – no, you're no drunkard, you've merely had a drop to drink . . ." And if one of us was boldly attacked by another, we could retort with supreme composure, "I'm a straightforward person, not a schemer," and add, consolingly, "Maybe it'll all turn out for the best."

Most mornings we were greeted by fitful flurries of snow – unsuitable conditions for practicing on the slopes – so we would huddle around the big stove in the corner and wait there, reading and singing, until the sky cleared. . . .

[Until], his hands busy kneading drips of wax from the candles, one of us brought the conversation around to hunger. It was, he said, a great mystery that so many people should feel no hunger for the things of the spirit. "Don't they ever wake up with a start and ask, Why? Where does it come from, this restlessness within me, this mild ache? Ah, but they always know of an instant remedy. . . .They bury the little voice inside them beneath a heap of stuff instead of simply standing still and asking, Why? If they would only once start with that 'Why?' it might be the beginning of hunger. But they seem to be asleep – indeed, they seem to have entirely forgotten how meaningless life can really be."

Wasn't that taking the mystery of spiritual hunger too far? retorted someone. What form did spiritual hunger take, when there was so much that derived from man himself, for instance the wide realm of art and literature, which was certainly capable of assuaging spiritual hunger as well? Think of Van Gogh, for a start. It wasn't as simple as that. . . .

"Or music!" Ulla chimed in, "Isn't that food for the soul?" At this point, two letters from Sophie have come to my aid, one of them written over a year ago, the other only recently. . . . They aptly convey the way I could have answered that question:

> . . . and, shortly afterward, Schubert's so-called *Unfinished*. I felt like a field that had been thoroughly plowed up, ready for sowing. . . .

> – And last night I heard some music on the radio, so strong and lucid and filled with joie de vivre that it could have been by Bach. I've thought a great deal about music, which is so essentially immaterial (painting and sculpture require images), and I've also imagined music among the angels. But it's intended solely for human beings, for their senses, and it's wonderful that an assortment of vibrations can conjure up such beauty and arouse such emotions. I found it easier to grasp how highly God values us, even if it's only a stool [for us to climb on] . . .

"That hunger," said Hans, " – that hunger can't be assuaged by music or any other form of art. Nothing derived from man can assuage it. The most it can do is indicate the bread [that can assuage it], that's all. . . ."

Why do they feel no hunger? We failed to find an answer to that question. Perhaps it's in the nature of many questions that they have to grow slowly like trees, year after year, until we can one day pluck the ripe fruit from their foliage. . . .

180. Reproduced by Inge Aicher-Scholl, op. cit., p. 99.

181. Hans Rogner.

182. *Des Epimenides Erwachen*, Act II, Scene 4.

183. Remarks like the one cited here can often be found in Hans Scholl's

letters after the fall of 1941. Compare the entry in his Russian diary dated August 22, 1942, page 254, and his letter to Otl Aicher of January 12, 1943, page 299. Theodor Haecker also recorded similar ideas in his *Tag-und Nachtbücher,* the journal he kept between 1939 and 1945, from which he sometimes gave readings in private. The following passages are typical:

> *December 13, 1939.* The Germans [want to be a nation like other nations, but they aren't succeeding. They're becoming far worse than the others. They] are becoming the abomination of the world. Prussian sourdough has made an utter mess [untranslatable pun] of the nation. Its mission is a fake.

> *January 1940.* In that partial history of Christian Europe, the history of Germany, this war may and will, one hopes, spell the end of Prussia's hegemony, which had reached its zenith when this war began.

> *February 20, 1940.* It's childish, trying to save Europe from decline merely by making changes in governments and economic systems. Our only hope is a complete change of mind, a metanoia. There can, of course, be no doubt that the greatest obstacle is "Prussia."

> *June 1–2, 1940.* German idealism in Kant and Fichte is a Prussian thing. . . . Hegel starts out as a great speculative [philosopher], but then, like many South German minds after him, becomes infected with and corrupted by Prussianism. Prussian idealism has deprived the Germans of fleshly hearts and given them iron and paper ones instead. The German heart now consists solely of iron and paper, action and claptrap. There lies the true 'inhumanity' of the German as a Prussian product. The real dehumanization of man consists in associating duty with claptrap, but it's a Prusso-German characteristic and invention.

184. A photograph of the putative face of Christ imprinted on the Turin Shroud. Compare note 157, Hans's letter of December 3, 1941, and the ensuing reprint of his *Windlicht* article on the subject. We know from letters and personal accounts that Hans presented several of his close friends and relations with copies of the same picture at the turn of the year (1941–1942). One of the recipients was Sophie, who wrote to thank him on January 20, 1942:

"Dear Hans, thank you for your letter and the photograph. I'm surprised the picture doesn't cause more of a stir, considering that Christians can't but regard it as the face of God, perceptible to their very own eyes. It's marvelous. And to think it had to be technology, of all things, that brought this picture to light."

Sophie Scholl, Winter–Spring, 1942

185. Goethe's five poems, *Urworte Orphisch*, in an edition illustrated by Karl Thylmann and published by H. Hohmann of Darmstadt in 1921.

186. Inge Aicher-Scholl is not alone in having recorded her impressions of this skiing vacation. Traute Lafrenz, who was then a girlfriend of Hans Scholl's, also wrote an account of it, and the last night in particular, for *Windlicht*:

> New Year's Eve.
> . . . A few sprigs of fir on the wooden tabletop lent it a festive air when we assembled for supper. Inge and Sophie had really outdone themselves in preparing this last communal meal. It was so good, and we were so replete, that no one said a word when Hans announced, with mathematical precision, "We won't celebrate according to summer time, of course, but at eleven o'clock, according to normal, Central European time." We were so replete that nobody spotted the glaring error. But there was still time – it was only just eight. Once again, as on every night, we crowded around the stove; once more we drew closer in readiness of heart; and once more the flickering, restless glow of burning logs mingled with peaceful candlelight. Voices were raised in song. Songs eliminate what separates people, and their harmony pervades those who sing them, so our hearts were receptive to the words of Novalis' *Hymnen an die Nacht*, that great Christian's joyous profession of faith [Novalis was the Baron Friedrich von Hardenberg, 1772–1801, early German romantic poet]. He opens with a loud paean to the light, only to extol the night more fervently still: night, that deep and unbounded darkness in which we become receptacles for pure spirit; in which we completely void our innermost selves and exclude all that seeks to penetrate by way of the senses; in which all that remains to us is an entirely empty consciousness (holy sleep) capable of being infused, by love, with the divine. This utter void must be conceived of as a great affliction, and the influx of percipient love is all the sweeter. Who can have failed to notice how seldom our conversations take their cue from what we have read? Are we fearful of breaking the spell of what we have heard with faltering words of our own?
> At midnight, that's to say, midnight Moscow time, we went outside the hut to await the new year in the open. There wasn't much to be seen. The landscape was swathed in a dense mist tinged with sulfurous yellow by the light of the moon. Not a star, not a mountain peak – just a pale, yellow glow.

Inge read two of the loveliest psalms aloud before we went to sleep. I lay awake for a long time, feeling as if Novalis' words were still resonating inside me, so powerful are they, and of such immediate concern to us.

187. See Inge Scholl's account in note 179.

188. Traute Lafrenz.

189. Dieter Rennicke, Klaus's younger brother. (See also Sophie's letter dated November 18, 1941, page 190.)

Hans Scholl, Winter–Spring, 1942

190. See Mario Krebs, op. cit., p. 115. Although Inge Aicher-Scholl and Hubert Furtwängler have only a vague recollection of the incident and think it was probably less a political offense than an infraction of military discipline, the comparatively serious nature of this dispute was also conveyed by a letter dated February 18, 1941, from Carl Muth to Otl Aicher: "Let us hope that the conflict in which he [Hans Scholl] is presently embroiled will turn out all right – a conflict that has worried me deeply and is still a source of concern." (See also Hans's letter of February 12, 1942, page 214.)

191. In the course of the winter semester 1941–1942, Hans Scholl and Alexander Schmorell had built up a loose-knit circle of friends – not confined to fellow students – who periodically met for communal readings and debates. (See also Hans's letter of February 28, 1942, page 215.)

192. A Russo-German cultural philosopher and author, he held a chair of sociology at Breslau from 1926 but was debarred from teaching in 1937. (See note 153.)

193. See note 179.

194. Because of Hans's confinement to barracks. (See note 190.)

195. *Oberkommando der Wehrmacht* [Armed Forces High Command].

196. Probably Alexander Schmorell, whom the authorities considered a rebel because of his individualistic and brazenly civilian attitude. (See also Krebs, op. cit., p. 78.)

197. See Hellmut Hartert's letter to Inge Aicher-Scholl in note 49. It is likely that Hans applied to work at the hospital there because he had friends at the local monastery.

198. According to information received from the Carl-Muth-Archiv, this manuscript has not survived. In this connection, however, see note 199 below.

199. Carl Muth's active participation in the debates of the *Windlicht* circle is attested by the following extracts from two of his letters to Otl Aicher:

> *February 18, 1942.* Last week I handed him [Hans Scholl] the copy of *Windlicht* you were kind enough to send me. I was already acquainted with much of the contents. I'm amazed, my dear young friend, that you manage to accomplish so much in such a thoroughly unintellectual environment. You'll have stirred up a hornet's nest by raising the question of poverty, so you mustn't be surprised to find complementary and contradictory replies buzzing around your ears before long. Arguments like these are a good thing, particularly if they benefit all concerned by prompting them to view the question increasingly, and even *exclusively,* in the light of the Gospel.

> *July 18, 1942.* The latest issue of *Windlicht* is fine, but I've yet to study the contributions in detail. It's proposed to include some of Gustav Thibon's aphorisms in the next, translated by myself.

200. A Hamburg medical student (b. 1919) and member of a reading circle run by Erna Stahl of the Lichtwark School, she later became a friend of Hans Scholl's at Munich.

Traute Lafrenz had met Alexander Schmorell back in 1939, while he was studying at Hamburg during the summer semester. In May 1941, having belonged during her time at Hamburg to a circle of dissidents centered on the pediatrician Rudolf Degkwitz, she transferred to Munich University. There Schmorell introduced her to Christoph Probst and Hans Scholl. By the end of 1942 she formed the liaison between the Munich and Hamburg resistance groups. Contrary to Judge Freisler's belief, it was she who managed to smuggle a White Rose handbill (the third, appealing for passive resistance) to Hamburg. Convicted of being an accessory at the second People's Court hearing on April 19, 1943, she was sentenced to twelve months' imprisonment.

201. An order devoted to the education of girls, founded in 1609 by the Englishwoman Maria Ward. The nuns were employed as teachers in the order's boarding schools until the National Socialists closed them down. They were then conscripted for hospital duty.

202. By 1942 there were many in Germany who hoped that the war would end in the foreseeable future. This frame of mind is conveyed by some of Carl Muth's letters to Otl Aicher:

> *July 18, 1942.* We all cherish the hope that the war will end as we must wish in the not too far distant future.

October 18, 1942. Everything will turn out as we must wish, if we love our native land and our people. The final decision is approaching with giant strides.

November 12, 1942. All manner of things are happening which permit one to hope that the end of this war is not far off.

203. Traute Lafrenz. (See note 200.)

204. Sausages.

205. Unascertainable.

206. All previous publications give the date of Sophie's arrival in Munich as May 9, 1942, her birthday, citing Inge Aicher-Scholl's account in *Die Weiße Rose.* Frau Aicher-Scholl has amended this date in the latest (4th) edition of her book. The university semester started at the beginning of the month, a further indication that Sophie arrived on or around May 1.

207. Describing the young Scholls' relations with Muth and Haecker, Inge Aicher-Scholl records that Muth was extremely hospitable and "kept open house. My sister spent her first few days at university at his home until a suitable room could be found for her."

Sophie Scholl, Summer 1942

208. *The White Rose: Munich 1942–1943,* p. 74.

209. Sophie had been officially enrolled at Munich University (registration number 83/28570) since May 18, 1942.

210. Essayist, feature writer, cultural commentator, and Roman Catholic convert, Sigismund von Radecki (1891–1970) was then resident in Munich and a member of Carl Muth's circle. His checkered career would have provided food enough for conversation in itself. Born at Riga and educated at St. Petersburg, he had worked by turns as a mining engineer at Freiburg, an irrigation engineer in Turkestan, and an electrical engineer with Siemens in Berlin. At the age of thirty-two he suddenly turned his hand to drawing and acting (he was a longtime friend of the Austrian playwright Karl Kraus), and ended by becoming a free-lance writer. In view of all this, one can well understand why Sophie found the conversation so "tiring," even though she makes no allusion to the political topics that almost certainly formed part of it.

211. Probably Josef Furtmeier. (See note 235.)

212. During vacations, all girl students had to do a minimum of two months' work in a munitions factory or forfeit their university places.

213. *June 17, 1942.* It is clear from a letter to her parents that Sophie failed in her aim:

> I'm going to write to the director of studies requesting that I be allowed to do my service at Ulm and start it a month later. Frau Kley [of Geislingen, wife of the painter Bertl Kley] has also put in a request [for me] because her one-year-service girl has left, but she'll doubtless have as little luck as a local woman doctor who asked to be assigned me as a receptionist.

214. Father Schwarz. (See note 234.)

215. Her request appears to have been promptly fulfilled. Ten days later, on June 17, 1942, she wrote to her parents to thank them:

> Professor Muth was absolutely delighted with the trout. We'll pay another visit to Passau for him – it's a great pleasure from our point of view. Haecker will probably be staying with him while Inge's here. When is she coming?

It is clear that the Scholl family often supplemented Carl Muth's rations, as witness a letter of thanks from Muth to Inge Scholl dated December 3, 1942:

> Hans was here a few days ago, and yesterday Sophie dropped in – not that I saw her in person – to deliver a fine joint of roast mutton on her dear mother's behalf. If I weren't able to invite Hans and Sophie to share it, I would find it hard to accept with an easy mind, because I'm sure it represents a sacrifice on your part. Please convey my most heartfelt thanks to your mother and tell me privately what I owe [her] for it.

216. Hans Scholl had met Radecki at Carl Muth's on April 24. See letter from Carl Muth to Otl Aicher dated April 23, 1942: "I expected Hans for supper, but he didn't turn up. He'll be here tomorrow, however, so he'll meet Sigismund von Radecki, whose books he admires. . . ."

217. After completing her Fröbel course and being drafted into the RAD in March 1941.

218. Dreams and dreamlike experiences figure repeatedly in Sophie's letters and notes. See her letters dated February 26, 1938, October 6, 1939, and August 9, 1942, likewise the following account of a dream she had the night before she was executed, as recalled by Else Gebel, a cellmate who had been detailed to keep an eye on her:

> You . . . told me your dream. It was a fine, sunny day, and you were taking a child in a long, white robe to be christened. The road to the church climbed steeply up a mountainside, but you held the child firmly and securely. All at once a crevasse yawned ahead.

You just had time to deposit the child safely on the other side. Then you plunged into the abyss.

You interpreted the dream as follows: the child in the white robe is our ideal, which will surmount every obstacle. We are privileged to be its pioneers, but we must die for it beforehand.

219. At Carl Muth's.

220. Otl Aicher had celebrated his birthday on May 13, so Sophie is here recalling her first few days in Munich as a guest of Carl Muth's.

221. Hans and Sophie Scholl owed their personal connection with Carl Muth to Otl Aicher. While still in school during the fall of 1940, Aicher had submitted a piece on Michelangelo's sonnets to *Hochland.* Though never published, this essay prompted the periodical's septuagenarian editor, Carl Muth, to invite its eighteen-year-old author to Munich. Their first encounter in March 1941 was a prelude to further meetings and discussions, some of them fiercely combative. By the time Aicher was compelled to join the army in the fall of 1941, Muth loomed large in his life. Anxious not to lose touch with the old man, he introduced Hans Scholl to him, and the resulting acquaintanceship blossomed into a friendship that embraced the entire Scholl family. Whenever friends of the Scholls' visited Munich, they would stay at Muth's house. In return, the Scholls strove to make his life easier by supplying him with scarce foodstuffs and doing him little favors.

Hans Scholl, Russia 1942

222. Willi Graf, Hans Scholl's friend and fellow conspirator-to-be, recorded the various stages of the journey in his diary:

> 7/23/42. Entrained at the Ostbahnhof 7 a.m., didn't pull out till 11. Our section is fine. I feel at home there. We've got enough room and can talk. That's worth a lot.
>
> 7/26/42. Noon in Warsaw, sweltering hot. Late this afternoon we went for a walk in the city, which looked wretched.
>
> 7/27/42. We went into town again, walked around, ate, then sat in the Blue Duck. Our money's running out. We drink our vodka in little sips.

223. See Willi Graf's diary:

> 8/3/42. We're staying together, assigned to the 252nd horse-drawn medical company, which is at Gshats [Gzhatsk], camped in the forest near the airfield. . . ."

8/4/42. Assignment: we're being split up. Hans and I are going to the isolation unit."

224. Willi Graf (b. 1918) lived with his family at Saarbrücken, where he underwent his formative religious and literary influences as a member of the Roman Catholic youth group Neu-Deutschland, and later of the illegal Grauer Orden. His first experience of a Gestapo prison cell dated from 1937, when the Nazis launched their major raids on everyone and everything connected with the free youth movements.

A medical student like Hans Scholl and his friends, Willi Graf had served as a medical orderly in France, Yugoslavia, and – from June 1941 onward – Russia before being assigned to Munich to continue his studies and attached to the second students' company there. On the advice of Hermann Krings, a friend from the Grauer Orden, he attended Professor Huber's lectures on the history of philosophy in addition to his medical courses. He also joined the Munich Bach Choir and took up fencing again. All these activities brought him into contact with fellow students who shared his dissident political outlook. Christoph Probst, a fencing acquaintance, eventually introduced him to Hans Scholl, who had by this time written and distributed the first of the White Rose handbills in collaboration with Alexander Schmorell. Scholl invited him to assist them in their work, and the ties between them were reinforced by their time together on the Russian front. When the students returned, Willi Graf participated in discussions with Falk Harnack (see the note on Hans Scholl's letter of December 6, 1942) regarding the possible expansion of the resistance movement and endeavored to recruit old friends from the Grauer Orden based in Munich, Freiburg, and Saarbrücken. After the Stalingrad debacle, he also joined Hans Scholl and Alexander Schmorell in their nocturnal efforts to mobilize the student population by daubing the walls of the university quarter with slogans ("Down with Hitler," "Freedom," etc.).

Willi Graf and his sister Anneliese, who was likewise studying at Munich, were arrested only hours after Hans and Sophie Scholl. On April 19 he was sentenced to death in the company of Alexander Schmorell and Kurt Huber by a People's Court presided over by Roland Freisler. Although Schmorell and Huber were executed on July 13, Gestapo interrogators pursued their attempts to induce Willi Graf to reveal the names of friends and accomplices until October. Staunchly silent to the last, he was guillotined at Stadelheim Prison on October 12.

225. A friend from the Munich students' company, Hubert Furtwängler (b. 1918) belonged to the Bach Choir like Willi Graf and accompanied

him, Hans Scholl, and Alexander Schmorell to Russia in the summer of 1942. He was a member of the White Rose circle and attended its evening meetings during 1942–1943 but did not participate in the handbill operations.

Although detained for questioning by the Gestapo after the events of February 18 and 22, Furtwängler escaped prosecution thanks to the vigorous efforts of his company commander.

226. Huber's lectures on Leibniz and the German idealist philosophers were attended by students from all faculties, most of them opposed to the regime. Many still testify to the fascination exerted by these lectures, which were wittily and enthrallingly delivered despite their author's speech impediment, their appeal enhanced by the boundless ingenuity of his subversive jibes and innuendoes.

It is probable that Huber first learned the identity of those responsible for the White Rose handbill operations in December 1942. An entry in Willi Graf's diary dated December 17, 1942, reads: "Very interesting talk with Huber." This heralded an analysis of the aims and objectives of the campaign, which the professor undertook to support. He edited the draft of the fifth appeal, *An alle Deutschen*. The last handbill, drafted under the impact of the Stalingrad fiasco and demeaning Party measures directed against members of the university, was written by him alone. Hans Scholl deleted only one paragraph before it was mimeographed. This enjoined students to "totally subordinate" themselves to the German armed forces, whose "magnificent achievements" had been irresponsibly abused by Hitler and the Party. This passage, which Huber himself called "peculiarly characteristic" of his political outlook, was firmly rejected by his student associates.

Kurt Huber was arrested on February 27, 1943, nine days after his handbill had been distributed. He was condemned to death at a People's Court hearing on April 19 and executed with Alexander Schmorell on July 13.

227. Hans and his brother Werner were often able to exchange visits. Commenting on the development of their mutual relations, Hans wrote to his parents on September 28, 1942: "Werner was here last night. He's growing very taciturn. What is there to talk about, anyway? We're imitators of a rare kind, and an entirely new language should be invented to freshen us up again."

228. This remark acquires significance when one recalls that the first four White Rose handbills had been drafted and distributed during Hans's "last few weeks in Munich."

229. See Willi Graf's diary entries:

> *9/1/42.* This morning came the unexpected news that we're to be switched around. Hubert and I are going to the 461st IR [infantry regiment], Hans and Alex are staying put, but we aren't in a hurry to leave. . . .

> *9/3/42.* Now we're really preparing to move out. Leaving for Staroye by horse-drawn ambulance . . . , then on foot to the 1st batl. [battalion], where we meet the regimental MO. Assignments: Hubert's going to the 3rd batl., I to the 1st, proceeding by track-layer's handcar.

230. *Quinta columna.* An ironic reference to the White Rose group. The term was coined by Franco during the Spanish Civil War when he said of his successful campaign against Madrid that he had four columns attacking the city from the outside and a fifth column inside.

231. Hans Scholl mentions this episode in his Russian diary on August 17, page 250, as a kind of preamble to his thoughts on melancholy.

232. Hans Scholl gave his sister Sophie a more equable account of the same incident:

> *Russia, 9/18/42.* The sun shines on and on, the fall wind chases the clouds away – and just now a medical officer annoyed me by condemning my unmilitary haircut. Yes, sir! But he can stuff it. There'll come a day when we see a different side of Russia – when we can let our beards grow down to the ground if it amuses us.

233. Ludwig Klages (1872–1956), philosopher and graphologist.

234. A priest and friend of Carl Muth's who had been transferred for disciplinary reasons, so Hans and Sophie Scholl informed their sister Inge, to a small village in the Bavarian forest. They visited him several times, impressed by his personality and the boxes full of manuscripts in his house. Father Schwarz supplemented Carl Muth's food rations whenever possible.

235. Hans Scholl's friendship with Josef Furtmeier, a legal officer with a wide knowledge of history and archaeology, dated from the spring of 1942, when they had met through Alfred von Martin, the Munich sociologist. Furtmeier formed the link between Hans and the architect Manfred Eickemeyer, from whom he and his friends received authentic information about the German atrocities in Poland. Before long, members of the White Rose circle were holding readings and discussions at Eickemeyer's secluded studio, and their handbills were printed in the cellar beneath it.

236. A formula devised by the Munich pediatrician Meinhard von Pfaundler (1872–1947) for calculating the daily intake of liquid nourishment required by an infant during its first six months of life: p/10 cow's milk + p/100 carbohydrate + water ad ¾ liter. (p = body weight in grams.)

237. When remanded for questioning in December 1937. (See Hans Scholl's letter of December 18, 1937, page 5.)

238. Ernst Reden had been killed in action in Russia during August 1942. Inge Aicher-Scholl, who was a close friend of his, recalls how Sophie heard the news at Ulm on August 23:

> Sophie was seated . . . at the piano. . . . When my mother told her the news, she got up, came into my room, and silently, after standing there for a moment, put the "Pietà d'Avignon" portfolio down in front of me. Then she quietly left the room. A little while later Lisa found her . . . standing beside the window. A tear was rolling down her cheek, and she said angrily, with almost ritual determination: "That's it. Now I'm going to do something." She also told Frau Rennicke, just as resolutely, that she would avenge his death.

239. Carl Muth to Otl Aicher on October 18, 1942: "The thought of his homecoming makes me very happy, not least because his sons are away in Russia."

240. A novel of educational development, published in 1857 by Adalbert Stifter (1805–1868).

Sophie Scholl, Autumn 1942

241. Probably letters and works by Goethe in the popular Reclam series. Otl Aicher recalls that he "had to read a lot of Goethe" because he had become embroiled in an argument with Hans Scholl and Carl Muth over their evaluation of "Goethe's liberal humanism." In this, Aicher had sided with the defenders of the "noncommittal 'both–and'" against the Kierkegaardian "either–or" position. "Muth's defense of Goethe," he wrote in 1983, "stemmed from an antiromantic attitude that formed part of the *Hochland* program. Where Hans was concerned, I felt he was more impressed by Goethe's unorthodoxy and capacity for continually changing his ground, and also, no doubt, by his visual mode of thought and receptivity to the world around."

242. All that exists of this planned contribution to *Windlicht* is the outline reproduced on page 207.

243. Elisabeth Scholl had worked for some time as governess to a parson's family at Suppingen in the Swabian Jura, not far from Ulm, where she received occasional visits from her brothers, sisters, and friends.

244. An allusion to the title of a piece by Ernst Wiechert in the *Frankfurter Zeitung* (May 15, 1937) thanking those readers who, heedless of any political consequences, had kept faith with him in the growing isolation to which he had been subjected since his Munich address of May 16, 1935. The Scholl family possessed the text of this speech in a special reprint that appeared shortly afterward (see note 19). In 1937, on the occasion of his fiftieth birthday, Wiechert had written:

> Thousands upon thousands of them are standing around my house . . . a dark, faithful, steadfast wall. They demand nothing, they ask nothing. They are there purely so that I shall know they are there. So that my house shall not be hemmed in by alien territory, solitude, or bitter desolation. . . . not a wall [built] of power or authority . . . , but a wall of love. And could anyone perish of whom love has partaken?

245. Sophie obviously changed her plans shortly afterward. Writing to a friend on October 4, 1942, she said: "Our trip to the Bohemian forest has been postponed. At present we're in Munich helping Professor Muth, whose house was damaged in the latest air raid. I'll probably be spending next week here as well."

246. Theodor Haecker's *Schöpfer und Schöpfung*, first published by Hegner of Leipzig in 1934.

247. Luke 16:22–25.

248. See notes 57 and 63.

249. At Blumberg.

250. See note 245.

251. Romans 8:2.

252. Romans 8:2.

253. The German boxer Max Schmeling (b. 1905), world heavyweight champion 1930–1932. Schmeling is best known to Americans as the only opponent to win a match from Joe Louis in his prime, June 19, 1936. Two years later, Louis won the rematch by a knockout in the first round.

254. It is apparent from Willi Graf's diary that he and his friends arrived in Munich on the evening of November 6 and traveled home the following day.

255. At the rear of 13 Franz-Joseph-Strasse, where Hans and Sophie had rented two rooms from Frau Dr. Schmidt, effective December 1, 1942.

Sophie Scholl, Winter 1942–1943

256. Sophie had already been to Stuttgart on December 3 and fixed a meeting with Susanne Hirzel:

> *Munich, December 1, 1942.* Dear Suse, I'm coming to Stgt. Thursday, Dec. 3. Can we meet? It would be so nice. I don't know my time of arrival yet. I'll call you when I get there.

257. Music was one of Sophie's staple needs in life, as her letters and her friends' recollections of her confirm. She played the piano well and devoted great attention to her progress in the field of music. The young Scholls often played together, and the family held musical soirées at home and regularly attended concerts. Sophie's appreciation of music is attested not only by this letter to Fritz Hartnagel but also by her draft essay for *Windlicht* (see page 207) and her letters to Otl Aicher (September 5, 1942) and Lisa Remppis (January 14, 1942). To assess her musical predilections correctly, the reader should bear in mind that "modern" composers such as Mahler, Schönberg, Hindemith, and Webern were not allowed to be performed in the Third Reich.

258. Inge Scholl, *The White Rose*, p. 89.

259. Wilhelm Geyer had come to Munich (through the good offices of Hans Scholl) to paint a portrait of Carl Muth.

260. See Sophie's letter of October 9, 1942, page 273, and note 247.

Hans Scholl, Winter 1942–1943

261. Hans Scholl had made the acquaintance of the novelist Werner Bergengruen (1892–1964) at Carl Muth's home in the late summer or fall of 1941. See Werner Bergengruen, "Erinnerungen an Carl Muth," op. cit., p. 79:

> I had no idea that Hans Scholl, the student whom I met at Carl Muth's house on Dittlerstrasse [in Munich-Solln, where Muth and Bergengruen had been neighbors since 1936], . . . was the author of the White Rose handbills which my wife and I typed out at night, and which I then, after carefully selecting their addresses, cycled

into town with and mailed in as many different postal districts as possible.

262. Hans Scholl appears to have expressed similar sentiments during his Christmas vacation at Ulm. Looking back on that period, Inge Aicher-Scholl recalls:

> Hans said he found it deeply satisfying to tend the sick. He loved the profession, he said, but if, after the war, nobody took the trouble to write a proper history of the National Socialist era, he would change horses in midstream and devote himself to setting the historical picture straight.

263. In 1968 Otl Aicher gave the following account of his visit to Munich:

> I went to Munich in the middle of February and stayed with Professor Muth. Before I could get in touch with Hans and Sophie, I received a call from Ulm asking me to let Hans know that the book *Machtstaat and Utopie* was out of print. [This message from Ulm was, Aicher realized, a coded warning from Hans Hirzel, but it almost certainly did not imply that the Gestapo had connected Hans Scholl with the handbill campaign.] We arranged to meet at eleven the following day at his lodgings at 13 Franz-Joseph-Strasse. At eleven I found the place locked up. When I returned half an hour later, I was greeted by the Gestapo. It was February 18, 1943.

Before Aicher came to Munich, he and Sophie had spent several days together at Ulm. He was visiting his parents after being discharged from the hospital; she had gone home to help her ailing mother.

264. See note 183.

Sophie Scholl, Winter 1943

265. Theodor Haecker (1879–1945), author, philosopher, and scholar, initially on the editorial staff of various periodicals. He made something of a name for himself as a writer and authority on the Danish philosopher Sören Kierkegaard, whose principal works he translated into German. Influenced by the writings of Cardinal J. H. Newman (1801–1890), he adopted the Roman Catholic faith in 1921.

It was Otl Aicher who introduced the Scholls to Haecker's chief works, *Vergil, Vater des Abendlandes* (1931), *Was ist der Mensch?* (1933), and *Schöpfer und Schöpfung* (1934). They became personally acquainted with him through Carl Muth, with whom Haecker had worked on *Hochland*. Although he had been forbidden to speak in public since 1935 and debarred from publishing works of his own since 1938, Haecker gave several readings to the White Rose circle in 1942, notably from the diaries he kept from 1939 on. These were published posthumously in 1947 under the title *Tag- und Nachtbücher.* Only his daughter's presence of mind saved the manuscript from discovery when his home was searched after the Scholls' arrest. Inge Aicher-Scholl has described how she copied this out during July and August 1944 at Bruderhof, a remote farm above the Wutachschlucht in the south of the Black Forest, which the family had employed as a refuge from the Gestapo and their threats since May of that year:

> Otl's father then made two watertight, damp-proof metal cylinders in which we planned to stow and hide two copies of the manuscript. I recall that my mother buried them under an oak tree in the garden while the rest of us were still debating the safest place to put them. Immediately after the war Otl cycled to Ulsterbach, near Augsburg, where Haecker had been evacuated, to deliver the cylinders to him. Haecker was already dead.

266. On the afternoon of February 4, 1943, Theodor Haecker read extracts from *Schöpfer und Schöpfung* and his unpublished diaries to an audience of around thirty-five people at Eickemeyer's studio. Several of those present have described the occasion. Willi Graf noted in his diary: "We met at four o'clock. Haecker read the first part of his *Schöpfer und Schöpfung.* He spoke for over two hours. Much of what I heard and understood was exceptionally interesting." Elisabeth Hartnagel-Scholl, who stayed at her brother and sister's Munich lodgings from the end of January to February 5, recalled: "On February 4, 1943, Theodor Haecker read to an invited audience of friends and acquaintances at Eickemeyer's studio." It was the day after the German surrender at Stalingrad had been announced.

267. Sophie was due to do some more war work during the university vacation.

268. Of the hospital at L'vov.

269. See Inge Aicher-Scholl, op. cit., p. 158 ff.

270. Inge Scholl, *The White Rose*, p. 91.

271. Ibid., p. 165.

Sophie Scholl, February 17

272. Born in Upper Bavaria on November 6, 1919, Christoph Probst was the son of a scholar and art lover. He and his sister Angelika, who was eighteen months older, continued to live with their father after his early divorce from their mother. His second wife being half

Jewish, the two adolescents found National Socialism a very palpable threat to their personal relationships from the day Hitler came to power. Their deep-seated and well-founded aversion to the regime was intensified by an education received at private boarding schools in the country.

Christoph Probst graduated from Schondorf, a boarding school on the Ammersee run in accordance with the educational theories of Hermann Lietz, in 1937. His final report described him as a pupil of outstanding maturity and refinement, mentally alert, keenly discriminating, and endowed with a special love of and bent for the sciences, notably astronomy, as well as literature. Motivated perhaps by his often-attested impulse to help and heal, he followed up his prescribed spells of Arbeitsdienst and military service by enrolling as a medical student at Munich in 1939. His membership in a Luftwaffe students' company enabled him to continue studying after the outbreak of war, initially at Munich and later at Strasbourg and Innsbruck. At twenty-one he married Herta Dohrn, daughter of Harald Dohrn, an anti-Nazi philanthropist whom the Nazis shot in the Perlacher Forest on April 25, 1945, only hours before Germany surrendered, together with his brother-in-law. (See Klaus Dohrn, *Von Bürgern und Weltbürger: Eine Familiengeschichte*, Verlag Günther Neske, Pfullingen, 1983, pp. 256–259.)

Hans Scholl first met Christoph Probst in 1941 at a reading at the home of Alexander Schmorell, with whom Probst had been on close terms since briefly attending the same Munich high school, the Neues Realgymnasium. Witnesses of this first encounter recall that they took to each other at once, and that their conversation unmistakably stamped them as kindred spirits whose instinctive affinity was enhanced by a common passion for mountaineering and skiing. This is confirmed by the few known letters from Christl, as his friends called him, to his newfound friend.

The paucity of documentary information about Christoph Probst's involvement in the White Rose ventures (printing and distribution of handbills, painting slogans on walls) is attributable mainly to his friends' endeavors to exclude him from such dangerous activities as far as possible and their subsequent refusal to divulge his name to the Gestapo. Not only was Probst a family man with three young children, but he had been transferred to a students' company at Innsbruck in December 1942 and could pay only sporadic visits to Munich thereafter. It is nonetheless probable that he contributed to the drafting and wording of some of the handbills. "Christl undoubtedly played a major part in drafting and formulating the texts," writes Inge Aicher-Scholl, op. cit., p. 34.

What is documented is that, when Hans Scholl was arrested and searched, the Gestapo found a sheet of paper torn into innumerable fragments. When reconstructed, they proved to be a handwritten draft by Christoph Probst. In sentencing him to death, Roland Freisler stated that this document had used:

> . . . [T]he heroic struggle at Stalingrad as an occasion for branding the Führer a military confidence trickster, indulging in craven defeatism, and then, adopting a proclamatory tone, calling for action in the form of honorable surrender, as he [Probst] styles it, coupled with opposition to National Socialism.

This draft proclamation cost Christoph Probst his life. He was arrested on February 19, 1943, when he went to pick up a leave pass to visit his wife, who was confined to bed with puerperal fever. His recent letters had testified to the steady growth of his Christian faith. Now, on the verge of death, he was baptized a Roman Catholic. Like Hans and Sophie Scholl, he was executed at Munich's Stadelheim Prison on February 22, 1943.

273. See note 72.

Index